BENTHAM'S THEORY OF LAW AND PUBLIC OPINION

This collection represents the latest research from leading scholars whose work has helped to frame our understanding of Bentham since the publication of H.L.A. Hart's *Essays on Bentham*. The authors explore fundamental areas of Bentham's thought, including the relationship between the rule of law and public opinion; law and popular prejudices or manipulated tastes; Bentham's methodology versus Hart's; sovereignty and codification; and the language of natural rights. Drawing on original manuscripts and volumes in *The Collected Works of Jeremy Bentham*, the chapters combine philosophical and historical approaches and offer new and more faithful interpretations of Bentham's legal philosophy and its development. As a coherent whole, the book challenges the dominant understandings of Bentham among legal philosophers and rescues him from some famous mischaracterizations.

XIAOBO ZHAI is Professor of Law at Zhengzhou University in China and Newton International Fellow at University College London.

MICHAEL QUINN is Senior Research Associate of the Bentham Project at University College London. His research focuses on Bentham's applications of the principle of utility to public policy.

BENTHAM'S THEORY OF LAW AND PUBLIC OPINION

Edited by

XIAOBO ZHAI

Zhengzhou University and University College London

MICHAEL QUINN

University College London

CAMBRIDGE
UNIVERSITY PRESS

CAMBRIDGE
UNIVERSITY PRESS

32 Avenue of the Americas, New York, NY 10013-2473, USA

Cambridge University Press is part of the University of Cambridge.

It furthers the University's mission by disseminating knowledge in the pursuit of education, learning, and research at the highest international levels of excellence.

www.cambridge.org
Information on this title: www.cambridge.org/9781107042254

First published 2014

Printed in the United States of America

A catalog record for this publication is available from the British Library.

Library of Congress Cataloging in Publication Data
Bentham's theory of law and public opinion / edited by Xiaobo Zhai, Michael Quinn.
p. cm.
Includes bibliographical references and index.
ISBN 978-1-107-04225-4 (hardback)
1. Bentham, Jeremy, 1748–1832 2. Law – Philosophy. 3. Utilitarianism. I. Zhai, Xiaobo, editor of compilation. II. Quinn, Michael, (research associate) editor of compilation.
K334.B465 2014
340′.1–dc23 2013040683

ISBN 978-1-107-04225-4 Hardback

CONTENTS

CONTRIBUTORS

EMMANUELLE DE CHAMPS is a lecturer in British history and civilisation at Université Paris 8 (France). Her publications include *La déontologie politique ou La pensée constitutionnelle de J. Bentham* (2008) and *Enlightenment and Utility: Bentham in France/Bentham in French* (forthcoming). She co-edited, with Jean-Pierre Cléro, *Bentham et la France. Fortune et Infortunes de l'utilitarisme* (2009).

DAVID LIEBERMAN is James W. and Isabel Coffroth Professor of Law and Professor of History at the University of California, Berkeley. He is the author of *The Province of Legislation Determined: Legal Theory in Eighteenth-Century Britain* (1989), and he edited Jean Louis De Lolme's *The Constitution of England; or, An Account of the English Government* (2007).

GERALD J. POSTEMA is Cary C. Boshamer Professor of Philosophy and Professor of Law, University of North Carolina at Chapel Hill. His publications include *Bentham and the Common Law Tradition* (1986) and *Legal Philosophy in the Twentieth Century: The Common Law World* (2011). He also edited the two-volume collection *Jeremy Bentham: Moral, Political, and Legal Philosophy* (2002).

MICHAEL QUINN is Senior Research Associate at the Bentham Project, UCL. He has edited Bentham's *Writings on the Poor Laws* (2 vols., 2001, 2010), and co-edited *Of Sexual Irregularities, and Other Writings on Sexual Morality* (2014). He is currently editing Bentham's writings on political economy.

FREDERICK ROSEN is Professor Emeritus of the History of Political Thought at UCL. He was Director of the Bentham Project and General Editor of the *Collected Works of Jeremy Bentham* from 1983 to 2003. His books include *Jeremy Bentham and Representative Democracy: A Study of the* Constitutional Code (1983); *Bentham, Byron, and Greece: Constitutionalism, Nationalism, and Early Liberal Political Thought* (1992); *Classical Utilitarianism from Hume to Mill* (2003); and *Mill* (2013).

PHILIP SCHOFIELD is Professor of the History of Legal and Political Thought at UCL, Director of the Bentham Project, and General Editor of the *Collected Works of Jeremy Bentham.* He has edited or co-edited nine volumes in the collected works, the most recent being *Of Sexual Irregularities, and Other Writings on Sexual Morality* (2014). His *Utility and Democracy: The Political Thought of Jeremy Bentham* (2006) won the prestigious W.J.M. Mackenzie Prize. He is also the author of *Bentham: A Guide for the Perplexed* (2009).

XIAOBO ZHAI is Professor of Law at Zhengzhou University and Newton International Fellow at the Bentham Project, UCL. His books include *The People's Constitution* (2009) and *The Chinese Model of Constitutional Implementation* (2009). He is the translator of five books on legal and constitutional theory.

contains a full discussion of the Continental debate in political ideas, and is original in showing both its nature and Bentham's eagerness to participate in it. Just as European academics nowadays feel the need to publish in English, philosophers in Bentham's day needed to address, and succeeded in addressing, a Continental European audience in French.

The starting point for Philip Schofield's essay on Bentham and natural rights is the composition of Bentham's 'Nonsense upon Stilts' in 1795. This work, previously known as 'Anarchical Fallacies', is considered by Schofield to be 'arguably the most profound critique of the theory of natural rights ever written'. Schofield's essay is carefully linked to the new text, published in the *Collected Works* as part of *Rights, Representation, and Reform: Nonsense upon Stilts and Other Writings on the French Revolution*,[8] and provides an excellent analysis of its main themes. Furthermore, Schofield develops a theoretical critique of the advocates of natural or human rights and a defence of utilitarianism. In the eighteenth-century context, he shows how Bentham could defeat Thomas Paine's arguments concerning the rights of man. He points out that both Paine and Bentham were responding in different ways to the Declaration of the Rights of Man and the Citizen of 1789. In relation to contemporary political philosophy, he provides a critique of Rawls's defence of human rights in a way which closely parallels Bentham's critique of Paine's theory of natural rights.

To conclude, this volume is an excellent introduction to Bentham as a philosopher, a legal theorist, and arguably the most important figure in the history of utilitarianism. It adds considerably to our knowledge of Bentham's life and times, as well as to our understanding of utilitarianism then and now. In addition, we can also learn from passing comments by these authors, as when Schofield, for example, notes that John Stuart Mill was present, as a young boy of approximately ten or eleven years of age, at Ford Abbey in Devon when Bentham lived there and was writing on sexual irregularities. Indeed, Mill's father, James Mill, shared the same large room as Bentham, where they would work on their various projects. Schofield believes that John Stuart Mill would have been too young to have had access to the manuscripts (and Mill apparently never subsequently mentioned them), but from his comments on Bentham and taste he would have known something of Bentham's ideas with regard to

[8] J. Bentham, 'Nonsense upon Stilts', in *Rights, Representation, and Reform: Nonsense upon Stilts and Other Writings on the French Revolution*, eds. P. Schofield, C. Pease-Watkin, and C. Blamires (Oxford: Clarendon Press, 2002 (*CW*)), 317–401.

liberty generally, and possibly with regard to free sexual expression. The striking image of young John Mill peeping at Bentham's manuscripts on sexual irregularities, then later sharing the irregular, though supposedly Platonic ménage à trois with John and Harriet Taylor, and participating in what appears to have been an unconsummated marriage with Harriet Taylor Mill, makes one wonder whether he was ever aware of these manuscripts and the ideas in them, or if he simply refused to pay such unconventional ideas much attention. One finds no discussion of the liberty of enjoying sexual irregularities, for example, in Mill's *The Subjection of Women*, and no discussion of the pleasures of pederasty elsewhere. Nevertheless, Bentham's overall position as a believer in liberty, particularly of consenting adults acting in private, including liberty for women, is developed by Mill in a legal and social context in the correspondence with Auguste Comte, *On Liberty*, *The Subjection of Women*, and elsewhere, and plays an important role in later social and legal thought concerning women and their rights.[9]

Frederick Rosen
University College London
28 June 2013

[9] See F. Rosen, *Mill* (Oxford University Press, 2013), 231–60, 281–5.

2

Law's Rule

Reflexivity, Mutual Accountability, and the Rule of Law

GERALD J. POSTEMA

'We are going to be a community of the rule of law',[1] announced C.H. Tung, the Chinese official appointed to govern Hong Kong, prior to China's assuming jurisdiction over the city. Tung's publicly uttered reassurance appealed to an ancient ideal. Already in the fifth century BCE, the core idea of the rule of law was captured on stone columns in the Cretan city of Gortyn. The first sentence of the Gortyn Law Code asserts the supremacy of the legal process, declaring 'if anyone wishes to contest the status of a free man or a slave, he is not to seize him before a trial'.[2] Law and the legal process were to rule the actions and interactions of citizens of Gortyn; but equally, they were to govern the exercise of power by officials and by those who acted under colour of law. Officials, even the city's highest official, the *kosmos*, were held accountable to the law. They could be fined if they failed to enforce the law properly.[3] Law was not to be merely an instrument of governance; law was meant to rule governors and citizens alike. This is the simple, central idea of the rule of law. 'If the law does not rule', Martin Krygier observed, 'we don't have the rule of law'.[4] The rule of law is first of all about *ruling* – the *law's* ruling.

This ancient ideal of *law's rule* is our subject. More precisely, this chapter focuses on the conditions for the realization of law's rule. Philosophical explorations of the rule of law ideal largely focus on principles of *legality* – the formal, procedural, and institutional aspects of the ideal – but I believe that these discussions are seriously incomplete. I argue that *fidelity* – the

1 'We Are Going to be a Community of the Rule of Law', *Business Week International Edition*, 23 December 1996, 20, quoted in B. Tamanaha, 'The Rule of Law for Everyone', *Current Legal Problems* 55 (2002), 97–122, at 100.

2 F.D. Miller, Jr., 'The Rule of Law in Ancient Greek Thought', in *The Rule of Law in Comparative Perspective*, eds. M. Sellers and T. Tomaszewski (Dordrecht: Springer, 2010), 11–18, at 11.

3 Ibid., 12.

4 M. Krygier, 'Four Puzzles about the Rule of Law: Why, What, Where? And Who Cares?', in *Getting to the Rule of Law: Nomos 50*, ed. J.E. Fleming (New York University Press, 2011), 64–104, at 68.

ethos of law – is essential to law's rule. Fidelity underwrites and makes possible law's rule. The rule of law is robust in a polity only when it is characterized by widespread fidelity, that is, only when its members, and not merely the legal or ruling elite, take responsibility for holding each other – and especially law's officials – to account under the law. This is the thought I explore and defend. To get our subject clearly in view, I begin with a vivid and troubling example of *in*fidelity.

Infidelity

Between 2003 and 2008, the presiding judge of the juvenile court in Luzerne County, Pennsylvania, summarily sentenced several thousand young people to extended detention in private facilities far from the young defendants' homes.[5] In hearings that lasted an average of four minutes, Judge Mark Ciavarella handed down harsh sentences for minor infractions or even innocent actions – for example, for throwing a steak at the defendant's mother's boyfriend, for calling the police when the defendant's mother locked him out of the house – with scarce attention to the evidence in the case, let alone any special features of the defendants' circumstances. In the U.S. juvenile justice system, the legally mandated aim is restorative rather than punitive. Court officials are charged with securing 'the best interest of the child'. This charge leaves a degree of discretion to judges to fashion arrangements to suit the needs and special circumstances of each defendant. Ignoring the law, however, Judge Ciavarella imposed sentences at his pleasure, in proceedings that mocked federal and state constitutional and statutory guarantees of due process. Although guaranteed the right to counsel through the whole process, defendants were systematically and illegally urged to waive their rights and to plead guilty. More than 50 per cent of defendants appearing before Judge Ciavarella waived their rights to counsel, and 60 per cent of those who did were placed in extended detention, whereas only 20 per cent of those who were represented by counsel were so placed. 'The judge's whim is all that mattered in that courtroom', said the legal director of the Juvenile Law Center (which was instrumental in finally exposing the practices of Ciavarella's court). 'The law was basically irrelevant.'[6]

5 W. Ecenbarger, *Kids for Cash* (New York: The New Press, 2012). All facts about this scandal discussed in this section are drawn from Ecenbarger's extended account, unless otherwise indicated.

6 Quoted in I. Urbina, 'Despite Red Flags about Judges, a Kickback Scheme Flourished', *New York Times*, 27 March 2009.

In early 2009, the public learned that Ciavarella's 'zero tolerance' policy was motivated by nothing more than venal sinister interest. Ciavarella and his fellow judge, Michael Conahan, had been paid handsomely – $2.6 million during this period – to send juveniles to two private detention centres, while working to eliminate the public detention centre run by the county. The judges were indicted and later convicted on a number of federal charges including conspiracy, money laundering, racketeering, and tax evasion. Judge Ciavarella denied that the money he received for juveniles he sent to the private detention centres in any way influenced his judgment. The Pennsylvania Supreme Court disagreed. In October 2009, the court expunged all the convictions, some 3,000, handed down by Ciavarella between 2003 and 2008.

Although the venal motive was not uncovered until 2009, the practices of systematic denial of constitutional due process rights, excessively harsh and arbitrarily imposed sentences, and utter disregard for the law went entirely unquestioned by hosts of people – other judges, district attorneys, public defenders, court officers and staff, police, probation officers, school administrators, teachers, counsellors, and the like – who saw and heard but did nothing to challenge them. The Interbranch Commission on Juvenile Justice, established by the state legislature to investigate the scandal, opened its proceedings in October 2009 with these words:

> This morning our Commission begins its public hearings to assess the breath-taking collapse of the juvenile justice system in Luzerne County. Two judges stand criminally charged for conduct that had the unmistakable effect of harming children . . . there is little doubt that their conduct, whether criminal or not, had disastrous consequences for the juvenile justice system. . . . Our concern, however, is not only the action of two Luzerne County judges. Our concern is also the inaction of others. Inaction by judges, prosecutors, public defenders, the defense bar, public officials and private citizens – those who knew but failed to speak; those who saw but failed to act.[7]

Many people personally witnessed hundreds of occasions on which the constitutional rights of children were violated; clear dictates of the law protecting children from abuse by adults and the state were ignored in their presence. For six years, no one spoke up or spoke out – or nearly no one. In 2004, the Wilkes-Barre *Times Leader* ran a series of stories on apparent irregularities in Ciavarella's court, but it fell on deaf ears in the public. Many in the community, especially school administrators,

[7] Opening statement of the Commission, quoted in Ecenbarger, 232.

liked the zero-tolerance stance of Judge Ciavarella; many others regarded irregularities as par for the course in Luzerne County, which had a long history of corruption, nepotism, and mob-influenced politics. Perhaps it was fear, uncertainty, indifference to familiar moral corruption, or approval of the end result that silenced their judgment and anaesthetized their will to challenge.

The list of wrongs done and evils inflicted on the children and families of Luzerne County is long and disgusting, but, without denying or minimizing any of the other wrongs, I want to draw attention to just one, not because it is the most important from a moral point of view, but because it is easily overlooked. In Luzerne County, there was not only a breakdown of justice and a failure of fairness, but also a collapse of law, a failure of law's rule. In crucial respects, for a significant stretch of time, for the children of the county, the law offered no protection. Law did not matter. It did not count.[8] In the words of the prophet Habakkuk, the law became slack, the wicked surrounded the righteous, and judgment came forth perverted.[9] The protections promised by the rule of law were not realized. The rule of law failed due to a failure of fidelity.

The Rule of Law: Core Idea

The rule of law is a powerful political idea and ideal. It supplies the architectural frame of a just and decent society and the infrastructure of democracy. It is the foundation stone of economic and political development, and establishing a robust rule of law is widely thought to be the first task in rebuilding nations shaken by civil wars or oppressed by authoritarian rule. Political ideals with this kind of scope, power, and visibility cannot escape controversy, and some believe, with Jeremy Waldron, that the rule of law is an essentially contested concept.[10]

Yet, it seems to me that the core of the idea, acknowledged from the time of its inception in ancient times, is simple and straightforward. Throughout its long history, the idea has been rooted in the thought that the law promises protection and recourse against the arbitrary exercise of power. This twofold orienting thought is that (a) a polity is well ordered,

8 For another extended example of the failure of fidelity in the Jim Crow era in the South of the United States, see G.J. Postema, 'Fidelity in Law's Commonwealth', in *Private Law and the Rule of Law*, ed. D. Klimchuck (Oxford University Press, in press).

9 Habakkuk 1: 4.

10 J. Waldron, 'Is the Rule of Law an Essentially Contested Concept (in Florida)?', *Law and Philosophy* 21 (2002), 137–64.

and its members are accorded the dignity demanded rightfully by them in the name of their common membership, when its members are secured against the arbitrary exercise of power, and (b) law, because of its distinctive features, is especially and perhaps uniquely capable of providing such security. One finds this thought expressed in the familiar voice of Locke when he contrasts power exercised in accord with 'settled standing laws' with power exercised 'arbitrar[il]y and at pleasure'.[11]

This notion has a distinctive structure. The focal and organizing aim is control of the exercise of power; the means of doing so is law, which seeks to constrain in advance the exercise of power (protection) and to offer means of holding those who exercise power accountable after the fact (recourse). This aim implies constraints on law itself, on its form and on its implementation, and it calls for an *ethos* as a necessary condition of the realization of law's rule. Several features of this account of the core idea of the rule of law need elaboration.

First, the rule of law concerns itself with *exercises of power*. Many forms of power are exercised in a polity.[12] It is useful to distinguish two broad sorts of power (or rather, two contexts in which power is exercised). *Political* power is wielded within government by one segment over another, by government over the governed, and in democratic polities by the governed over their governors; *social* power, which comes in many forms, is wielded by members or corporate entities in a polity over other members or entities. The rule of law includes all forms of power wielded in a polity within the scope its concern. Joseph Raz once maintained that the rule of law concerns only the abuses of law,[13] but this too narrowly conceives the focus and scope of the rule of law.[14] The rule of law sets its face against all abuses of power in the polity. The aim of the rule of law, E.P. Thompson wrote, is to impose 'effective inhibitions upon power and the defence of the citizen from power's all-intrusive claims'.[15]

The rule of law is typically thought of as a mode of governance. The United Nations report on the rule of law in transitional societies, for example, begins with the claim that the term 'rule of law refers to a

[11] J. Locke, 'Second Treatise of Government', in *Two Treatises of Government*, ed. P. Laslett (Cambridge University Press, 1988), 265–428, at 359, 360 (§ 137).

[12] I restrict attention here to exercises of power in a polity. Power, of course, can be exercised in intimate interpersonal relations as well, but I will not consider here whether the rule of law may properly extend its concern to this domain.

[13] J. Raz, *The Authority of Law* (Oxford: Clarendon Press, 1979), 224.

[14] See J. Waldron, 'The Concept and the Rule of Law', *Georgia Law Review*, 43 (2008), 1–61, at 11.

[15] E.P. Thompson, *Whigs and Hunters* (Harmondsworth: Penguin, 1977), 266.

principle of governance in which all persons, institutions and entities, public and private, including the State itself, are accountable to laws'.[16] In this same vein, Bentham wrote extensively about 'securities against misrule'.[17] But the rule of law also prescribes a *mode of association*. In addition to defining a distinctive mode of exercising political power, it defines a distinctive social ordering.[18]

Second, the rule of law promises not protection against violence and cruelty, but rather protection and recourse against the *arbitrary* exercise of power. What makes an exercise of power 'arbitrary'? An exercise of power is arbitrary in the rule-of-law-relevant sense if it is the expression of the *liberum arbitrium*, the free decision or choice, of its agent. Philip Pettit observes: 'An act is perpetrated on an arbitrary basis . . . [if] the agent was in a position to choose it or not choose it, at their pleasure.'[19] The act is arbitrary, even if it is reasonable, reasoned, or justified, if it is undertaken entirely at the will or pleasure of its agent. The *dominus* – owner and master – exercised this kind of power or *dominion* over his estate according to medieval understanding of Roman law; the use and disposition of property was entirely at his pleasure. He answered only to his own *arbitrium*. Arbitrary power is unilateral power. The only relevant perspective on the action is that of the agent; no other side or perspective need to be considered. Arbitrary power is not necessarily unreasoned, or unpredictable, or even in a strict sense unruly. Rather, it is unaccountable. Gloucester captured this sense of arbitrariness when he uttered the bitter lines, 'As flies to wanton boys are we to th' gods, They kill us for their sport'.[20] It is not that no norms or rules apply to the gods, that they are utterly wanton, but rather that divine nature is so far beyond us that we are to them as flies are to us; we are not worth bothering about, utterly without standing to demand an accounting, at the mercy of divine whim. To us their behaviour is at their pleasure, unilateral, unaccountable. The

[16] *The Rule of Law and Transitional Justice in Conflict and Post-Conflict Societies – Report of the Secretary-General*, United Nations Security Council, 23 August 2004, S/2004/616, 4.

[17] J. Bentham, *Securities Against Misrule and Other Constitutional Writings for Tripoli and Greece*, ed. P. Schofield (Oxford: Clarendon Press, 1990 (*CW*)). See Postema, 'The Soul of Justice: Bentham on Publicity, Law, and the Rule of Law', Chapter 3 in this volume, 42–7.

[18] This aspect of the rule of law is discussed at greater length in Postema, 'Fidelity in Law's Commonwealth'.

[19] P. Pettit, *Republicanism: A Theory of Freedom and Government* (Oxford University Press, 1997), 55.

[20] Shakespeare, *King Lear*, IV. i. 37–8.

rule of law sets its face against exercises of power that are arbitrary in this sense. This is its core, defining aim.

Third, the core idea of the rule of law holds that it is law that promises protection and recourse against arbitrary exercises of power. Law is the instrument of this protection and recourse. Note that *the law* as a whole makes this promise – not merely positive legal *rules*, but rather law understood as a systematic mode of ordering, as a co-ordinated system of institutions and procedures for administration and adjudication, and as an argumentative system of deliberative discourse.[21] If we think of law simply as a set of formal rules (and thus regard law merely as 'the enterprise of subjecting human behaviour to the governance of rules'),[22] we overlook distinctive features of law that are enlisted in the struggle to harness the exercise of power. Law provides institutions, procedures, and a mode of discourse with and in which power can be called to account. 'He who commands that the law should rule', Aristotle maintained, commands that 'God and reason alone should rule'.[23] Law's governance is not governance by that which is rational, reasonable, or right, but rather by reason, that is disciplined deliberative *reasoning*, by the disciplined giving and taking and assessing of reasons. Law's rule is, in an important part, the rule of deliberative reason. In the words of Justice Brandeis, we look to law to help us govern ourselves because we want 'deliberative forces [to] prevail over the arbitrary'.[24] Law's distinctive discipline of systemic, deliberative reasoning, along with posited rules, and formal institutions of administration and adjudication, constitute the arsenal of its promised rule over arbitrary power.

Fourth, a word should be said about the notion of accountability invoked by the notion of law's rule. Accountability finds its home in a *normatively structured interpersonal relationship*. A is accountable *to* B *for* some X – where A and B are individual or collective agents, B is usually a relatively determinate party, who may act in and for a wider public, and X is A's decision, act, activity, performance, or policy. This interpersonal relationship is *normatively structured* in three respects: (1) A is normatively *liable* to be called to account by B, and B not only can expect but also has the normative *power* to call for or demand an accounting from A

21 Waldron, 'The Concept and the Rule of Law', 19–36.

22 L. Fuller, *The Morality of Law*, revised edn. (New Haven: Yale University Press, 1969), 106.

23 *The Politics of Aristotle*, trans. and ed. E. Barker (Oxford: Clarendon Press, 1946), 146 (Bk. III, Ch. 16; 1287a29).

24 *Whitney* v. *California*, 274 U.S. 357, at 375 (Brandeis concurring).

for X, and B has a *claim* to that accounting which A is *obligated* to provide; (2) the liability, power, claim, and obligation all presuppose norms which authorize or provide warrant for B's claim and underwrite A's obligation; (3) A's act is norm governed in the sense that the accounting offered is expected to be articulated in terms of norms that warrant and justify it. Answerability – public answerability – to a charge or count is at the heart of the notion of accountability. B is authorized to demand both an *explanation* and a *reckoning*, a narrative and reasons or arguments connecting the act to relevant standards that could provide warrant and grounds for the act. B also has standing to assess the explanation and reckoning, and to utter a judgment of the action in light of his assessment of them.

Authorization to impose sanctions may be included in the remit of the party holding an agent to account, but it is not central to the concept of accountability. The opposite of accountability is not impunity (freedom from punitive response) but immunity (freedom from answerability). Accountability may 'lack teeth' without liability to formal sanctions, but that is not to say that accountability does not exist in the absence of enforcement. Adverse public judgment or denunciation of an accountable agent is usually undesirable from the point of view of that agent, and so accountability in its core sense will typically involve, not unintentionally, something akin to a sanction – Bentham misleadingly called it 'the moral sanction'[25] – but this informal consequence of adverse public judgment should not be confused with the explicit exercise of coercive force imposing a criminal or civil penalty. The former may be an inevitable and often intended consequence of acts of accountability-holding, but the latter is not.

It is worth noting that bureaucratic management is not a form of accountability in the sense relevant to the rule of law. Reporting relationships within a hierarchical bureaucratic structure may involve a kind of answerability, but the aim of bureaucratic supervision is adequate performance of a task defined by the bureaucracy's policy, not accountability to public norms. Moreover, supervision typically operates, and is meant to operate, out of the public eye. But the accountability that the rule of law insists upon is meant to be public. The rule of law calls for answerability *in* public and *to* some relevant public, although determinate individuals or agencies may have primary responsibility (and so authorization) for holding accountable agents publicly to account.

[25] See, for instance, Bentham, *Constitutional Code: Volume I*, ed. F. Rosen and J.H. Burns (Oxford: Clarendon Press, 1983 (*CW*)), 24; and Postema, 'Soul of Justice', Chapter 3 in this volume, 50–62.

Interlude: Harnessing the Unruly Horse

Whereas the core aim of the rule of law is protection and recourse against the arbitrary exercise of power through the instrumentality of law, the content of the ideal is typically thought to comprise a number of canonical standards or norms. The United Nations Secretary-General's Report of 2004 offers a familiar litany of such standards. The rule of law constitutes

> a principle of governance in which all persons, institutions and entities, public and private, including the State itself, are accountable to laws that are publicly promulgated, equally enforced and independently adjudicated, and which are consistent with international human rights norms and standards. It requires, as well, measures to ensure adherence to the principles of supremacy of law, equality before the law, accountability to the law, fairness in the application of the law, separation of powers, participation in decision-making, legal certainty, avoidance of arbitrariness and procedural and legal transparency.[26]

It would not be difficult to draw lines from the core aim of the rule of law to many of these component standards, although I will not do so here. They tend to fall into three groups. The first set includes standards governing the form of laws, and thereby of successful law-making – standards that require law to be general, consistent, prospective, accessible, intelligible, stable, and possible to comply with. The second set includes standards governing the institutions, procedures, and practices by which formally adequate laws are administered, adjudicated, and enforced. For example, they require that official enforcement of the rules be congruent with the publicly accessible rules of law and subject to official oversight and review; that adjudicative institutions be independent of the executive and legislature, widely accessible, open, impartial, and bound to reach judgments based on evidence and argument presented to them. They require that those called before such institutions have rights to representation by competent counsel, to present evidence and arguments and confront witnesses, to hear reasons from the tribunal for its decisions which are responsive to the evidence and arguments presented to it, and to appeal to a higher tribunal. In addition, all citizens and officials alike

[26] *Rule of Law and Transitional Justice*, 4. For similar lists (with notable exclusions and additions) see, for example, Fuller, *Morality of Law*, Ch. 2; Raz, *Authority of Law*, 214–18; J. Finnis, *Natural Law and Natural Rights* (Oxford: Clarendon Press, 1980), 270–3; J. Waldron, 'The Rule of Law and the Importance of Procedure', in *Nomos 50: Getting to the Rule of Law*, 3–31, at 5–7; T. Bingham, *The Rule of Law* (London: Penguin, 2010), Chs. 3–9.

are subject to the same law ('equality before the law'). These two sets of standards of legality are accepted by most defenders of the rule of law.

A third set of standards, imposing constraints on the content of laws and the policies it is designed to serve, has been more controversial. Indeed, Sir Ivor Jennings once called the idea of the rule of law 'an unruly horse',[27] because the content of the rule of law has been hotly disputed, not only by philosophers and legal theorists, but also public figures, politicians and government officials, domestic watchdog groups, and international development organizations. Some who have insisted on 'thicker' conceptions of the rule of law have sought to incorporate robust substantive standards of equality; others have insisted on including substantive civil rights or welfare rights; still others find 'Asian' or communitarian values essential to the rule of law, or argue for the inclusion of key institutions of democracy.[28] These disputes have been especially unsatisfying, typically relying on argument by stipulation, and frequently motivated by attempts to plant the flags of a favoured ideology in the soil of an allegedly universal value.

It is not part of my project in this chapter to enter this debate, but I do wish to point out that the reflections already undertaken here suggest a promising approach to harnessing this 'unruly horse' and moving the dispute from its current impasse. In the place of pitting stipulated lists of canonical standards against each other with selective appeals to intuition, might we not rather look for some organizing principle that will guide our choice of component principles. The core idea proposed earlier – that the *aim* of the rule of law is to provide protection and recourse against the arbitrary exercise of power through the instrumentality of distinctive

[27] I. Jennings, *The Law and the Constitution*, 5th edn. (University of London Press, 1959), 60.

[28] The list of standards set out in the United Nations Secretary-General's Report quoted earlier is echoed in M. Agrast, J. Botero, A. Ponce, and C. Pratt, *WJP Rule of Law Index 2012–2013* (Washington, DC: World Justice Project 2012–13), 7–9. According to the World Justice Project, the rule of law is a system in which the following four universal principles are upheld:

1. The government and its officials and agents as well as individuals and private entities are accountable under the law.
2. The laws are clear, publicized, stable and just, are applied evenly, and protect fundamental rights, including the security of persons and property.
3. The process by which the laws are enacted, administered, and enforced is accessible, fair, and efficient.
4. Justice is delivered timely by competent, ethical, and independent representatives and neutrals who are of sufficient number, have adequate resources, and reflect the makeup of the communities they serve.

For discussion of various competing conceptions of the rule of law in contemporary China, see R. Peerenboom, *China's Long March toward Rule of Law* (Cambridge University Press, 2002), Ch. 3.

features of law – provides a basis for determining which standards are eligible for inclusion in a conception of the rule of law, and which, despite their intrinsic appeal, are not eligible. It also provides an organizing principle that can give structure and coherence to a proposed conception.

We are also encouraged to push our enquiry deeper. The core idea captures an attractive, middle-level political aim, but we can ask why seek protection and recourse against the arbitrary exercise of power, and what values or principles ground this core aim? Several answers suggest themselves. Some believe that it is necessary to protect individual freedom of choice and action (so-called negative liberty); others locate its value in the distinctive way in which it respects and serves individual human dignity; others are attracted to it because it respects and promotes the republican value of liberty as non-domination. It might also be seen to serve communitarian values that protect and promote thick communal values and community control.

Although I personally find the republican defence the most compelling,[29] the point I wish to emphasize here is that the rule of law's defining aim can be defended from a number of different quarters. There is nothing necessarily individualist or Western about the core idea itself. The aim of protecting against abuse of power, providing securities against misrule, and defining a framework of secure communal relations has broad cross-cultural appeal. The rule of law is a powerful political idea and ideal, but it is not an essentially Western one. Its institutions are meant to hold power accountable – not just the political power of big governments, not just the economic and social power of large corporate entities, but exercises of power wherever they can be found in the polity. Of course, the ideal of the rule of law represents a challenge and hence a threat to power wherever it is established and entrenched, but this challenge is not alien to political communities; it is indigenous wherever and for whatever reason corruption, abuse, and unchecked *arbitrium* are seen as cancerous evils in the body politic. This is not to say that different accounts of the grounds of the rule of law ideal will not reasonably influence the choice of standards and institutions that are thought directly to serve this idea. But disputes about such implications of the ideal are more manageable if the core idea and its proposed, albeit competing, grounds

[29] On the republican notion of freedom see Pettit, *On the People's Terms* (Cambridge University Press, 2013), Ch. 1. On the relationship between republican freedom and the rule of law, see Pettit, 'Republican Legal Theory', in S. Besson and J.L. Martí (eds.), *Legal Republicanism* (Oxford University Press, 2009), 39–59. See also N. Simmonds, *Law as a Moral Idea* (Oxford University Press, 2007), 101–4, 109–10, 142–3.

are explicitly acknowledged and taken as bases for further exploration and deliberation.

The focus of this chapter, however, is not on the grounds or content of the ideal of the rule of law, but rather on the conditions of its realization. For this purpose, it is possible to take as our starting point the core idea of the rule of law, understood as a middle-level political value, capable of being defended in a number of different ways from different ideological perspectives, and at least committed to, but not necessarily restricted to, a relatively 'thin' conception of the rule of law.

Legality and Fidelity

The idea of the rule of law is the idea of a *realized condition*, like Kant's *rechtlicher Zustand*. 'A rightful condition', Kant wrote, 'is that relation of human beings among one another that contains the conditions under which alone everyone is able to *enjoy* his rights'.[30] This rightful condition is not the mere idea of right or rights, or even of a universal scheme of reciprocal rights; it is the realization of this idea. In this condition, individual right-bearers *enjoy* their rights, not in the sense that the rights are always and necessarily respected, but rather in the sense that practices and institutions needed for effective claiming of the rights and recourse against infringements of the rights exist, and, therefore, they are widely respected and function as the ground rules for the relations among participants in this condition. The rule of law, I maintain, is likewise a necessarily realized ideal. For it to exist, it must be realized in a given polity. Conditions of its realization are conditions of its existence in that polity – of course, it can be more or less robust, and it can exist in a severely diminished or marginal form. To say that the rule of law is robust in a polity is not to say that political or social power is never abused, but rather that such abuses, when they occur and the rule of law equilibrium is disturbed, are addressed, parties responsible are held accountable, and equilibrium is restored.

To understand the conditions necessary for the realization of the rule of law in a polity, we must look beyond the canonical formal and procedural standards widely accepted as components of the rule of law ideal, and even beyond the more controversial substantive principles often proposed. We

[30] I. Kant, 'The Metaphysics of Morals', 'Part I. Metaphysical first principles of the doctrine of right', § 41, in Kant, *Practical Philosophy*, trans. and ed. M.J. Gregor (Cambridge University Press, 1996), 370–506, at 450.

must look to and explore what I have called the dimension of *fidelity.* The rule of law, I maintain, comprises not only (a) a set of standards for laws and for the conduct of governmental agents, and (b) a set of core legal institutions and procedures for administration of these laws, but also and crucially a third component: (c) an *ethos,* a set of relationships and responsibilities rooted in core convictions and commitments. I refer to the sets of standards and institutions constituting and articulating the rule of law as components of the idea of *legality*; I refer to the set of relationships, responsibilities, convictions, and commitments constituting the ethos of the rule of law as the ideal of *fidelity.* Legality and fidelity combine to form the ideal of the rule of law. My thesis is that we cannot adequately understand the ideal of the rule of law without giving full credit to fidelity to law.

This is not an original idea. Philip Selznick and many legal theorists after him have argued for the importance to the rule of law of 'a culture of lawfulness'.[31] 'Power and culture, not law and institutions, form the roots of a rule of law state',[32] writes Rachel Kleinfeld for the Carnegie Endowment for International Peace. Evaluating nation-building efforts in the last few decades, development theorists have come to realize that 'without a widely shared cultural commitment to the idea of the rule of law courts are just buildings, judges are just bureaucrats, and constitutions are just pieces of paper'.[33] Similarly, Brian Tamanaha argues:

> For the rule of law to exist, people must believe in and be committed to the rule of law. They must take it for granted as a necessary and proper aspect of their society. This attitude is not itself a legal rule. It amounts to a shared cultural belief. When this cultural belief is pervasive, the rule of law can be resilient, spanning generations and surviving episodes in which the rule of law has been flouted by government officials. . . . When this cultural belief is not pervasive, the rule of law will be weak or non-existent.[34]

[31] P. Selznick, 'Legal Cultures and the Rule of Law', in *The Rule of Law after Communism*, ed. M. Krygier and A. Czarnota (Aldershot: Ashgate, 1999), 21–38, at 37. See also R. Kleinfeld, *Advancing the Rule of Law Abroad* (Washington, DC: Carnegie Endowment for International Peace, 2012), 20, 243–4n.

[32] Kleinfeld, *Advancing the Rule of Law Abroad*, 15.

[33] J. Stromseth, D. Wippman, and R. Brooks, *Can Might Make Rights? Building the Rule of Law after Military Interventions* (Cambridge University Press, 2006), 76. In their chapter 'Creating Rule of Law Cultures' they write: 'the rule of law can neither be created nor sustained unless most people in a given society recognize its value and have a reasonable amount of faith in its efficacy' (310).

[34] B. Tamanaha, 'The History and Elements of the Rule of Law', *Singapore Journal of Legal Studies* (2012), 232–47, at 246.

But I want to argue that what is needed is not merely a faith in the idea and efficacy of the rule of law, but rather a shared commitment among officials and citizens to make it work. The task is to explore what is involved in this shared commitment.

Lon Fuller offered a useful point of departure. In his argument for the moral significance of the rule of law (the inner morality of law, as he called it), Fuller maintained that rule of law presupposes and reinforces a partnership, a set of robust reciprocal commitments, between government officials and ordinary citizens.[35] The eight canons, he argued, articulate this partnership, rulers pledging to rule by and to be ruled by law, and ordinary citizens allowing their conduct to be governed by those who so pledge. Reciprocal compliance with the law is at the core of his notion of fidelity. Fuller took it to be a distinctively moral virtue, because it involved faithfulness to a matrix of shared responsibilities that are taken seriously and practised with commitment in a political community.

But reciprocal compliance is not the whole of fidelity; fidelity also entails positive efforts on the part of citizens that complement those of officials. In Bentham's view, the law's rule ultimately 'depends upon the spirit, the intelligence, the vigilance, the alertness, the intrepidity, the energy, the perseverance, of those of whose opinions Public Opinion is composed'.[36] Similarly, Adam Ferguson argued:

> the influence of laws, where they have any real effect in the preservation of liberty [depends on] . . . the influence of men resolved to be free; of men, who, having adjusted in writing the terms on which they are to live with the state, and with their fellow-subjects, are determined, by their vigilance and spirit, to make these terms be observed.[37]

Fidelity is expressed not only in compliance with law and with the standards of legality, but also in active taking of responsibility for 'making the terms' of law's rule 'be observed'. This involves taking responsibility for holding partners in the relationship to their respective duties. Fidelity involves mutual accountability as well as reciprocal compliance.

The focus of legality is formal and institutional, but the focus of fidelity is *ethical* in two ways. First, it is concerned with the ethos or culture of a

35 See Postema, *Legal Philosophy in the Twentieth Century: The Common Law World* (Dordrecht: Springer, 2011), 157–8 and references to Fuller's work there.

36 Bentham, *Securities Against Misrule* (*CW*), 139.

37 A. Ferguson, *An Essay on the History of Civil Society* (first published 1767), ed. F. Oz-Salzberger (Cambridge University Press, 1995), 249.

polity, the mutual understandings and associated practices of people in a community in which the rule of law is realized. Second, it is concerned with the mutual responsibilities borne by members of law's ethos, including the responsibility to hold each other to faithful execution of these responsibilities. Thus, the rule of law is robust in a polity just when its members take responsibility for holding each other, and especially law's officials, to account under the law. Fidelity of citizens and officials alike, properly speaking, is a matter of fidelity neither *to law* nor *to government*, but rather of fidelity *to each other*.

It is possible to argue for the necessity of fidelity for the realization of the rule of law – for law's rule – on empirical grounds, but the argument in this chapter is conceptual and normative. To focus the argument, it will help to see how the problematic of law's rule arises. This problematic was familiar already to ancient and medieval legal theorists.

Bulwark, Bridle, and Bond

In his *History*, Thucydides wrote that when people want to impose their wills on others, they first seek to 'destroy without a trace the laws that commonly govern such matters', not realizing that 'it is only because of these that someone in trouble can hope to be saved, and anyone might be in danger some day and stand in need of such laws'.[38] Thus, it is imperative that, as Heraclitus observed: 'The people... fight for the law as they would for the city walls.'[39] Law, on this ancient idea, is a bulwark against domination by others. In this vein, some, such as Hobbes,[40] thought of law narrowly as a 'hedge' against power wielded by one's fellows, whereas others, such as Locke,[41] construed it more broadly as a framework of common rules giving equal status in the community to each member. But

[38] Thucydides, *History* 3. 84; quoted in *Early Greek Political Thought from Homer to the Sophists*, eds. M. Gagarin and P. Woodruff (Cambridge University Press, 1995), 108.

[39] Quoted in Gagarin and Woodruff, *Early Greek Political Thought*, 152.

[40] T. Hobbes, *Leviathan* (first published in 1651), 3 vols., ed. N. Malcolm (Oxford: Clarendon Press, 2012 (*The Clarendon Edition of the Works of Thomas Hobbes: Vols. III–V*)), ii. 540 (Ch. 30). In 1660, the authors of the Preamble to the *Book of the General Lawes and Libertyes* [of Massachusetts] wrote, 'Laws are the people's Birth-right.... By this Hedge their All is secured against the Injuries of men.' (Quoted in John Phillip Reid, *Rule of Law: The Jurisprudence of Liberty in the Seventeenth and Eighteenth Centuries* (DeKalb: Northern Illinois University Press, 2004), 51.)

[41] Locke, 'Second Treatise', 283–4 (§ 22), 304 (§ 54), 305–6 (§ 57).

in either case, law's first task on this view was not to structure governing power, but to articulate a mode of social ordering, to constitute a mode of association.

For law to succeed in this task, that is to say, for law to rule in this dimension, it is not enough for formally valid laws to be enacted and in some sense in place; law must be used in the right way in the community governed by it.[42] It must play a vital role in the day-to-day normative economy of its members; it must be regularly used and commonly expected to be used, not just as restraint upon choice and action, but also as a resource for vindication of their own actions and for justification of anticipations and assessments of the actions of others. Law must not merely *exist* as measured by conventional positivist criteria, law must also *count*.[43]

For laws to function, they must be to a large extent self-executing. Those to whom the laws are addressed must be capable of grasping, and expect most others to grasp, their import across a large range of their application. Not only would laws collapse of their own weight if they depended at virtually every point of their application on official interpretation, but they would fail to function *as laws*, providing general normative guidance. Nevertheless, it has been understood from ancient times that public norms can function as laws only if they are underwritten by institutions for their interpretation, application, enforcement, and enactment. So we charge political authorities with the task of executing law and ordering social relations through law. But, this creates a new problem. 'In framing a government which is to be administered by men over men', James Madison observed, 'the great difficulty lies in this: you must first enable the government to control the governed; and in the next place oblige it to control itself'.[44] To Juvenal's question, '*Sed quis custodiet ipsos custodes*?'[45] the ancient answer was, again, *the law*.

Of course, it was expected that the guardians would rule with and through the law. Indeed, it has been easy for power to grasp the political

[42] For an analysis of what is involved in law's being 'used in the right way', see G. J. Postema, 'Conformity, Custom, and Congruence: Rethinking the Efficacy of Law', in *The Legacy of H.L.A. Hart: Legal, Political, and Moral Philosophy*, ed. M. Kramer, C. Grant, M. Colburn, and A. Hatzistavrou (Oxford University Press, 2008), 45–65.

[43] M. Krygier, 'The Rule of Law: Legality, Teleology, and Sociology', in *Re-locating the Rule of Law*, ed. G. Palombella and N. Walker (Oxford: Hart, 2000), 45–70, at 60.

[44] A. Hamilton, J. Madison, and J. Jay, *The Federalist Papers*, ed. L. Goldman (Oxford University Press, 2008), (No. 51), 256–60, at 257.

[45] That is, 'Who guards the guardians?', Juvenal, *Satires*, in *Juvenal and Persius*, ed. and trans. S.M. Braund (Cambridge, MA: Harvard University Press, 2004), 266 (vi, 347–8).

advantages of rule *by* law and embrace it publicly.[46] Edward I, the legendary 'English Justinian', Hume tells us, 'took care that his subjects should do justice to each other; but he desired always to have his own hand free in all his transactions, both with them and with his neighbours'.[47] Ruling powers have often thought they had good reason to follow the advice of Justinian's prince: 'Although we stand above the laws . . . we live by the laws.'[48] But, Ferguson observed, laws embraced on grounds of political prudence 'serve only to cover, not to restrain, the iniquities of power: they are possibly respected even by the corrupt magistrate, when they favour his purpose; but they are contemned or evaded, when they stand in his way'.[49]

The rule *of* law demands more. Bracton, the thirteenth-century English jurist, wrote: 'The king must not be under man but under God and under the law, because law makes the king, [Let him therefore bestow upon the law what the law bestows upon him, namely, rule and power.] for there is no *rex* where will rules rather than *lex*.'[50] 'Let him, therefore, temper his power by law, which is the bridle of power, that he may live according to the laws'.[51] In Plato's view, law must be master over the rulers, and rulers slaves of the law.[52] Law is not only power's instrument, but law is also power's *bridle*. The rule of law obtains in a polity just when *law rules* those who purport to rule with law. *Reflexivity* – law ruling those who rule with law and in its name – is the rule of law's sine qua non.

However, Bracton's image of a bridle is revealing. The idea at the core of the rule of law is not merely that laws *apply* to those who exercise political

46 Hobbes was a vigorous advocate of rule *by* law (see *Leviathan*, ii. 414–97 (Chs. 26–8), 520–53 (Ch. 30). So too were Hans Feizi and the Legalist tradition of Chinese legal theory: see Peerenboom, *China's Long March*, 32–3; K. Winston, 'The Internal Morality of Chinese Legalism', *Singapore Journal of Legal Studies* (2005), 313–47. Neither embraced the rule *of* law.

47 D. Hume, *The History of England from the Invasion of Julius Caesar to the Revolution in 1688* (first published 1754–63), 6 vols. (Indianapolis: Liberty Classics, 1983), ii. 143.

48 *Justinian's Institutes*, trans. P. Birks and G. McLeod (London: Duckworth, 1987), 78–9 (II. xvii. 8).

49 Ferguson, *Essay on the History of Civil Society*, 249.

50 H. de Bracton, *Bracton on the Laws and Customs of England*, ed. and trans. S.E. Thorne, 4 vols., (Cambridge, MA: Belknap Press, 1968–77), ii. 33.

51 Ibid., 305.

52 See Plato, *Laws*, trans R.G. Bury, 2 vols. (London: Heinemann, 1926) i. 292–3 (IV: 715D). Likewise, Richard Hooker writes: 'Though no manner person or cause be unsubject to the king's power, yet so is the power of the king over all and in all limited that unto all his proceedings the law itself is a rule.' R. Hooker, *Of the Laws of Ecclesiastical Polity* (written in the 1590s, Bk. VIII first published in 1648), ed. A.S. McGrade (Cambridge University Press, 1989), 147 (Bk. VIII, Ch. 3. § 3).

power (as well as ordinary members of the polity), or offer normative guidance to those who fall within their scope, but in addition that those who fall within its scope are *subject to* the law. And with this thought, our problem returns: for the bridle directs the horse only when it is in the hands of the rider. How, then, are we to understand law's claim to rule? For, after all, laws don't rule, only people do.

At this point, Bracton fell back on what was then a famous, albeit much debated, passage of the *Corpus Iuris Civilis*, writing: 'it is a saying worthy of the majesty of a ruler that the prince acknowledge himself bound by the laws. Nothing is more fitting for a sovereign than to live by the laws, nor is there any greater sovereignty than to govern according to law.'[53] In Machiavelli's story, Pluto, chief of the princes of Hell, insisted that he 'cannot be bound by any judgment whatever, be it earthly or heavenly'; but nevertheless accepted that 'it is a sign of great wisdom when they who have supreme power allow themselves to be ruled by law'.[54] This seems to fall well short of what Bracton and the *Codex* had in mind. In contrast, Bracton insisted that the 'majesty' of those in power calls for them to *acknowledge and profess* themselves to be bound by law. That is, law rules just insofar as those to whom it applies *submit* to its rule.[55]

How are we to understand this thought? It suggests that law rules when those whom law purports to govern *impose* its rule *on themselves* (when it is not or cannot be imposed by others). Law's rule is *self-imposed*. However, early commentators on the *Codex*, Accursius for example,[56] rejected this reading. To be bound by self-imposed resolves, or self-commands, they argued, is not to be bound *by law*. The problem is not that personal resolves are, as a psychological matter, difficult to keep, but rather that submission to law cannot be a matter of submission to *oneself*. We have

53 *Bracton on the Laws and Customs of England*, ii. 305–6, closely paraphrasing Justinian's *Codex*, I. xiv. 4. See *Codex Iustinianus*, ed. P. Krüger (Berlin: Weidmann, 1877/Goldbach: Keip, 1998), 103: '*Digna vox maiestate regnantibus legibus alligatum se principem profiteri: adeo de auctoritate iuris nostra pendet auctoritas, et re vera maius imperio est submittere legibus principatum.*'

54 N. Machiavelli, 'Balfagor Arcidiavolo', in *La Mandragola, La Clizia, Belfagor, Classici del Ridere*, ed. A.F. Formiggini (Rome, 1927), 133–4. The passage is translated by Inez Kotterman-van de Vosse in her 'Hayek on the Rule of Law', in *Hayek, Co-ordination and Evolution*, eds. J. Birner and R. van Zijp (New York: Routledge, 1994), 255–72, at 255.

55 Hobbes, who insists on rule *by* law, but decisively rejects the notion that the sovereign is subject to the (civil) law, makes a point of rejecting Bracton's *Codex*-inspired dictum. See *Leviathan*, ii. 520 (Ch. 30): 'he deserteth the Means, that being the Soveraign, acknowledgeth himselfe subject to the Civill Lawes; and renounceth the Power of Supreme Judicature'.

56 See B. Tierney, '"The Prince is Not Bound": Accursius and the Origins of the Modern State', *Comparative Studies in Society and History* 5 (1963), 378–400, at 391.

now come to the crux of the problem of law's rule. To understand law's rule, we must understand what it is to be subject to law, and in particular what it is to submit to law, that is, to undertake the commitment to be ruled by law.

The thesis of this chapter is that law can rule only when those who are subject to it, the prince and officials of government and citizens alike, are bound together in a thick network of mutual accountability with respect to that law. The rule of law is robust in a polity only when the members of that polity undertake and carry out commitments of mutual faithfulness to a set of differentiated and interconnected responsibilities, core among them being the responsibility to hold each other accountable under law. That is, law rules only when planted firmly in the rich soil of fidelity.

The Necessity of Mutual Accountability[57]

The rule of law insists that any exercise of power in the polity, including any act of holding another accountable under the law, must be subject to law; its agent must have warrant from law to do so, warrant that provides the agent *standing* to exercise power over the other party and (typically, if not in every case) a *standard* guiding that exercise of power. Likewise, someone subject to the exercise of power thus authorized is expected to obey, that is, not only to comply, but also to act in response to and recognition of the warrant. The relationship between the parties is essentially normative, defined by law. Not only is each party governed by the law that defines this relationship, but also each is subject to that law; and to be subject to the law, which authorizes holding another accountable, is necessarily to be accountable to others participating in a network of accountability. The central thesis of this paper is that to submit to law's bridle is to submit to a network of mutual accountability.

The first step we must take in defence of this thesis is to prove *Hobbes's Thesis.* In the course of his argument that the sovereign cannot be subject to the civil law, Hobbes maintained that he that 'setteth the Lawes above the Soveraign, setteth also a Judge above him'.[58] To commit to law, on Hobbes's view, just is to undertake a commitment to others and thus to allow oneself to be held accountable by others. Aquinas argued the contrary thesis, that although the sovereign ruler is not exempt from the

57 I summarize here the argument set out in full in 'Fidelity in Law's Commonwealth'.

58 Hobbes, *Leviathan*, ii. 504 (Ch. 29).

directive power of law, he or she is exempt from its *coercive power* (and, presumably, from accountability more generally).[59] *Aquinas's Thesis* is that one can be subject to the law but not accountable to any other judge. But one who claims to submit to the law but denies accountability to any other party claims exclusive standing to judge one's own interpretation of its applications to particular cases. We must reject Aquinas's Thesis because the notion of exclusive standing to judge the validity and application of a norm entails a contradiction.[60]

Suppose that someone claims to hold another person accountable, and in that way exercise authority over that person. To do so is to claim to act with warrant of some law. That entails a complex judgment, P, to the effect that one's action properly falls under some legal norm and that that norm is in some relevant sense valid or binding on one. As a *judgment*, P points behind the person making the judgment to the matter judged of; it claims to be a judgment *of* that matter (the relationship between the person's conduct, the norm, and some ground of the validity of the norm). P is necessarily *judgment-maker-transcending*. So, to judge that one's act is warranted is, necessarily, to claim *self-transcending* warrant. However, simultaneously to claim exclusive standing to judge the matter is, in effect, to say that one's saying ('judging') makes it so – ipse dixit, as Bentham was fond of saying. It is to deny the claim implicit in the judgment to transcend the assessor's making of the judgment. To deny the office of others to assess one's assessments, to judge one's judgments, is simultaneously to claim and deny self-transcending warrant.

Thus, self-validating judgments are not merely false judgments, they are failed judgments – utterances that fail as judgments. So, submission to law can never be a matter of self-imposition or self-authorizing; *self-authorizing is failed authorizing.* The problem is not that we cannot count on such people to follow through, because their self-professions or self-judgments are escapable, but rather that there is a contradiction between the explicit and implicit claims made by such an alleged authority. To be *solely self*-accountable is to be accountable *to no one.* Thus, we must reject Aquinas's Thesis and embrace Hobbes's Thesis: to be subject to the law entails that one is accountable to others. An unaccountable accountability-holder is a contradiction in terms.

59 See Thomas Aquinas, *Summa Theologiæ: Volume 28 Law and Political Theory*, ed. T. Gilby (Cambridge: Blackfriars, 1966), 134–7 (ɪaɪɪae, Qu. 96, Art. 5, Resp. 3).

60 Bentham also rejected the notion of self-imposed legal restrictions. See Postema, 'Soul of Justice', Chapter 3 in this volume, 58–9.

According to Hobbes's Thesis, to submit to law is to submit to *another*, to acknowledge the standing of another to hold one accountable. Kant extended this thesis when he wrote that 'no one can rightfully bind another to something without also being subject to a law by which he in turn can be bound in the same way by the other.'[61] According to *Kant's Thesis*, to submit to law, is, necessarily, to submit to *reciprocal* (or at least *mutual*) accountability. If A claims to bind S and to hold S accountable to this obligation, A is also subject to network of accountability to others in which S also participates.

The argument for Kant's Thesis emerges from a dilemma to which Hobbes's Thesis leads us. Note, first, that one can embrace Hobbes's Thesis but reject Kant's, for one party might be subject to another party without that other being reciprocally accountable to them (directly or indirectly), so that accountability relationships could be linked in a transitive but non-reflexive chain: A could accountable to B, B to C, C to D and so on. Indeed, Hobbes thought this must be the case, because in his view to be subject (i.e., accountable) to another party is to be *subordinate* to that other party. In his view, accountability relationships are necessarily transitive and non-reflexive. With respect to Hobbesian chains of accountability, we face two options: either the series goes on infinitely or it stops at some point. An infinite series would be a conceptual, or at least a practical absurdity. So, Hobbes argued, we are forced to accept the other option: the series must stop at some point.[62]

But that is to say that any such chain of accountability relationships must end with an unaccountable accountability-holder. Hobbes embraced this result, concluding that the ruling sovereign *cannot* be subject to the civil law. But the result is not a happy one, and we cannot coherently embrace it because the notion of an unaccountable accountability-holder is incoherent. Of course, it is not incoherent or impossible for someone to stand outside the accountability-holding nexus and exercise arbitrary coercive power; but it is impossible for someone to claim to *hold another accountable* and to claim to be unaccountable. For to claim to hold another accountable is to claim to participate in a normatively structured accountability relationship and to claim warrant for one's accountability-holding in some norm presupposed by that relationship,

[61] I. Kant, 'Toward Perpetual Peace', in Kant, *Practical Philosophy*, 311–51, at 323n (original emphasis removed).

[62] See *Leviathan*, ii. 504 (Ch. 29). See also Hobbes, *On the Citizen*, eds. R. Tuck and M. Silverthorne (Cambridge University Press, 1998), 88 (Ch. 6. § 18).

a norm to which one thereby is subject. But to be subject to a norm, as we have seen, is to be accountable to another. An unaccountable accountability-holder is not something to be feared; it is strictly impossible. It appears, then, that Hobbes's Thesis leads us either to one absurdity (an infinite series of accountability relationships) or to another (an unaccountable accountability-holder).

But it need not. For we are forced to these absurd results only if we accept Hobbes's implicit *Hierarchy Thesis*, the view that to be subject to another party is to be *subordinate* to that other party, and hence, that accountability relationships are necessarily transitive and non-reflexive. We can avoid incoherence by embracing the modified version of Kant's Thesis: If the rule of law is to be conceptually possible, accountability must be at least *mutual*. S's submission to A does not preclude A's submission – direct or perhaps indirect – to S. It may not be that A is *reciprocally* accountable *to S*, but A and S must be participants in what we might call an *accountability loop* or *accountability network*. Thus, law's rule requires submission of all in a polity – officials of all ranks and citizens alike – to the law, but, as we can now see, that entails that all submit to and participate in a network of mutual accountability.

A limiting case of this accountability loop can be found in the medieval doctrine of 'double sovereignty', championed by the glossator, Azo of Bologna in the early thirteenth century.[63] Applying the Roman law doctrine of corporations to the polity itself, Azo argued that although the emperor was superior to every individual, he was subordinate to the people regarded as a corporate whole (*universitas*): 'The emperor does not have more power than the whole people but than each individual of the people.'[64] (The prince is *major singulis universis minor.*) Here the loop is tight: the emperor holds the people regarded in *sensu diviso* accountable, but they, participating in the corporate whole, in turn hold the emperor accountable. Thus, S is accountable to A, but A is accountable S* – the *universitas* in which S participates. This, however, is a limiting case of mutual accountability, since the hierarchical assumption is retained, as was made clear by Jacques de Révigny's gloss on Azo's doctrine: 'It is true that the emperor is superior to each one of the people, but he is not superior to the people', he wrote, 'the people has no superior'.[65] The emperor

[63] See B. Tierney, *Religion and the Growth of Constitutional Thought 1150–1650* (Cambridge University Press, 1982), 56–60.

[64] Quoted in ibid., 58.

[65] Quoted in ibid., 58.

retains sovereignty over individuals, but the people is sovereign over the emperor. Sovereign authority on this view is still hierarchical.

Another limiting case is suggested by Philip Hunton, a seventeenth-century contemporary of Hobbes.[66] The king is limited by law, and hence subject to judgment of the people, he argued. Such limitation is not absurd, as Royalists such as Filmer argued, because 'this power of judging argues not a superiority of those who Judge, over him who is Judged'. This seems to reject the Hierarchy Thesis, but then Hunton embraces it again, explaining that no superiority is assumed since the power

> is not Authoritative and Civill, but morall, residing in reasonable Creatures and lawful for them to execute, because never devested and put off by any act in the constitution of a legall Government, but rather the reservation of it intended: For when they define the Superiour to a Law, and constitute no Power to Judge of his Excesses from that Law, it is evident they reserve to themselves, not a Formall Authoritative Power but a morall Power.[67]

Hunton locates ultimate, albeit only moral, authority in the people, but leaves in place the *Hierarchy Thesis* underwriting the doctrine of sovereignty, authority, and accountability.

However, if our argument above is compelling, we must push the idea of mutual accountability beyond these limiting cases, for if such sovereignty, wherever it is located, entails an unaccountable accountability-holder, then it is vulnerable to the *reductio* we set out earlier. Mutual accountability in a wide network is not ultimately an expression of popular sovereignty, but an alternative to it. The accountability at the core of the ideal of law's rule appears to be incompatible with the notion of sovereignty.

Accountability Networks, Some Examples

What would such an accountability loop look like? Formally speaking, it might take the form of some extended analogue of the children's game rock-paper-scissors: scissors cut paper; paper covers rock; rock blunts scissors.[68] More likely, the relationships of accountability will intersect in

66 P. Hunton, *A Treatise of Monarchy* (London, 1643). Jean Hampton discusses Hunton's argument in 'Democracy and the Rule of Law', in *Nomos 36: The Rule of Law*, ed. I. Shapiro (New York University Press, 1994), 13–45, at 20–3.

67 Ibid., 21.

68 See C.D. Kenney, 'Horizontal Accountability: Concepts and Conflicts', in *Democratic Accountability in Latin America*, ed. S. Mainwaring and C. Welna (Oxford University Press, 2003), 55–76, at 65.

many different ways, forming a network rather than a circle. One familiar example is available in the constitutionalist doctrine of intragovernmental checks and balances. Governmental powers are not only divided and allocated to different, relatively autonomous, branches, but the jurisdiction of each given branch also penetrates to some extent the jurisdictions of other branches. Mutual accountability-holding requires more than power sharing, and not every form of power limiting is also a mode of accountability-holding. Requiring that legislation be passed by both houses of a bicameral legislature limits the power of each house, and so 'balances' their power, but it does not make the exercise of the power of one house accountable to the other house. Accountability entails the liberty and power to demand an accounting for the exercise of power. Intragovernmental accountability depends on a network of agencies empowered to hold each other accountable.

'Bottom-up' accountability in the 'vertical' political dimension is also familiar. Where the rule of law is adequately realized, the exercises of power by civil authorities taken under colour of law can be challenged in court. Not only can demands be made for a public showing of the alleged operative facts on which the exercise of power is premised, but those subjected to this exercise of power can also demand that the authorities' warrant for so acting be produced publicly, and can challenge its validity, interpretation, and application. Citizens are accountable to authorities, but so too are authorities accountable to citizens, through the offices of the court.

Courts play an essential role in public accountability of both governmental and non-governmental power. But they are only one, albeit a prominent, node of a healthy network of accountability. Media, social groups and associations, non-governmental or non-profit institutions and the like also play critical roles. One example of such accountability-holding occurred in 2004 in Greensboro, North Carolina.[69] Twenty-five years earlier, members of the Ku Klux Klan and the American Nazi Party attacked labour union activists and members of an organization with ties to the Communist Workers' Party during the latter's demonstration in a low-income neighbourhood in Greensboro. The city police were notably absent from the demonstration. Five demonstrators were killed and ten severely injured. In subsequent trials, all Klan and Nazi defendants were

[69] See D.K. Androff, Jr., 'Can Civil Society Reclaim Truth? Results from a Community-Based Truth and Reconciliation Commission', *The International Journal of Transitional Justice*, 6 (2012), 296–317.

acquitted. City officials sought to move on after what had come to be called the 'Greensboro Massacre', and the local media did little to resist their efforts, but racial and civic tensions kept resentment alive. In 2004, a group of citizens sought support from the city council to establish a truth commission on the model of the Truth and Reconciliation Commission of South Africa. The city council refused to support the attempt and sought to stifle it. But the Greensboro citizens persisted. They set up an ad hoc truth commission with financial support from a local private foundation. At the commission hearings, evidence was presented documenting and exposing failures of the city police department, city government, and the criminal and civil justice systems.[70] This citizen-initiated, privately funded effort illustrates how a community's sense of responsibility to hold officials accountable, even twenty-five years after the fact, can be given concrete form. The 'kids for cash' scandal discussed at the opening of this chapter illustrates the failure of fidelity in a community; this case illustrates fidelity at work.

Two Latin American scholars offer another example.[71] The body of a high school student was found on the outskirts of an Argentine city in a province in which political corruption, nepotism, and clientelism were widespread. Police and city officials ignored the case, but people in the city were outraged and organized a large number of silent demonstrations – *marchas de silencio* – to demand an investigation and a speedy trial. The protest engaged the local media and, as national media took up the case, marches were organized in other cities around the country. Eventually officials were forced to investigate and bring the case to trial. Through the efforts of the murdered child's father, a 'Commission for Justice and Truth' was established consisting of nuns, human rights activists, trade unionists, teachers, neighbours, and others. This Commission kept watch over the police investigation and trial. During the trial, the judges repeatedly made decisions systematically favouring the defence, compromising the impartiality of the court. The Commission and national media kept the spotlight on the proceedings and, after massive demonstrations, the trial was suspended and a new trial was begun some months later. In this case, individuals, social organizations, ad hoc institutions, and eventually

70 The Commission's Executive Summary is available at www.greensborotrc.org/exec_summary.pdf.

71 C. Smulovitz and E. Peruzzotti, 'Societal and Horizontal Controls: Two Cases of a Fruitful Relationship', in *Democratic Accountability in Latin America*, ed. Mainwaring and Welna, 309–31, at 317–23.

formal institutions of law worked together and on each other to hold individuals and public authorities accountable.

Fidelity: Ethics and Institutions

Fidelity is the *ethos* of law; it is first of all a matter of ethics, that is, a matter of personal and collective mutual commitments and the practices that give them concrete content, but institutions are also needed to support and underwrite this ethos. Let us consider first some dimensions of the ethics of fidelity.

With regard to judges, for example, fidelity calls for impartiality, fairness to parties in litigation, openness to evidence and argument from all quarters, a commitment to make reasoned, principled decisions based on the evidence and argument presented in court. Judges must see to it that law, rather than personal relations, is the lingua franca of the courts. It also calls for a deep, jealously guarded conviction regarding their independence from other branches of government. In some legal systems, institutional dependence of the judiciary on executive or legislative branches of government is secured through training judges to regard themselves as bureaucrats administering government policy, rather than independent professionals interpreting public laws. As a result, correction of the institutional obstacles to judicial independence in such countries will not succeed without fundamental change in the judicial ethos.[72] A similar commitment to professional independence amongst lawyers is critical for robust fidelity.

Fidelity also makes demands on the attitudes of ordinary citizens and the practices that express and nourish those attitudes. As noted earlier, for law to rule in a polity law must *count* among ordinary citizens as well as officials; it must occupy a prominent place in the normative economy of members of the polity. Law cannot rule where apathy due

[72] Failures of this ethical sort were evident, for example, in apartheid South Africa. See D. Dyzenhaus, *Judging the Judges, Judging Ourselves* (Oxford: Hart, 1998). The report of the Truth Commission for El Salvador offers a second chilling example. The Commission highlighted the 'appalling submissiveness' of the El Salvador judiciary during period of war and dictatorship in the 1980s, and 'the glaring inability of the judicial system either to investigate crimes or to enforce the law, especially when it comes to crimes committed with the direct or indirect support of State institutions'. See UN Security Council, Annex, *From Madness to Hope: the 12-year war in El Salvador: Report of the Commission on the Truth for El Salvador*, S/25500, 1993, posted by the United States Institute of Peace at www.usip.org/publications/truth-commission-el-salvador, 163, 168.

to alienation or indifference is the dominant popular attitude. Martin Krygier reports the Bulgarian saying to the effect that 'the law is like a door in the middle of an open field. Of course, you could go through the door, but only a fool would bother'.[73] This attitude eviscerates the rule of law. No less debilitating is popular tolerance, or resigned acceptance, of corruption. Paula Dobriansky, U.S. Undersecretary of State for Global Affairs, observed that 'corruption is not just a government problem, it is also a social problem'.[74] It is a social problem in two respects: corruption of government officials which is expected or tolerated is allowed to grow unchecked and unchallenged, and toleration of governmental corruption tends to nourish a like corruption in relations among ordinary citizens.

It is also difficult for fidelity to flourish in a culture of unqualified deference to governmental authority. According to Philip Pettit, a 'contestatory citizenry' is one of three pillars of classical Republican political theory, and the disposition to challenge concentrations and exercises of power is a core republican civic virtue.[75] Fidelity, and hence law's rule, also depends on this civic virtue. Bentham argued that a free government should *cherish*, *encourage*, and *enable* the popular disposition to resistance: 'Of a government that is not despotic, it is therefore the essential character even to *cherish* the disposition to eventual resistance.'[76] He conceded that the system of public responsibility (akin to the notion of fidelity defended in this chapter) could be seen as 'a system of *distrust*'.[77] This characterization is unfortunate, for trust is among the critical constituent attitudes of fidelity; yet, Bentham is right that fidelity calls for a disposition to challenge, to call to account, to demand warrant for any exercise of power in the polity. Deference that is too readily or unconditionally given is inconsistent with this constituent disposition.

But, although fidelity is ultimately a matter of personal commitment and community culture, it can sink deep roots into a community only with the help of civic and legal institutions and practices that facilitate and structure responsible accountability-holding. Although fidelity is in

[73] M. Krygier, 'Legality, Teleology, and Sociology', 60.

[74] Quoted in Kleinfeld, *Advancing the Rule of Law Abroad*, 100.

[75] See P. Pettit, *On the People's Terms*, 5, 225–9.

[76] J. Bentham, *Of the Liberty of the Press, and Public Discussion, and Other Legal and Political Writings for Spain and Portugal*, eds. C. Pease-Watkin and P. Schofield (Oxford: Clarendon Press, 2012 (*CW*)), 30. For more extensive discussion see Postema, 'Soul of Justice', Chapter 3 in this volume.

[77] *Political Tactics*, eds. M. James, C. Blamires, and C. Pease-Watkin (Oxford: Clarendon Press, 1999 (*CW*)), 37.

part an individual responsibility, political accountability-holding is never simply an individual activity, and it is likely to be dangerous if it is the activity of an unorganized and undisciplined mob. Institutions and organizations are needed to perform three key fidelity-supporting tasks. First, they are needed to encourage and nurture the *ethos* of fidelity. Educational institutions – schools, universities, civic associations, and professional organizations – provide citizenship training for members of the polity and professional training for judges, lawyers, and government officials. Second, they are needed to empower, enable, and facilitate accountability-holding. Institutions such as public media and civic associations inform, mobilize, organize, and direct citizen accountability efforts. Formal legal institutions like courts facilitate individual as well as community accountability efforts. Third, institutions and practices are needed to discipline accountability-holding efforts. They structure, focus, restrain, and economize efforts and provide facilities for articulating grievances and their grounds.

Among these essential institutions we must include the following: first, constitutional and legal guarantees of transparency of all aspects of government; second, a vigorous, independent, and legally protected press, and broadly protected freedom of speech and assembly; third, universal and affordable access to independent, impartial, competent, and efficient courts that carry on proceedings in a language ordinary people understand[78]; fourth, a competent, well-trained, rule-of-law-minded and professionally disciplined legal corporation. Also a critical component of the infrastructure of fidelity is a rich, diverse, and civically minded civil society, including diverse religious organizations, non-profit and non-governmental organizations, universities and other educational institutions, professional associations, business organizations, trade unions, community watchdog groups, and the like. Governmental accounting offices, formal or informal ombudsman offices, human rights commissions, and similar organizations can also inspect and monitor governmental activities and inform, enable, and facilitate accountability efforts.

Law's Sovereignty and the Rule of Judges

It is often thought that the rule of law is the special responsibility of judges. 'Judges', Brian Tamanaha writes, 'are the ones whose specific task

[78] Informal, community-based rather than state-based, adjudicative institutions may be adequate or even preferred in some societies, as long as they can guarantee adequate impartial, fair, and law-focused accountability.

is to insure that other government officials are held to the law. The ultimate responsibility for maintaining a rule of law system therefore rests with the judiciary'.[79] But, although the judiciary plays a crucial role in realizing the rule of law, it is a mistake to assume that judges are the sole guardians of the law, and even a greater mistake to believe that the rule of law is ultimately the rule of judges. For that is just to confer on the judiciary the incoherent status of an unaccountable accountability-holder.

The U.S. Supreme Court made this mistake in *Walker* v. *Birmingham*.[80] The case arose out of a demonstration in Birmingham, Alabama, by members of the Southern Christian Leadership Council (SCLC) in the middle of the civil rights struggle in the United States.[81] In early April 1963, the SCLC leadership was twice denied a permit to parade in the city by Bull Connor, who had recently been removed from his position as Birmingham city commissioner, but who had refused to leave office. Connor then secured an ex parte injunction from a local magistrate forbidding the SCLC from demonstrating as planned. Two days later, the group demonstrated in defiance of the permit denial and the injunction. Judge Jenkins, who issued the injunction, jailed and fined the demonstrators for criminal contempt. The U.S. Supreme Court upheld the criminal contempt conviction, despite accepting the defendants' contention that the denial of the parade permit and the injunction were constitutionally invalid. The Court argued that even a demonstrably invalid court order is binding until determined otherwise by a court, and hence those who violate it are criminally liable. In the heart of its opinion, the Court argued:

> In the fair administration of justice no man can be judge in his own case, however exalted his station, however righteous his motives. . . . This Court cannot hold that the petitioners were constitutionally free to ignore all the procedures of law and carry their battle to the streets. One may sympathize with the petitioners' impatient commitment to their cause. But respect for the judicial process is a small price to pay for the civilizing hand of law.[82]

This argument relied on the following argument by Justice Frankfurter in the *United Mineworkers* case decided twenty years earlier:

> Only when a court is so obviously traveling outside its orbit as to be merely usurping judicial forms and facilities, may an order issued by a

[79] B. Tamanaha, 'History and Elements of the Rule of Law', 244.

[80] 388 U.S. 307 (1967). For an insightful discussion of this case, see D. Luban, 'Difference Made Legal: The Court and Dr. King', *Michigan Law Review*, 87 (1989), 2152–2224, at 2152, 2162–86.

[81] Dr. Martin Luther King, Jr., wrote his famous 'Letter from the Birmingham Jail' while incarcerated for defying a court injunction against this demonstration.

[82] 388 US 320–1 (1967).

> court be disobeyed and treated as though it were a letter to a newspaper. Short of an indisputable want of authority on the part of a court, the very existence of a court presupposes its power to entertain a controversy, if only to decide, after deliberation, that it has no power over the particular controversy. Whether a defendant may be brought to the bar of justice is not for the defendant himself to decide.... There can be no free society without law administered through an independent judiciary. If one man can be allowed to determine for himself what is law, every man can. That means first chaos, then tyranny.[83]

The *Walker* Court here offers an incoherent argument for a general thesis in deep conflict with the rule of law. The argument begins (as does Frankfurter's) with the principle *nemo judex in causa sua* – no one can properly claim to be a judge in his or her own case. From this venerable rule-of-law principle, the Court infers that citizens must obey court orders, even if they are demonstrably invalid, until the matter is settled by the courts themselves – unless, the Court adds, the orders were 'transparently invalid'[84] (or, in Frankfurter's language, they indisputably lacked authority). It is for the courts, not individuals, to determine the validity of actions or decisions taken under colour of law, the Court argues, because 'the civilizing hand of law' is exclusively that of the courts, and any alternative to locating final authority there invites, in Frankfurter's vivid language, 'chaos' and 'tyranny'. Thus, individuals must comply with them as if valid until officially and finally told otherwise.

Except for the invocation of a Hobbesian hell[85] at the end, this argument turns entirely on the *nemo judex* principle. But that principle is absurdly misapplied in this context. It is misapplied because its natural habitat involves cases in which individuals seek to make final (judicial) determinations of legal matters in which they have a personal stake. That, of course, is not what the SCLC demonstrators sought to do. Even more, they did not act, as Frankfurter's argument assumes, as if the orders had no more claim to authority than a letter to the editor. On the contrary, the SCLC leadership took seriously the orders' claims to authority, assessed them, and found them demonstrably wanting. That is, they did not take the mere assertion of the claim of validity by officials as enough to settle the matter. They assessed it by their best lights. However, in doing so, they did *not* seek thereby to *settle* anything; and they certainly did not claim

83 *United States* v. *United Mineworkers*, 330 U.S. 258, 309–10, 312 (1947) (Frankfurter concurring).

84 *Walker*, 338 U.S. 316.

85 This argument is remarkably similar to Hobbes's argument for the necessity of a sovereign above the law in *Leviathan*: see note 62 above.

sole standing to determine the matter with finality. They assumed only standing sufficient to make the assessment and act on it, an assessment which they implicitly recognized was itself vulnerable to challenge and could stand only on its merits. To that extent, they acted at their peril on their judgment of the orders' invalidity, in order publicly to challenge them, and by doing so hold to account for their exercise of official power officials who used the law to prevent them from engaging in what they took to be lawful activity.

The *Walker* Court's use of *nemo judex* is absurd, because to do the work, it was meant to do in the Court's argument, the principle must hold that *no one* is ever legitimately in a position to act on his or her best judgment of the law's interpretation or validity. This is an absurd view, because if it were true, law would be impossible. For law can do its ordinary normative-guidance work only if, in most cases, it is possible and legitimate for those addressed by law to act on their best judgment (or that of their legal advisers) of the law's interpretation and validity. It is absurd on its face also because the Court's own conclusion, that it alone is the sole determiner of the validity of official acts and decisions, including its own, violates the principle on which it rests.

The more serious problem with the argument, however, is that the lemma it seeks to prove is itself incoherent. The proposition the Court endorses is that *it* is the sole determiner of the legal validity of official acts taken under colour of law. But that is to claim that it is an unaccountable accountability-holder, and this notion, we have seen, is incoherent and clearly in violation of the core idea of the rule of law. Of course, the Court qualifies its lemma: the court is the sole determiner, *unless* invalidity is 'transparent' or 'indisputable'. But it is not clear that there is any genuine logical space for this exception. If 'transparency' and 'disputability' are matters that turn on the merits of arguments about legal validity, then the Court's mere assertion that the injunction and permit denials were not transparently invalid is highly implausible, since three of the dissenting justices insisted that they *were* transparently invalid. Moreover, if such matters do inevitably turn on assessments of the merits, then inevitably everyone *must* be a judge in his or her own cause as the Court understands *nemo judex*, even if a high bar is set for acting on one's judgment.[86] If 'disputability' is not a matter of the merits, but rather a matter of fact about whether someone actually does dispute the matter, and if the invalidity could be made non-transparent merely by brazenly acting under colour

[86] Luban makes this point; see 'Difference Made Legal', 2172.

of law, then the exception rules out nothing of significance. The view is that the court alone is determiner of all claims of validity including its own, except when it does not make any attempt to disguise the fact of its lack of power.[87]

The upshot of this analysis and critique of *Walker* is twofold. First, we can conclude that civil disobedience, conscientious action in violation of what officials claim to be valid law, must be recognized by law and the courts. It is one more critical part of the institutional infrastructure of fidelity. That is not to say that that those who act in violation of what they take in their best judgment to be legally invalid are, in virtue of this judgment (acting on their legal conscience, as it were), invulnerable to law's penalties, but only that such penalties are warranted only when warranted on the merits, that is, only when the disobedients' judgment proves unsustainable. The rule of law requires this conclusion because first, the contrary view, that the courts have sole standing to determine legal validity, is logically incoherent according to the argument we rehearsed earlier. Second, on practical grounds, the rule of law drives us to this conclusion because the legal recognition of civil disobedience is an essential component of the infrastructure of fidelity. Fidelity is a polity-wide mutual commitment to hold each other accountable under the law. Holding accountable in some cases requires challenging official actions and decisions taken under colour of law, and challenging the validity of laws under colour of which officals act. Publicly acting in violation of those actions, decisions, and laws may be the only way in which their validity can be challenged in courts of law.

Second, it follows from the above argument that the rule of law must not be understood as reducible to the rule of judges. From the point of view of law's rule, courts and judges have no more sustainable claim to sovereignty – that is, unilateral and unaccountable authority – than any other branch of government. But, equally, the same is true for *the people.* Popular sovereignty – if 'sovereignty' is committed to Hobbes's Hierarchy Thesis – is no more acceptable from the point of view of the rule of law for being *popular.* The upshot of the analysis of *Walker*, and of the entire argument of this essay, is that, the homespun wisdom to the contrary notwithstanding, it is not people that rule, but only the law. The ideal of the rule of law challenges fundamentally the doctrine of sovereignty, wherever it is located. The logic of the rule of law drives

[87] Frankfurter, after all, was willing to think that 'the very existence of a court' presupposes its validity to determine such issues.

out sovereignty, because it rejects the assumption of hierarchy of power that lies at its centre. The ideal of the rule of law, properly understood, is a rival to the doctrine of sovereignty. It calls for complex, reciprocal accountability-holding. Thus, the core argument of this essay is not an argument for shifting sovereign governing power from the executive to the parliament, or from parliament to courts, or even from government to the people. Rather it is an argument for the widest sharing of the reciprocal responsibility characteristic of fidelity to law, which, I have repeatedly maintained, is ultimately and fundamentally a matter of each member keeping faith with every other member in the political community.

Conclusion

In this essay I have urged that, when we think of the rule of law, we must think not only of *legality* but also of *fidelity*, not only of the standards that apply to laws and the corpus of law, and to the institutions and officials that apply, interpret, and execute them, but also of the convictions, commitments, and reciprocal responsibilities of all who claim its warrant, resources, and protection. Law's rule depends on mutual commitments among parties in robust authority relationships to hold each other to account. These commitments run in both vertical/political and horizontal/societal directions. Fidelity to law is ultimately a matter of fidelity of all (official or lay) members of the polity to each other. It depends on each taking responsibility for his or her conduct and for the law's proper functioning (to the extent that it is within their power to do so). Thus, it depends on their holding each other, and the officials who claim to govern them, to the standards found in and argued from the law.

3

The Soul of Justice

Bentham on Publicity, Law, and the Rule of Law

GERALD J. POSTEMA

> Publicity is the very soul of justice. . . . It is through publicity alone that justice becomes the mother of security.[1]

Publicity is a central concept of Bentham's theory of law and governing. In Bentham's view, security of society and its individual members is the focal aim and fundamental task of law.[2] But law must be made, administered, adjudicated, and enforced; so if law is introduced into a political community, human beings must be entrusted with making, applying, and enforcing that law. Although law is the primary mode or instrument of governing, law governs only through the efforts of those who govern with it. But then, even as it seeks to secure us against the abuse of power, it creates new opportunities and resources for such abuse. Law introduces a new and especially worrisome form of insecurity arising from the potential for abuse of the power that we entrust to governing officials. Who is to guard the guardians? In Bentham's view, the only effective solution to this problem lies in publicity, a robust and comprehensive system of public oversight of public power in all its forms. 'Publicity is the very soul of justice [that is law]. . . . through publicity alone . . . justice becomes the mother of security.'

The problem just described is the core problem of the rule of law. The *rule of law* is that state or condition of a political community in which *law rules*. When the rule of law is robust in a political community, when

[1] J. Bentham, 'Draught of a New Plan for the organisation of the Judicial Establishment in France: proposed as a Succedaneum to the Draught presented, for the same purpose, by the Committee of Constitution, to the National Assembly, December 21st, 1789' (henceforth 'Judicial Establishment in France'), printed in London, 1790, 25–6 (Bowring, iv. 285–406, at 316–17).

[2] For a defence of this claim see G. J. Postema, *Bentham and the Common Law Tradition* (Oxford University Press, 1986), Ch. 5.

law effectively rules in that community, members of the community are protected against the arbitrary exercise of power, in the first instance, by public officials, but also by fellow members (individual, corporate, and collective). Law rules, we might say, when law is not just an instrument in the hands of those who govern, but also guides, directs, and controls those who govern with it. However, at this point an ancient and still troubling question arises: how can *law* rule if, as Plato taught, only *men* rule? The ancient answer is that law can rule only when those entrusted to rule with law submit to its governance, that is, only when they commit to be guided and controlled by it.[3]

I have argued elsewhere that this commitment is not personal but political, and that law can rule only when there is among officials and subjects of law a rich ethos of reciprocal responsibilities and commitments to holding each other accountable under that law.[4] However, one might reasonably object that this answer is at best incomplete. It speaks only of attitudes, activities, and internalized responsibilities. It articulates an ethics of the rule of law, but we need an articulated account of the infrastructure of the rule of law, of the social conditions in which it thrives and the institutions that enable and empower it. Bentham's reflections on publicity promise to address this need and offer something of value to the long tradition of thinking about the rule of law.

Yet, it may not be obvious from his extensive writings on the merits of publicity that Bentham has much to say about the rule of law. He never explicitly used the language of the rule of law. That is not in itself surprising, since that language is of more recent vintage, although the idea and ideal have ancient origins. But more seriously, a more than casual acquaintance with Bentham's jurisprudence might reasonably lead one to think he was not sympathetic to the idea of the law's ruling those who hold and exercise sovereign political power. Early in *Of the Limits of the*

[3] This answer finds classic expression in Roman Law. See *Codex Iustinianus*, ed. P. Krüger (Berlin: Weidmann, 1877/Goldbach: Keip, 1998), 103 (I. xiv. 4), and the translation by B. Tierney in '"The Prince Is Not Bound": Accursius and the Origins of the Modern State', *Comparative Studies in Society and History* 5 (1963), 378–400, at 391: 'It is a statement worthy of the majesty of a ruler for the Prince to profess himself bound by the law. So much does our authority depend on the authority of the law. And indeed it is greater for the imperium to submit the principate to the laws.'

[4] I argue for this thesis in 'Law's Rule: Reflexivity, Mutual Accountability, and the Rule of Law,' Chapter 2 in this volume, which develops a theme first argued on slightly different terms in Postema, 'Law's Ethos: Reflections on the Public Practice of Illegality', *Boston University Law Review* 90 (2010), 101–22.

Penal Branch of Jurisprudence, shortly after offering his definition of law as a command of a sovereign, Bentham famously wrote,

> The mandate of the sovereign, be it what it will, can not be illegal: it may be impolitic; it may even be unconstitutional: but it can not be illegal. It may be unconstitutional, for instance, by being repugnant to any privileges that may have been conceded to the people whom it affects: but it would be perverting language and confounding ideas to call it *illegal*.[5]

This passage suggests that Bentham was hostile to the idea of legal limits on governing power. But if that is correct, then one might ask whether Bentham's discussion of publicity offers an *alternative to* the idea and ideology of the rule of law, rather than an elaborated *conception of* the rule of law. The answer to this question is complex and nuanced. I return to it at the conclusion of this essay. But we must first explore the role that the notion and manifold devices of publicity play in Bentham's theory of law and governing.

Publicity and Its Progeny

Security Against Misrule

Two strategies for securing ordinary subjects of law against the arbitrary exercise of power at the hands of ruling officials have commonly been deployed in the Western rule-of-law tradition. One conceives of a law *above*, standing in judgement on, the ordinary law, a law which entrenches certain fundamental rights; the other insists on sharply separating the powers of government, and thereby securing the independence of the judiciary, which is itself charged with keeping the other branches of government within the limits of their respective constitutional powers.[6] Bentham rejected both strategies out of hand. Notoriously, he rejected the idea of natural rights as nonsense.[7] He also rejected the strategy of American and French constitution writers to incorporate fundamental natural rights into their respective constitutions or basic laws. His objections were many and detailed, but the following two are among the most important and most familiar. First, he argued that the notions to which

[5] *Of the Limits of the Penal Branch of Jurisprudence* (henceforth *Limits* (*CW*)), ed. P. Schofield (Oxford: Clarendon Press, 2010 (*CW*)), 38.

[6] As, for example, Montesquieu argued in *The Spirit of Laws* (trans. and eds. A.M. Cohler, B.C. Miller, and H.S. Stone (Cambridge University Press, 1989)), 156–66 (Bk. XI, Ch. 6).

[7] See, for instance, 'Nonsense upon Stilts', in *Rights, Representation, and Reform: Nonsense upon Stilts and Other Writings on the French Revolution*, eds. P. Schofield, C. Pease-Watkin, and C. Blamires (Oxford: Clarendon Press, 2002 (*CW*)), 317–401, at 330.

the constitutional provisions appealed were hopelessly vague, and that entrenching them in the nation's basic law made them no more concrete or publicly accessible.[8] Second, he argued that it was a grave mistake to make the validity of legislation depend on the enacted law's adherence to some standard of respect for fundamental rights. Doing so, he argued, in effect transferred legislative power to the judiciary, which is a recipe for tyranny.[9] Bentham had no difficulty in distinguishing between legal duties and legal limits on legislative power; he simply opposed subjecting the legislative branch of government to such (Hohfeldian) disabilities. Limiting legislative power in this way put untrammelled power into the hands of judges.

A similar objection lay at the core of his rejection of Montesquieu's constitutional doctrine of separation of powers. He argued that it was a fundamental mistake of government institution-building to limit the powers of governing institutions and to subject them to competition and constraint by other such powers. The more rational and effective strategy, he argued repeatedly, was to give government institutions all the power they needed to be effective while, at the same time, subjecting them to comprehensive, relentless, and unavoidable *public* oversight, that is, by subjecting them to what he called 'constant responsibility'.[10]

Rather than relying on appeals to natural rights, and embedding them in a legal system's basic law, or designing an elaborate scheme for the separation of powers, Bentham proposed a carefully engineered system of 'securities against misrule' to counteract the real and pervasive threat of abuse of power by officials. *Security against misrule* was his mantra and his singular aim; *publicity* was his most powerful tool for achieving such security.

Moral Aptitude

Bentham thought that political rule can misfire in three ways, which correspond to failures of the three components of 'official aptitude': there can be (1) failure of intellectual aptitude – of knowledge or (non-normative) judgment; (2) failure of active aptitude – of attendance and attention; and (3) failure of moral aptitude – of moral or legal judgment and, more

[8] See Bentham, *Securities against Misrule and Other Constitutional Writings for Tripoli and Greece*, ed. P. Schofield (Oxford: Clarendon Press, 1990 (*CW*)), 231.

[9] See Bentham, 'A Fragment on Government' (henceforth 'Fragment'), in *A Comment on the Commentaries and a Fragment on Government*, eds. J.H. Burns and H.L.A. Hart (London: Athlone, 1977 (*CW*)) (henceforth *Comment/Fragment* (*CW*), 391–551, at 485–8.

[10] 'Constitutional Code', Bowring, ix. 62.

fundamentally, of motivation to act on right judgment. By far the most important concern, on which Bentham spent most of his energy in his numerous writings on the topic, was failure of moral aptitude on the part of governing officials. The 'misrule' he primarily sought to secure against was failure of moral aptitude, manifested in what he called the 'sinister sacrifice' – that is the sacrifice of the public interest to the private interests of those in power. His overarching aim was to engineer institutional devices that would 'maximize official moral aptitude'.[11]

Bentham understood 'moral aptitude' in terms of the judgment-shaping and motivating interests of agents – their private or personal interests and their universal or public interests.[12] When an individual's interests lead her to act in a way that is likely to work against the interests of others, and especially public interest generally (and thus, to sacrifice the public interest), Bentham called such private interests 'sinister'. Accordingly, Bentham characterized moral aptitude, first of all, in a negative mode as the absence of a certain characteristic disposition, namely 'a certain propensity universal in human nature . . . to sacrifice all other interests to that which at each moment appears to him to be his own preponderant interest'.[13] In the political context, Bentham thought that the contrary of 'appropriate moral aptitude' is the 'disposition to exercise arbitrary power'.[14]

There are two ways to counteract the sinister interests of officials, and thereby encourage or enable moral aptitude in them, according to Bentham. It can be done either by providing officials with weighty considerations of public interest, or by denying them opportunities to act on their conflicting private interests.[15] The first way is feasible only if officials are naturally socially minded, and are typically moved by a kind of sympathy for the well-being of others such that they are willing to sacrifice their own happiness for the happiness of others. Although Bentham thought such motivations were available to human beings, he thought

[11] See Bentham, *First Principles Preparatory to Constitutional Code*, ed. P. Schofield (Oxford: Clarendon Press, 1989 (*CW*)), 13–76, 270–324; *Official Aptitude Maximized, Expense Minimized*, ed. P. Schofield (Oxford: Clarendon Press, 1993 (*CW*)), 21–38; *Securities Against Misrule* (*CW*), passim.

[12] On Bentham's distinction between universal and particular (private or personal) interests, as well as the related notions of public interests and sinister interests, see Postema, 'Interests, Universal and Particular: Bentham's Utilitarian Theory of Value', *Utilitas*, 18 (2006), 1–25.

[13] Bentham, *First Principles Preparatory* (*CW*), 13.

[14] 'Lord Brougham Displayed', Bowring, v. 549–612, at 556.

[15] See Bentham, *First Principles Preparatory* (*CW*), 236.

they were relatively rare among people generally, and especially among those who held political power. So he thought that it would be a grave mistake to rely on that sort of public spirit when designing legal and political institutions, especially given the unavoidable temptations of power. The only safe institutional design strategy, in his view, was to assume that officials will make the sinister sacrifice, if they are given the opportunity.[16] The wiser course, he argued, would be to 'render [officials] unable to do wrong, yet sufficiently able to do right'.[17] This is done either by making the 'wrong' unavailable,[18] or by making it ineligible (because too personally costly), that is, by 'bringing . . . the particular interest of rulers into accordance with the universal interest'.[19]

What motive remains when desire is denied hope of fulfilment and an official's private interest no longer stands opposed to the public interest? Bentham sometimes says that aligning private and public interests (i.e., giving the official sufficient personal incentive to act in the public interest) neutralizes the 'sinister' dimension of the official's private interest. However, at other times he suggests that when an official's private interest has been denied hope of fulfilment, it is his concern for the public interest that drives his action. Having thereby been 'virtually divested of all such sinister interest', he argued, there 'remains as the only interest whereby his conduct can be determined, his right and proper interest, which is . . . to say that interest which is in accordance with the universal interest taken in the aggregate'.[20] Thus, Bentham seems to recognize that 'moral aptitude' has a *positive* aspect; it involves a disposition to act in the public interest, at least insofar as one recognizes that one's own interest is an integral part of the public interest.[21] On the whole, Bentham tended to focus his attention on the negative characterization, but at times he sought to mobilize this positive dimension as well. His account of the 'moral sanction', as we shall see later, seems to rely in part on something more than the addition of extrinsic disincentives to outweigh countervailing, potentially sinister, personal or private interests.

16 See ibid., 15, 234. On Bentham's 'strategic egoism', see Postema, *Bentham and the Common Law*, 383–93.

17 *First Principles Preparatory* (*CW*), 15.

18 See ibid., 236; 'Constitutional Code', Bowring, ix. 100; Postema, *Bentham and the Common Law*, 391.

19 *First Principles Preparatory* (*CW*), 235.

20 Ibid., 236.

21 For a fuller discussion of these two understandings of moral aptitude and their relationship to the moral sanction, see Postema, *Bentham and the Common Law*, 376–83, 393–402.

Publicity

To maximize official moral aptitude, Bentham proposed a number of institutional devices including, for example, minimizing the amount of money at an official's disposal and, where feasible, subjecting officials to legal punishment for violation of their official duties.[22] But by far the most important device for Bentham was *publicity*. Indeed, in *Securities Against Misrule*, he insisted that publicity is the *only* effective check on official power: 'Those who desire to see any check whatsoever to the power of the government under which they live, or limit to their sufferings under it, must look for such check and limit to the power of the Public Opinion Tribunal . . . to this place of refuge or to none.'[23] At other times, Bentham admitted that other devices might also serve the purpose, but publicity remained, in his view, the indispensable condition of the success of any other institutional strategy for control of official exercise of power. 'Without publicity, all other checks are fruitless; in comparison of publicity, all other checks are of small account.'[24] 'Without publicity, no good is permanent', he argued, whilst 'under the auspices of publicity, no evil can continue'.[25] Moreover, once law is clearly and publicly articulated, 'for every practical purpose, appropriate *moral* aptitude [of a judge] must be considered as exactly proportioned to the strictness of his dependence upon public opinion'.[26]

Bentham sought to subject governmental action of every sort – legislative, administrative, enforcement, and judicial – to (nearly unlimited)[27] publicity. He enlisted every kind of device and facility he could imagine for this purpose. He included laws requiring openness and disclosure of governmental actions among these devices, but he thought equally about the physical and social structures of public spaces, and of the buildings and

[22] *First Principles Preparatory* (*CW*), 30–73.

[23] *Securities Against Misrule* (*CW*), 125; see also *First Principles Preparatory* (*CW*), 241; *Political Tactics*, eds. M. James, C. Blamires, and C. Pease-Watkin (Oxford: Clarendon Press, 1999 (*CW*)), 29; and *Constitutional Code: Volume I*, ed. F. Rosen and J.H. Burns (Oxford: Clarendon Press, 1983 (*CW*)), 36: 'To the pernicious exercise of the power of government it [i.e. public opinion] is the only check; to the beneficial, an indispensable supplement'.

[24] 'Judicial Establishment in France', 26 (Bowring, iv. 317); and see also 'Lord Brougham Displayed', Bowring, v. 555.

[25] *Political Tactics* (*CW*), 37.

[26] 'Lord Brougham Displayed', Bowring, v. 555 (emphasis original).

[27] There is an extended discussion of the necessary limits of publicity in adjudication, at least regarding the taking of evidence, in Bentham's *Rationale of Judicial Evidence, Specially Applied to English Practice* (first published in 5 vols., 1827), Bowring, vi. 189–585, and vii. 1–644, at vi. 351–65 (Bk. II, Ch. 10).

rooms where public matters were debated and public affairs transacted. He was an engineer of publicity, and, even more, he was literally an *architect of publicity*. He also sought to design formal and informal institutions that promoted, and provided opportunities for, public inquiry into public affairs, public activities, and the activities of public officials. Among the most important of these quasi-formal institutions were the free press and what he called the 'quasi-jury'. In his vision, the quasi-jury was an institution modelled after the English jury in criminal trials, except that he denied the quasi-jury the responsibility or power to decide particular cases.[28] The primary task of the quasi-jury was to oversee the judge's conduct of civil and criminal trials. Publicity 'keeps the judge himself, while trying, under trial. . . . [U]nder the auspices of publicity, the original cause in the court of law and the appeal to the court of public opinion, are going on at the same time'.[29] Bentham sought not merely to make governmental actions of all kinds transparent, but also to encourage, enable, educate, and empower the Public Opinion Tribunal's oversight of governmental actions. Public opinion, he thought, was 'more powerful than all other tribunals'.[30]

The Public Opinion Tribunal

The *public* whose opinion Bentham sought to mobilize through deploying these devices of publicity was the indeterminate aggregate of 'unassignable' individuals which might be regarded as a kind of unofficial and informal tribunal. In his constitutional writings, he gave it official status, treating it as a 'committee' of the 'supreme constitutive' power.[31] Bentham admitted that the Public Opinion Tribunal, strictly speaking, is fictional or 'imaginary',[32] at least insofar as we are inclined to view the 'whole aggregate' of the public as if it were a formally constituted body, exercising conferred powers ('with the formalities of a Judge').[33] But he insisted that it is a harmless and useful fiction – indeed, a necessary one.[34]

28 See 'Principles of Judicial Procedure, with the outlines of a Procedure Code', Bowring, ii. 3–188, at 141–61; 'Constitutional Code', Bowring, ix. 41, 554–67.

29 'Rationale of Judicial Evidence', Bowring, vi. 355 (Bk. II, Ch. 10).

30 *Political Tactics* (*CW*), 29.

31 See *Constitutional Code: I* (*CW*), 35–9.

32 *Securities Against Misrule* (*CW*), 212.

33 Ibid., 28.

34 See *First Principles Preparatory* (*CW*) 70; 'Constitutional Code', Bowring, ix. 41; *Securities Against Misrule* (*CW*), 28, 121.

And he thought the fiction can be largely avoided by focusing on the subset of members who take an active role in public matters, even more so when, like his proposed 'quasi-jury', a subset of the whole is institutionalized and given a specific quasi-legal function. Thus, while the relevant *public* consists of all members of the community, Bentham took the membership of the Public Opinion Tribunal proper – that 'quasi-judicial' body – to consist of all those who actively take cognizance of public matters. He liked to think of them as a kind of self-designated 'committee of the whole', that is, a determinate but not officially determined subset of the whole which takes upon itself the task of doing the work of the whole.[35]

Bentham took the membership in the Public Opinion Tribunal to be very broadly based. He did not limit it to members of the enfranchised 'supreme constitutive'; on the contrary, all adult members of the community, men and women, were eligible. He thought that those who wrote and published would play a major role, but others could participate through reading; even the illiterate were eligible, in Bentham's expansive picture. The only conditions of eligibility were a seriousness of purpose and a willingness to observe and scrutinize the actions of public officials, and on the basis of these observations to form and publicly express opinions and join others in sharing views on public matters. Bentham even opened this public sphere to persons and groups outside the community who might also take cognizance of such matters and engage actively in discussion of them.[36] Publicity was meant to expose governmental exercises of power to the light of day which illuminated these actions for *any* interested observer.

The key institution for making such actions public, and for informing the broad membership of the Public Opinion Tribunal, was the press. A free press was, in Bentham's view, essential to the vigour and vitality of this wide-open public sphere. 'The liberty of the press, and the liberty of public discussion by word of mouth' are 'indispensable, at all times and every where . . . to everything that can, with any propriety, be termed good government'.[37] In a remarkable passage in his second letter on the liberty of the press, Bentham wrote,

[35] Ibid., 121.

[36] See ibid., 28, 57–8, 121; *First Principles Preparatory*, 57, 283; *Constitutional Code: I* (*CW*), 35; 'Constitutional Code', Bowring, ix. 41.

[37] Bentham, *Of the Liberty of the Press, and Public Discussion, and Other Legal and Political Writings for Spain and Portugal*, eds. C. Pease-Watkin and P. Schofield (Oxford: Clarendon Press, 2012 (*CW*)), 4.

> Instruments necessary to the existence of such a disposition [of resistance], in a state adequate to the production of the effect, are *instruction, excitation, correspondence.* To the understanding applies instruction; to the will, excitation: both are necessary to appropriate action and correspondent effect: instruction and excitation, in the case of each individual taken separately: correspondence for the sake of concert amongst the number of individuals requisite and sufficient for the production of the ultimate effect. Co-extensive with the instruction and excitation must be the correspondence.... When, to a national purpose, exertions on a national scale are necessary, exertions made without concert (need it be said) are made without effect.[38]

The role of the press was not merely to expose and inform, for it was vital in Bentham's view to enable co-ordinated, collective action of general, public 'resistance'.

The primary function of Public Opinion Tribunal, according to Bentham, was 'censorial'. Its aim was to 'maximize [the] responsibility' of government officials of all kinds.[39] The wide variety of devices of publicity was designed in various ways to enable, promote, underwrite, and provide resources for this activity. An important secondary function, in his view, was educational. Public access to, and oversight of, legislative and judicial activities offers the general public a 'school of justice', where the most important concerns of morality are held up, discussed, and enforced.[40] He thought that by observing and participating in public argument and debate, people learn that the primary currency of public discourse is not private (sinister) interests, but rather the public or universal interest – not the interests of the community that stand *opposed to* interests of individuals, but rather those interests of the community in which all individual members have a significant stake.[41]

Bentham did not idealize this public; he recognized that the public is ignorant, self-absorbed, undisciplined, and subject to manipulation.[42] To these problems, his solution was even more publicity. With greater publicity, there will be greater access to information to correct ignorance; modelling of public argument will educate the public in public interest. And so, although the public is not at present fully enlightened, publicity is the

38 Ibid., 30.

39 *First Principles Preparatory* (*CW*), 28.

40 See *Political Tactics* (*CW*), 31; 'Principles of Judicial Procedure', Bowring, ii. 143, 148, 149–50; 'Rationale of Judicial Evidence', Bowring, vi. 355 (Bk. II, Ch. 10).

41 'Principles of Judicial Procedure', Bowring, ii. 144; see also Postema, 'Interests, Universal and Particular', 117–19.

42 See 'Constitutional Code', Bowring, ix. 42.

best means of enlightenment of the public. 'Though this tribunal may err, it is incorruptible . . . [and] it continually tends to become enlightened'.[43] The Public Opinion Tribunal is 'incorruptible' not because it is infallible or because it is supremely virtuous, but because its interests are, by definition, interests of the whole, so that its dictates coincide, for the most part, with dictates of 'the greatest happiness of the greatest number', and, given greater publicity, deviations from the latter will decrease and eventually vanish.[44] This is not true, however, of certain sectors of the public. In particular, the 'unproductive', 'aristocratical class', which in the England of his time was also the ruling class.[45] The interests of this class were, in Bentham's view, directly opposed to those of the majority, the 'productive', 'democratical class'. Publicity was meant to expose the subterfuges, manipulations, corruption, and 'sinister sacrifices' typical of the work of the aristocratical class. But we might wonder whether the money and power at the disposal of this class would enable them to manipulate the mechanisms of publicity (the press, for example) as well. Bentham seemed to worry about this. His solution, entertained but not entirely endorsed, was to deny membership in the Public Opinion Tribunal to members of the aristocratical class.[46] However, even if Bentham were serious about this proposal, there seems to be no way in which they could be excluded, since by his account the Public Opinion Tribunal has no official eligibility criterion, no licencing protocol, and no process of disciplinary exclusion. Moreover, officially excluding them would not eliminate, but possibly only mask, their ability to manipulate the devices of publicity for their own purposes.

Maximize Responsibility

We noted that Bentham gave publicity an educational and disciplinary role in securing against misrule. His view of the 'educational' role of publicity is rarely acknowledged and worth extended discussion, but that must be taken up on another occasion. Here I focus attention on the disciplinary function of publicity.

We have seen that the central aim of this disciplinary function was 'responsibility'. 'For security against breach of trust, the sole apt

[43] *Political Tactics* (*CW*), 29.
[44] See *Constitutional Code: I* (*CW*), 36.
[45] See *First Principles Preparatory* (*CW*), 68–76; *Securities Against Misrule* (*CW*), 67–8.
[46] See *First Principles Preparatory* (*CW*), 76.

remedy is . . . constant responsibility . . . on every occasion and at all times, the strictest and most absolute dependence' on the public.[47] Bentham regarded this responsibility in two complementary ways[48]: (1) as *accountability*, that is, subjection to the legitimate demand for explicit, public accounting of the reasons for actions taken or proposed; and (2) as *liability* to punishment, that is, subjection to the moral sanction on analogy to legal liability.[49] Because he so closely associated responsibility (and obligation) with sanctions, it is easy to overlook the accountability dimension, and with it the subtlety of Bentham's notion of official responsibility. But we will consider responsibility as liability to sanction first, and then explore the complementary notion of accountability.

Bentham observed that public opinion typically involves more than mere opinion – it also engages the good or ill offices of the public[50] – and he recognized and welcomed the fact that such ill offices might extend well beyond private or even public condemnation. He recognized that it would also extend to withdrawal of obedience and even collective opposition to, and obstruction of, official action.[51] Indeed, Bentham argued that a free government should *cherish*, *encourage*, and *enable* the popular disposition to resistance: 'Of a government that is not despotic, it is therefore the essential character even to *cherish* the disposition to eventual resistance.'[52] Does this not, Bentham asked, make the system of public responsibility nothing more than 'a system of *distrust*'? Yes, indeed, he replied. But 'every good political institution is founded upon this base', for 'whom ought we to distrust, if not those to whom is committed great authority, with great temptations to abuse it?'[53] In 'Fragment', Bentham unfurled his jurisprudential banner: '*obey punctually and censure freely*',[54] but as his thoughts about the devices necessary for security against misrule developed, the Public Opinion Tribunal – the 'tribunal of free criticism'[55] – took an ever more active role. He came to believe that free censure

47 'Constitutional Code', Bowring, ix. 62.

48 See Postema, *Bentham and the Common Law*, 367–8.

49 See *Constitutional Code: I* (*CW*), 24; 'Constitutional Code', Bowring, ix. 50–1, 151–2; 'Principles of Judicial Procedure', Bowring, ii. 31.

50 See 'Constitutional Code', Bowring, ix. 41.

51 See 'Fragment', in *Comment/Fragment* (*CW*), 485.

52 *Liberty of the Press* (*CW*), 30.

53 *Political Tactics* (*CW*), 37.

54 'Fragment', in *Comment/Fragment* (*CW*), 399.

55 'Papers Relative to Codification and Public Instruction', in *Legislator of the World: Writings on Codification, Law, and Education*, eds. P. Schofield and J. Harris (Oxford: Clarendon Press, 1998 (*CW*)), 1–185, at 98.

could, and sometimes must, qualify and limit obedience, and even excite resistance. Although he designed institutions for regular election of law-makers and government officials at all levels (including all judges), the participation of the public in disciplining – holding accountable – public officials was not limited to replacing them with other officials. He designed devices of publicity to enable and empower active accountability-holding by the public subject to the laws made and administered outside the electoral process. They enabled the public to limit or qualify their general compliance with the law, and hence to oversee and limit the power of those who sought to rule with law.

Although conscientious disobedience and even resistance were part of the public's armamentarium, the primary leverage used by the public, in Bentham's view, was manipulation of reputation or esteem. Public condemnation threatened an official's reputation. The 'Judge is a man of honour: he has a rich fund of reputation to preserve and to improve'.[56] Knowing this, judges and other officials internalize anticipated judgments of the public. They anticipate the unexpressed judgment entertained by the people,[57] and this in turn engages their self-esteem. Officials are thereby forced to find a public language in which to articulate the grounds for their actions. This drive for vindication in the eyes of the public engages the second mode of responsibility – accountability, liability to the demand for an accounting in the language of public reasons for actions taken in the name of the public. In Bentham's vision, the moral sanction, when mobilized for this legal-political function, involves a discursive, reasons-demanding and reasons-assessing dimension.

Bentham offers one example of how this might work in his discussion of the moral forces operative in adjudication. One of the most salutary consequences of full and unconstrained publicity of 'judicature', in Bentham's view, was that it forced the judge to seek publicly to explain and justify each decision and action. 'By the power given to the jury, the judge finds himself under the necessity of addressing his discourse to them explanatory of the nature of the case and of the ground on which his advice and recommendation, if any is given them, has been founded.'[58] Publicity has the 'natural and in experience customary' – if not absolutely necessary – consequence of forcing the judge into 'the habit of giving

56 UC lvii. 9.

57 See 'Constitutional Code', Bowring, ix. 42.

58 'Principles of Judicial Procedure', Bowring, ii. 141–2; see also ibid., 147.

reasons from the bench'.[59] It order to avoid the impression that he has taken advantage of obscurity in the law or the evidence presented in court, or complexity of legal arguments made at trial, the judge feels pressed to 'state, in the presence of the [observers] . . . the considerations – reasons – by the force of which the decision so pronounced by him has been made to assume its actual shape, in preference to any other that may have been contended for'.[60] 'Specifying reasons is an operation, to the performance of which, under the auspices of publicity, the nature of his situation will . . . naturally dispose him to have recourse.'[61] In this way, not only is the unjust decision exposed, but so too 'the injustice of it is to a certain degree manifest. . . . [T]he exposure is in this case effected either by the utter absence of all attempt at exhibiting reasons, or by what may be still better, the weakness and absurdity of his reasons'.[62] While this necessity is not (and Bentham thought must not be) a matter of *legal* obligation, it is nevertheless a *moral* obligation, enforced by the moral sanction imposed by the Public Opinion Tribunal.[63]

This is equally important in other institutional contexts in which government officials must act in the full light of publicity: 'In legislation, in judicature, in every line of human action in which the agent is or ought to be accountable to the public or any part of it, – giving reasons is, in relation to rectitude of conduct a test, a standard, a security, a source of interpretation.'[64] Already in 'Fragment', Bentham had insisted that the *responsibility* of governors consisted in the 'right which a subject has of having the reasons publicly assigned and canvassed of every act of power that is exerted over him'.[65] Bentham directly linked this demand of public, reason-giving accountability with constraints on arbitrary power. 'That which constitutes *arbitrary power* in judicature is', he wrote, 'exemption from the controul of a superior, – from the obligation of assigning *reasons* for his acts, – and from the superintending scrutiny of the public eye'.[66] One of the key means of securing 'responsibility' of officials was

59 'Rationale of Judicial Evidence', Bowring, vi. 357 (Bk. II, Ch. 10).
60 Ibid., 356.
61 Ibid., 357.
62 'Principles of Judicial Procedure', Bowring, ii. 147.
63 See 'Rationale of Judicial Evidence', Bowring, vi. 357 (Bk. II, Ch. 10); 'Constitutional Code', Bowring, ix. 147, 555.
64 'Rationale of Judicial Evidence', Bowring, vi. 357 (Bk. II, Ch. 10).
65 'Fragment', in *Comment/Fragment* (*CW*), 485.
66 'Lord Brougham Displayed', Bowring, v. 556.

for the public to expect and demand an accounting of the grounds for any exercises of power. Full and comprehensive publicity makes such accountability possible and provides the tools the public needs to bridle the power of those who govern.

Although reason-giving is seen here largely in its power-bridling, accountability-holding mode, there is some reason to think that Bentham also welcomed participation of the public in a debate over the values and principles underwriting the reasons offered by judicial or legislative officials. Bentham seems to have recognized the potential for active involvement of the Public Opinion Tribunal in deliberative public debate on the matters of which its members take cognizance. This is implied in his characterization of the Public Opinion Tribunal as 'the tribunal of free criticism'. At one point in 'Fragment' Bentham makes this recognition even more explicit. In the course of arguing that it would be a mistake to give judges the power to overturn legislation, Bentham acknowledged that doing so would have one very valuable consequence: it would promote vigorous public debate over the law. 'A public and authorized debate on the propriety of the law is by this means brought on. The artillery of the tongue is played off against the law, under cover of the law itself.'[67] This, he thought, was likely to serve the interests of the people. Likewise, his discussion of the role of the free press in government oversight suggests a more robust and active (if not exactly Habermasian) 'public sphere'. Taking part in that public sphere are those who read, write, and publish, but also those who, although illiterate, nevertheless engage with others speaking on public matters.[68] Moreover, the 'school of justice' established and funded by the publicity of major political institutions, in Bentham's view, prepares members of the public for this kind of active participation. Thus, it appears Bentham understood to some degree the potential for, and importance of, more active public participation in deliberation on public matters.

Public Reasons and Law

As we return to the question of whether Bentham offers a robust conception of the rule of law, we could do well to look carefully at his view of the relationship between reason-giving and law. In fact, public reason-giving lies at the core of Bentham's view of law's proper functioning. Governing

[67] 'Fragment', in *Comment/Fragment* (*CW*), 488n.
[68] See *Securities Against Misrule* (*CW*), 58.

through law, according to Bentham, is sharply distinguished from the exercise of brute force, which elicits compliance out of fear. Law involves the public expression of will (of the sovereign), he insists, but it does not involve only that. Law's typical mode of governing, in his view, is to *address* clear, public, systematically organized directives to a people capable of understanding and applying them to their own case. This is not a matter of one will imposing itself on another, or even issuing directives with some claim to doing so with authority, but rather it is a matter of the understanding of the law-maker and law-applier addressing the understanding of their constituents.[69] 'Power gives existence to a law for the moment', Bentham wrote in 'Judicial Establishment in France', 'but it is upon reason that it must depend for its stability'.[70] Governing by will alone is, inevitably, power answering only to sinister interest. As a mode of governing, it cannot function in the full light of publicity, because a rational, aware, and informed public will not willingly comply with its commands. Rejecting the authoritarian motto *sic volo, sic jubeo, stet pro ratione voluntas*,[71] Bentham insisted that law governs not by substituting will for reason, but rather by conjoining expressions of will (law's commands) with public articulation of the rational grounds of the directives publicly announced. These reasons, we have seen, provide 'a standard, a security, [and] a source of interpretation'. 'Those who are able to convince men, will inevitably treat them like men; those who only command, avow their inability to convince',[72] and lose their legitimate claim to command. This is the conclusion he draws from his critique of eighteenth-century common law practice. Common law, he charged, had lost its legitimacy for just this reason. It was 'dog-law', imposing penalties with no warning and no public rationale, treating citizens like creatures who understand only the lash.[73]

With this understanding of Bentham's notion of publicity and its role in law, we can return to the question I posed at the opening of this essay: Does Bentham offer us a distinctive conception of the rule of law, or does he offer rather a distinctive alternative to that ideal?

[69] See UC cxxvi. 1; 'Codification Proposal, addressed by Jeremy Bentham to all nations professing liberal opinions', in *Legislator of the World* (*CW*), 241–384, at 248–9; Postema, *Bentham and the Common Law*, 368.

[70] 'Judicial Establishment in France', 11 (Bowring, iv. 310).

[71] See 'Essay on the Promulgation of Laws, and the reasons thereof; with a specimen of a Penal Code', Bowring, i. 155–68, at 159.

[72] Ibid., 160.

[73] See 'Truth *versus* Ashhurst; or, Law as it is, contrasted with what it is said to be', Bowring, v. 231–7, at 235; Postema, *Bentham and the Common Law*, 275–8.

Publicity and the Rule of Law

The Rule of Law

The rule of law is a complex ideal. It includes formal and procedural standards that apply to legal norms and institutions.[74] If law is to rule in a political community, law must not only be a tool that public officials use to manage that community, but it must also rule those who propose to rule with it. We might call this the *reflexive* dimension of the rule of law. Those in power as well as those subject to that power must be subject to the law. The rule of law is not robust in a community – law does not effectively rule there – if some of those who wield political power and hold others accountable to the law are not themselves accountable under law. The question is whether Bentham's views regarding 'securities against misrule' and the central role of publicity in law offer resources for a robust notion of the rule of law, and in particular whether it has room for this reflexive dimension of the rule of law.

I think the answer is yes. In his extended discussion of securities against misrule we have a sustained, articulated exploration of the necessary infrastructure of the rule of law. Other theorists have contributed greatly to our understanding of the formal and procedural elements of the rule of law, but to my knowledge no major legal theorist before the twentieth century has contributed more to our understanding of its informal infrastructure. He analyzed the background conditions and engineered the supporting institutions needed for a comprehensive and effective architecture of accountability.

Legal Limits on the Sovereign

However, we noted at the opening of this essay that in his early jurisprudential writings Bentham seems to have set himself resolutely against any suggestion that the sovereign is subject to the law. Recall, he insisted that there will, of course, be political and possibly even 'constitutional' limits to the sovereign's power, but the notion that the sovereign could be subject to *legal* limits was nonsense.[75] Alleged limits on sovereign law-making (like limits on sovereign exercises of power) may rest on matters of political fact (popular obedience always has its limits), and attempts

[74] See, for example, J. Waldron, 'The Concept and the Rule of Law', *Georgia Law Review*, 43 (2008), 1–61.

[75] See *Limits* (*CW*), 38.

to transgress them may be 'impolitic', or they may rest on what Austin would later call 'positive morality' – social rules or customs enforced by the 'moral sanction' – but they cannot be legal limits enforced by the 'political' or 'legal' (that is law-warranted, coercive) sanction. Legal limits on sovereign power, on this view, are not just unwise, they are impossible. If this was his view, then, whatever we say about Bentham's discussions of 'accountability', we must conclude that his theory of law has no room for the idea of *law* limiting or ruling those with sovereign power. We might say that in the place of a robust theory of the infrastructure of the rule of law, Bentham offers a politically realistic alternative to the ideal of the rule of law. However, I believe this conclusion does justice neither to Bentham's view of the nature of law, nor to his view of role of the 'moral sanction' and 'popular opinion' in the ordinary and proper functioning of law.

My main reason for thinking this turns on a closer look at the passage from *Limits* that we have just considered. But before we do so, we should consider the evolution of Bentham's understanding of law. Bentham's reluctance to regard 'constitutional' constraints as legal seems to follow directly from his command model of law. However, soon after setting out his command model in *Limits*, he began to back away from it. First, he relaxed (or enhanced and reshaped) his notion of what constitutes an individual law, qualifying his command model. Much of *Limits* was devoted to working out the logical and conceptual resources needed to construct a complete and integral body of law – a 'pannomion', as he called it. Sovereign commands, decrees, and even statutes are discrete historical events with canonical linguistic formulations, but laws, on Bentham's considered view, are ideal wholes. *A* law – as opposed to a statute enacted by law-makers – is a part of an integrated system of laws. 'The idea of a law, meaning one simple but entire law, is in a manner inseparably connected with that of a compleat body of laws: so that what is a law and what are the contents of a compleat body of the laws are questions of which neither can well be answer'd without the other.'[76] By taking as his central concept that of a *complete law*, Bentham left behind any simple understanding of his command model.

Second, although Bentham distinguished *legal* sanctions from *moral* sanctions, he gave moral sanctions an integral role to play in the ordinary functioning of law proper. Early on, he recognized the possibility of divided sovereignty in a polity, where supreme legislative and executive

76 Ibid., 21n.

power (and all but supreme judicial power as well) is located in one body, and the power to hold that body accountable is located in another.[77] And he elaborated that idea in subsequent work as he developed the role of the Public Opinion Tribunal in securing official responsibility. Much of what we have seen earlier regarding the reliance of law on the operation of public opinion and the moral sanction makes clear that Bentham thought that political power could not be exercised in a distinctively law-like and law-governed way unless it engaged public opinion in the right way in its ordinary operations. Public opinion was, in Bentham's view, integral to law; no jurisprudential inquiry into the foundations of law could ignore the role of the public in law's ordinary functioning

Leges in principem

This close interdependence of law and public opinion is especially clear in his discussion of constitutional constraints on sovereign ruling power in *Limits.* In the recent new edition of Bentham's early jurisprudential manuscripts (published earlier under the title *Of Laws in General*),[78] the editor, Philip Schofield, points out that in a marginal comment on the passage quoted earlier (in which Bentham says that limits on the sovereign can be political or constitutional, *but not legal*), Bentham wrote: 'Alter. These are laws not *in populum* indeed, but [they are laws] *in principem.*'[79] That is, they are not laws addressed to the people generally, but rather are laws addressed to the ruling body. Since writing the original passage, Bentham had significantly refined his thoughts on the status of sovereign-guiding, sovereign-limiting constitutional norms.[80] He had developed a more nuanced view of the nature and force of such constraints. He began where Roman Law and Canon Law theorists had traditionally begun,[81] by thinking of such constitutional constraints as self-imposed, that is, as sovereign commitments to respect certain limits on its power. Yet Bentham understood these commitments to be quite different from personal policies or self-addressed commands; rather, they engaged parties other

[77] See ibid., 91n. Strictly speaking, he noted, we should say that in that case sovereignty is held jointly although most of us would be inclined to say that the former is *the* sovereign.

[78] *Of Laws in General*, ed. H.L.A. Hart (London: Athlone, 1970 (*CW*)).

[79] P. Schofield, 'Editorial Introduction', in *Limits* (*CW*), xi–xl, at xxii.

[80] The discussion can be found in *Limits* (*CW*), 85–93. For a discussion of the concept of *leges in principem*, and the development of Bentham's concept of sovereignty, see Postema, *Bentham and the Common Law*, 250–6.

[81] In their commentary on *Codex*, I. xiv. 4; see note 3 of this chapter.

than the sovereign itself and empowered those other parties to judge the actions of the sovereign. What he had earlier styled mere 'concessions',[82] he here labels '*leges in principem*'. They are *laws*, to be sure, but 'transcendent' ones,[83] transcendent because they 'prescribe to the sovereign what *he* shall do: what mandates *he* may or may not address to *them* [subjects]; and, in general, how he shall or may conduct himself towards them'.[84] Bentham was initially inclined to think of these commitments on analogy with promises or 'covenants',[85] but he realized that the promise model itself was not entirely adequate. It restricted the scope of the commitment to the promise-issuing sovereign, while the constitutional limitations he had in mind typically bound successive rulers over time. So, he thought of such sovereign acts of commitment as having two analytically separable but implicit aspects: at the same time as the sovereign engages himself through entering a covenant, he commits his successors through addressing to them, as it were, a 'recommendatory mandate'.[86] Both commitments have the status as *leges* in virtue of issuing from the sovereign and engaging the public in holding the sovereign to them.[87]

This way of conceptualizing constitutional limits on ruling power was not original with Bentham, of course, but if we set this strategy in the context of his principle of publicity and the foundational jurisprudential role he assigns to public opinion, we can better appreciate its jurisprudential significance. First, Bentham asks, what sense can we give to the idea that these constitutional limits are self-imposed; how can one impose an obligation upon oneself?[88] He answered that there is no more difficulty in this kind of case than in a case in which a subject binds himself to another subject. In neither case are the obligations simply self-imposed. In the case of an ordinary promise, the subject binds himself just in case there is some party or force to hold him to this commitment; and, Bentham maintains, the same is true in the case of the sovereign's commitment. In the simple promise case, the law, strictly speaking, is the work of both the covenanter and the guarantor of the covenant. In the latter case, the guarantor is public opinion, exercising the moral sanction.[89]

82 *Limits* (*CW*), 38; see also *Securities Against Misrule* (*CW*), 138.
83 *Limits* (*CW*), 86.
84 Ibid.
85 Ibid., 87; see also *Securities Against Misrule* (*CW*), 138–41.
86 *Limits* (*CW*), 87.
87 See ibid., 90.
88 See ibid.
89 See ibid., 92; and also *Securities Against Misrule* (*CW*), 139–40.

Second, Bentham's explanation of the binding force of recommendatory mandates further stretches the promise/covenant analogy and integrates his account of *leges in principem* into his larger theory of the foundations of law.[90] He argues that sovereign covenants, motivated initially by considerations of political expediency, tend to shape the expectations of the subjects of law to such an extent that, when a change in sovereign takes place, the new sovereign will be custom-bound to adopt the same covenants. Indeed, it will not be necessary for the new sovereign explicitly to adopt the previous sovereign's covenants, for he will simply be held to have done so.[91] Thus, while historically specific constitutional limitations on sovereign power may have originated in some concession or promise of a sovereign, their current status and force do not depend on that origin, but rather on present-day custom, rooted in the expectations of subjects that are binding on the sovereign. Moreover, Bentham adds, the expectation of compliance with such covenants over time will become integrated into the law-constituting, law-grounding convention ('habit') of obedience. 'This expectation may even become so strong', he wrote, 'as to equal the expectation which is entertained of the prevalence of that disposition to obedience on the part of the people by which the sovereignty *de facto* is constituted: insomuch that the observance of the covenant on the one part shall be looked upon as a condition *sine quâ non* to the obedience that is to be paid on the other'.[92]

The expectations and opinions underwriting and enforcing *leges in principem* are all of a piece with expectations at the foundations of law as Bentham understood them. These expectations are 'constitutional' in the literal sense of being law-constituting – that is, constituting the system or body of law as a whole – because, on Bentham's view, the existence and unity of any legal system depend on the law-making (and law-executing and law-adjudicating) efforts of the sovereign, and the sovereign has such power just in virtue of the co-ordinated expectations of the subjects of law in the jurisdiction to recognize that power and to tender their compliance to those efforts. Law exists just in virtue of the 'habit of obedience' of subjects, but this 'habit' is not a thoughtless, rote, and strictly singular responsiveness to commands, but rather a

[90] See *Limits* (*CW*), 88–9.

[91] See ibid., 89.

[92] Ibid.

co-ordinated collective response to the efforts of those in power.[93] It depends on a kind of convention or 'custom', the content and shape of which is determined by the collected and uttered opinions of the public. At one point, Bentham was even willing to say explicitly that the rules and standards issuing from firm expectations of public opinion themselves constitute a kind of *law*. 'Public Opinion may be considered as a system of law, emanating from the body of the people', he wrote at the opening of his *Constitutional Code*.[94] Its rules may have no explicitly articulated, canonical formulations, 'no individually assignable form of words', but in this respect it is no different from English common law, except that, since it issues from the people rather than from a part of the ruling elite, it is not subject to the kind of abuse which was endemic to common law. The customs at the foundations of law, customs that shape and give nuance to the law-constituting dispositions to obedience of subjects of law, are no less law and no less obligatory for resting ultimately on the moral sanction of public opinion, that is, on the willingness of law subjects to hold sovereign power accountable.

Conclusion

Thus, unlike Hobbes and Austin, Bentham did not think it impossible for law to bind a sovereign. Law, properly understood, binds not only its immediate subjects, but also those entrusted to make, administer, and enforce it. And Bentham integrated his account of the jurisprudentially necessary constraints on legally authorized officials, and the devices and institutions that made it possible for these officials to be held accountable, into his account of the foundations of law. His analysis of the conditions for the existence of law at the same time, and in his view necessarily, was an analysis of the conditions of *law's ruling* in a political community. Moreover, this analysis led him to the conclusion that for law to rule – in his terms, for there to be adequate security against misrule – the sovereign's self-limiting commitments must be matched by an equal commitment on the part of those subject to the sovereign's rule to hold the sovereign

[93] For a general discussion of Bentham's expectation-based, 'interactional' understanding of the 'habit of obedience', see Postema, *Bentham and the Common Law*, 232–7.

[94] *Constitutional Code: I* (*CW*), 36. Although this is the only passage of which I am aware in which Bentham makes this point explicitly, it is hard to dismiss as a slip of the pen, since, it appears in a very prominent position near the opening of the work.

to those commitments. In Bentham's view, the law's ruling ultimately 'depends upon the spirit, the intelligence, the vigilance, the alertness, the intrepidity, the energy, the perseverance, of those of whose opinions Public Opinion is composed'.[95] And public opinion can work its constraining magic only if at every point the exercise of governmental power is public. As he said, publicity is the soul of the law, and through publicity alone law becomes the mother of security. It is an essential part of the infrastructure of the rule of law.

95 *Securities Against Misrule* (*CW*), 139.

4

Popular Prejudices, Real Pains

What Is the Legislator to Do When the People Err in Assigning Mischief?

MICHAEL QUINN

Introduction

This chapter attempts to investigate the status in a utilitarian calculus of the pleasures and pains arising from the moral, sympathetic, and antipathetic biases of human beings. Assuming that your action inflicts no objective harm on me or anybody else, does the real pain I feel in contemplating that action require to be taken into account in the calculation of the pleasures and pains consequent upon that action, with a view to deciding whether to apply deterrent sanctions, legal or moral, to it?

Most commentators agree that the idea that the infliction of harm was a necessary (although not of itself sufficient) condition for the imposition of punishment (legal or moral) was the 'very simple principle' advanced by J.S. Mill in *On Liberty*.[1] Mill's simple principle has been interpreted in a complex variety of ways, but many scholars would effectively endorse Riley's statement that the essential Millian claim is that the pain and disgust I feel in consequence of your objectively harmless activity does not constitute harm to me.[2] Like Mill, Bentham argued that simple aversion to a mode of behaviour constituted no good reason for punishing it, but he was also conscious of the pains consequent on challenging and attempting to change popular perceptions. In what follows, Bentham's attitude to legal and moral restraint on the basis of aversion or antipathy is examined in two areas. First, does the utilitarian count all pains, from

[1] See J.S. Mill, *On Liberty, in Essays on Politics and Society* (*The Collected Works of John Stuart Mill*, vol. xviii), ed. J.M. Robson (Toronto and London: University of Toronto Press/Routledge & Kegan Paul, 1977), 213–310, at 223. For a rejection of this interpretation, see J. Wolff, 'Mill, Indecency and the Liberty Principle', *Utilitas* 10 (1998), 1–16.

[2] See J. Riley, 'One Very Simple Principle', *Utilitas* 3 (1991), 1–35, at 23; R. Wollheim, 'John Stuart Mill and the Limits of State Action', *Social Research* 40 (1973), 1–30, at 8–9; C.L. Ten, *Mill on Liberty* (Oxford: Clarendon Press, 1980), 14–15.

whatever source, in his or her calculations? Second, what is the relation between the legislator and the public, or, in other words, between the political and the moral sanction? What is a legislator to do when public opinion not only disregards objectivity and reason in applying the moral sanction, but also demands that he or she do likewise in applying the political?

Bentham's Position: Conflicting Evidence

For Bentham, a conclusive justification for making any act an offence punishable by law could only lie in its 'tendency' (that is in its predicted consequences for the pleasures and pains experienced by sentient beings)[3] to produce mischief (that is to give rise to pain, or loss of pleasure).[4] Since punishment consisted in the infliction of pain (official, state-inflicted pain in the case of legal punishment; informal, but nevertheless deliberately inflicted and organized pain in the case of punishment by the moral sanction), and was therefore an evil, its justification in turn lay in its capacity 'to exclude some greater evil'.[5] Where an act gave rise to no pain, there was simply, in utilitarian terms, no case for punishment.

Of course, humans indulge in many acts which bring short-term pain – labour in general, and writing papers in particular, for instance – with a view to producing greater pleasures or averting greater pains. For Bentham, the fact that an act had a tendency to produce pain was a necessary, but not a sufficient condition for intervention to prevent it. To attract the proscriptive attention of the legislator, an act must satisfy more exacting criteria:

> to constitute such a mischief as for the prevention of which the legislator would be justifiable in employing coercive measures, three things will be necessary – 1. that the mischief be shown to have existence in some specific assignable shape . . . 2. that the practice by which it is produced be not attended with any beneficial effects capable, when taken together, of operating as an over-balance or exact counterpoise to it: 3. that the measures taken for the exclusion of it be not productive of evil to an

[3] J. Bentham, *An Introduction to the Principles of Morals and Legislation* (first published 1789), ed. J.H. Burns and H.L.A. Hart, with a new introduction by F. Rosen (Oxford: Clarendon Press, 1996 (*CW*)) (henceforth *IPML* (*CW*)), 74.

[4] See ibid., 49: 'Is an offence committed? It is the tendency which it has to destroy, in such and such persons, some . . . pleasures, or to produce some . . . pains, that constitutes the mischief of it, and the ground for punishing it.'

[5] Ibid., 158.

> amount superior or equal to the good resulting from the exclusion of it, in so far is it is excluded.[6]

The legislator must thus set the pains resulting from the act against the corresponding pleasures, and, even if the act is found mischievous (is found, that is, to produce a net balance on the side of pain), must then be satisfied that her intervention does not produce more pain than it removes.

So far, so good. However, no answer has yet been offered to the central question at issue: do all pains get taken into account in the calculation, or are some pains disregarded? In investigating Bentham's attitude to this question, a problem arises insofar as there is textual evidence to support each of the following contradictory positions: (1) My pain at the knowledge of your engagement in a particular action which causes no harm (that is, no significant pain other than mental pain dependent on disapproval of the action), and the pleasure I might derive from the coercive intervention of the law to stop you from so engaging, should be disregarded in the calculations of the legislator. (2) My disapproval-dependent pain at the knowledge of your engagement in such action, and the pleasure I might derive from its prohibition, should be included in the calculations of the legislator.

Let us begin with some support for position (1). Bentham clearly limited offences to acts which inflict injury on person, property, reputation or condition in life (that is, the four branches of security).[7] That seems to narrow down the sorts of pains which can give rise to injury. How can my distress at your harmless action injure my security? Further, in discussion of whether the law should intervene to prevent self-regarding offences, Bentham urged the legislator to be very sure that her intervention would not be unprofitable, that is, cause more pain than it prevents. Thus, in such cases, the pain-producing properties of such acts 'should show themselves at first glance, and appear to belong to the subject beyond dispute'.[8]

[6] 'Of Sexual Irregularities', in *Of Sexual Irregularities, and Other Writings on Sexual Morality*, eds. P. Schofield, C. Pease-Watkin and M. Quinn (Oxford: Clarendon Press, 2014 (*CW*)), 1–45, at 35–6 (UC lxxiv. 149).

[7] *IPML* (CW), 193.

[8] Ibid., 196. Self-regarding offences could only be, for Bentham, the result of faulty prudential reasoning on the part of the individual. That errors could occur in my calculation of the pains and pleasures accruing to me from my acts was indubitable, but Bentham's general position was that their correction was the province of advice rather than law, of the deontologist rather than the legislator. Bentham also clearly viewed many self-regarding offences punished by English law as not properly offences at all, but as the innoxious victims of asceticism and caprice.

Further, in discussion of cases where punishment is unjustified because needless, Bentham was explicit that consent constituted the strongest possible evidence for the absence of harm: 'This consent, provided it be free, and fairly obtained, is the best proof that can be produced, that, to the person who gives it, no mischief . . . is done.'[9] Bentham provided the general basis for this assertion elsewhere: 'Every person is not only the most proper judge, but the only proper judge of what with reference to himself is pleasure: and so in regard to pain.'[10] In developing this position, he was pellucidly clear that no justification for preventing you from seeking pleasure in your own way could be drawn solely from my disapproval of your judgment about which actions best supply pleasure:

> To say of any act, from this [act] no pleasure, . . . were the act exercised by me . . . would be reaped by me . . . , therefore, although from the like act, if exercised by you, pure or preponderant pleasure would be reaped by you, the act is not fit or not proper to be exercised by you, is folly: and, if followed up by acts having for their object the applying evil in any shape to you, injustice and, in so far as public power or influence is employed to that end, tyranny. . . .
>
> On every man who, whether by misrepresentation of the natural consequences, or by erroneous argumentation in any other shape, or by fear of punishment at the hands of any one or more of the tutelary sanctions, viz. physical, popular or moral, political, or religious, is dissuaded from the reaping of any pleasure, an injury is inflicted, an injury as great as would be done to him by causing him to suffer pain in any shape to an equivalent amount.[11]

Note that Bentham's condemnation of coercive interference encompassed not only the use of the legal sanction, but that of the moral also: if public opinion punished me because it disapproved of my choice of pleasures to pursue, when those pleasures inflicted no assignable mischief, it acted unjustly. In his sex writings, he argued trenchantly that cleaving to prejudiced antipathy when presented with contrary evidence was itself tyranny:

> If, as above, the enjoyment be so much pure good, all punishment in whatever shape endured in consideration of it . . . so much pure evil, every man by whose instrumentality any such punishment . . . is produced is, to

[9] Ibid., 159.

[10] J. Bentham, 'Deontology', in *Deontology, A Table of the Springs of Action, and Article on Utilitarianism*, ed. A. Goldworth (Oxford: Clarendon Press, 1983 (*CW*)), 117–281, at 150.

[11] Ibid., 151–2.

> the amount of the quantity of gratification thus prevented from coming into existence, the author of the injury.... But let warning, as here, have been given – by the man, whoever he be, who, being apprized of the alleged innoxiousness of these gratifications, and of the alleged existence of the fullest and clearest proof of it, persists in shutting his ears and eyes against these proffered proofs: by this man, ignorance of that . . . the means of knowing which are offered to him, operates not in any degree in the character of an extenuation of the injury: in proportion and to the amount of the evil of which . . . he is the author, a tyrant and a persecutor.[12]

It is true that these strong statements came comparatively late in Bentham's career, but even in 1780 he was quite clear that mere dislike of an action could never justify punishment:

> 'I feel in myself', (say you again) 'a disposition to detest such or such an action in a moral view; but this is not owing to any notions I have of its being a mischievous one to the community. I do not pretend to know whether it be a mischievous one or not: it may be not a mischievous one: it may be, for aught I know, an useful one.' – 'May it indeed?' (say I) 'an useful one? but let me tell you then, that unless duty, and right and wrong, be just what you please to make them, if it really be not a mischievous one, and any body has a mind to do it, it is no duty of yours, but, on the contrary, it would be very wrong in you, to take upon you to prevent him: detest it within yourself as much as you please; that may be a very good reason (unless it be also a useful one) for your not doing it yourself: but *if you go about, by word or deed, to do any thing to hinder him, or make him suffer for it, it is you, and not he, that have done wrong: it is not your setting yourself to blame his conduct, or branding it with the name of vice, that will make him culpable, or you blameless.* Therefore, if you can make yourself content that he shall be of one mind, and you of another, about that matter, and so continue, it is well: but *if nothing will serve you, but that you and he must needs be of the same mind, I'll tell you what you have to do: it is for you to get the better of your antipathy, not for him to truckle to it.*'[13]

The Benthamic origins of Mill's harm principle emerge here in a striking fashion. A less liberal utilitarian might argue that if permitting your distasteful but unmischievous act were to result in the imposition of severe distress, that is, mental pain, on a vast disapproving majority, whilst delivering pleasure, however intense, to only a tiny minority who wished to indulge in it, the utilitarian should endorse its coercive prevention, at least where the majority's resulting relief from pain and receipt of pleasure

12 'Sextus', in *Of Sexual Irregularities* (*CW*), 47–115, at 92–3 (UC lxxiv. 180).

13 *IPML* (*CW*), 28–9n (emphasis added).

outweighed the corresponding loss of pleasure and subjection to pain of the minority of pleasure-dissidents.

Bentham, however, seemed to declare that no such calculation could, in fact, ever issue in the endorsement of prohibitive sanctions. Towards the end of his career, he laid down the following as an axiom, so called because it met the conditions of incontestableness, comprehensiveness, and clearness: 'The pleasure derivable by any person from the contemplation of pain suffered by another, is in no instance so great as the pain so suffered.'[14] For our moral majority utilitarian, however, this declaration that the calculation can only produce one result, far from being incontestable, looks like an attempt to rig the calculation. The axiom might well be true when comparing one person's vindictive pleasure against the pain of sufferance endured by one frustrated eccentric pleasure-seeker. However, the value of any pleasure or pain is the product of its intensity and its duration, discounted by its uncertainty and temporal distance, multiplied by its extent, or the number of people whose sensation it is.[15] In this case, the dimension which might well tip the scales in favour of prohibition is extent, that is, the sheer weight of the number of people who would derive pleasure from punishing harmless acts which they detest.

Further, even if, for argument's sake, our moral-majoritarian were to accept Bentham's axiom as regards the inability of antipathetic pleasure to outweigh pain of sufferance, the axiom confines itself to comparison between the antipathetic pleasure – the anticipation of which constitutes the motive of an act – and the pain imposed by it. When the act in question is the coercive prohibition of a mode of behaviour, this comparison omits relevant sensations, namely the antipathetic pain experienced by the moral majority, and the corresponding pleasure of enjoyment experienced by the eccentric pleasure-seeker, in the absence of that prohibition. If we compare these sensations – even where sexual behaviour is concerned, which Bentham viewed as delivering the purest, most extensive and most intense of all sensual pleasures[16] – might not the majority's antipathetic pain outweigh the pleasure accruing to the minority of

[14] Jeremy Bentham, 'Pannomial Fragments', in *Jeremy Bentham: Selected Writings*, ed. S.G. Engelmann (New Haven and London: Yale University Press, 2011), 240–79, at 269 (Bowring, iii. 211–30, at 225). Bentham had, in passing, laid down the same axiom forty years earlier in *IPML* (*CW*), 3n: '*The suffering of a person hurt in gratification of enmity, is greater than the gratification produced by the same cause*' (emphasis original).

[15] See ibid., 38–41.

[16] See 'Sextus', in *Of Sexual Irregularities* (*CW*), 111 (UC lxxiv. 217), and 'Editorial Appendix. Sextus', in *Of Sexual Irregularities* (*CW*), 145–9, at 148–9 (UC clxi. 8–11).

sexual dissidents? Only by discounting those pains completely could the outcome of the calculation become axiomatic, and since Bentham did regard it as axiomatic, he must have excluded them.

Let us turn to textual evidence in support of proposition (2). Bentham was adamant that mischief was simply pain, or loss of pleasure, and included in his catalogue of pains and pleasures those of both sympathy and malevolence.[17] If these are not morally relevant, and are disqualified from counting towards the calculation of the tendency of an action, what are they doing there? Bentham also cautioned that among the circumstances which may render a particular punishment 'unprofitable' – that is, productive of more evil than it prevents – is unpopularity, or 'The displeasure of the people; that is, of an indefinite number of the members of the same community, in cases where . . . they happen to conceive, that the offence or the offender ought not to be punished'.[18] Now the displeasure of the people, which impacts on the legislator's calculation, can only be constituted by the pains which the punishment would inflict, not on the offender, but on the people in general, or at least enough of them to render that punishment unpopular. However, if this applies to punishments which would otherwise accord with the principle of utility, does it not equally apply to the converse situation? That is, couldn't its unpopularity render similarly unprofitable the legislator's decision *not to punish* acts which, according to the principle of utility, do not call for punishment?

Further, Bentham included among offences against the person 'simple mental injuries', so that mischief is certainly not limited to bodily pain.[19] Just after writing *An Introduction to the Principles of Morals and Legislation* (*IPML*), in an essay intended to form a continuation thereof, he noted, in discussion of 'simple mental injuries', that the pains arising from an action depended on the susceptibilities of those who experienced them: 'Those sights, those discourses, which would give pain to the inhabitant of one country would not, in every instance, be productive [of] a similar sensation to the inhabitant of another.'[20] In other words, the circumstances influencing sensibility play a huge role, whilst included in the primary circumstances influencing sensibility are moral, religious, sympathetic

[17] *IPML* (*CW*), 44, 48.

[18] Ibid., 163–4.

[19] Ibid., 223–4.

[20] 'Place and Time', in *Jeremy Bentham: Selected Writings*, ed. Engelmann, 152–219, at 155 (Bowring, i. 169–94, at 174).

and antipathetic biases and sensibilities.[21] Because these factors do have an impact directly on the value of pleasures and pains, it would surely be absurd to exclude them from the utilitarian calculation. It should come as no surprise then, that Bentham did not exclude them, noting, for instance: 'The votary of every sect may receive a cruel wound from any discourse or exhibition which tend[s] to reflect contempt on any of the objects of his veneration.'[22]

Much later in his career, with reference to simple mental injuries, Bentham noted both that 'pain of mind is liable to be produced' by expressions of contempt for religious opinions, and that '[a]ccording to the amount of it . . . the act, by which it is produced, may . . . be with propriety regarded and dealt with as injurious'.[23] Since moral and religious sensibilities vary, and vary according to moral and religious beliefs, among the basic tools for a legislator seeking to transplant laws, that is, to apply laws to a different cultural context from that in and for which they were drafted, was precisely 'a general table of the circumstances influencing sensibility: tables, or *short accounts, of the moral, religious, sympathetic and antipathetic biases of the people for whose use the alterations are to be made*'.[24]

Abstract versus Net Utility

Is Bentham being inconsistent, or careless in expression? What does the textual evidence reveal about his utilitarianism? The thesis of this chapter is that these apparent contradictions reveal a distinction, and a tension, between abstract and final or net utility. Abstract utility is not a term Bentham used frequently.[25] However, it would appear to denote the pains

21 See *IPML* (*CW*), 57–8.

22 'Place and Time', 159 (Bowring i. 174).

23 'Codification Proposal, Addressed by Jeremy Bentham to All Nations Professing Liberal Opinions' in *Legislator of the World: Writings on Codification, Law, and Education*, eds. P. Schofield and J. Harris (Oxford: Clarendon Press, 1998 (*CW*)), 241–384, at 292.

24 'Place and Time', 156–7 (Bowring, i. 173) (emphasis added).

25 For Bentham's use of the term in the sense in which it is understood in this paper, see 'Place and time', 174 (Bowring, i. 181). Elsewhere, Bentham discussed the contrasting requirements for departure from the dictates of abstract utility in relation to publicity in monarchies and republics respectively (see *Rationale of Judicial Evidence, Specially Applied to English Practice* (first published in 5 vols., 1827), Bowring, vi. 189–585, and vii. 1–644, at vi. 371–2 (Bk. II, Ch. 10)); equated abstract utility with both 'benefit' and 'expediency' (*A Plea for the Constitution* (first published 1802), Bowring, iv. 249–84, at 260); contrasted grounds or reasons derived from 'abstract aptitude' with reasons 'which have reference to local jealousies and partialities'

and pleasures liable to be experienced by human agents as such, which are embodied in the empirical generalizations about human psychology which he termed axioms of mental pathology, and defined thus: 'By an axiom of pathology, understand a proposition declarative of a connexion as having place between any event or state of things in the character of a cause, and pain or pleasure, or both, in the character of effects of that same cause.'[26] Bentham rejected the idea that the range of pleasures available to human beings differed according to context: 'in this point at least human nature may be pronounced to be everywhere the same'.[27] However, although pleasures and pains remain constant, sensibilities to particular sensations do vary according to circumstances, and it is from this variation that the grounds for departures from the dictates of abstract utility are derived: 'In the catalogue, then, of these circumstances we shall find the sum total of the principles . . . which, in our enquiry concerning the influence of place and time on matters of legislation, are to serve us as a guide.'[28] For present purposes, the central point is that my beliefs play a central role in determining my sensibilities.

The utilitarian legislator must attend not only to the pains and pleasures of human beings as such, but also to the pains and pleasures liable to be experienced by particular populations sharing particular geographical and historical contexts, and, in consequence, particular sensibilities (crudely, contingent liabilities to affective reactions) which are a product of shared understandings or interpretations of meaning. These understandings are themselves beliefs, derived in large measure from particular cultural (including moral and religious) inheritances.[29] In short, the

('Papers Relative to Codification and Public Instruction', in *Legislator of the World* (*CW*), 1–185, at 33); and, finally, provided the following gloss on law in the abstract: 'We still want a work, unfolding the true principles of Law in the abstract, as derived from the nature of man, and the necessary structure of society – the beau-ideal of law, such as it never yet has been in any state, such as it never will be, but such as every state ought, as near as possible, in its own case, to make it' ('Codification Proposal', 327). Bentham also used the designation 'primitive utility' to denote that which is here called 'abstract' utility. See 'A General View of a Complete Code of Laws', Bowring, iii. 154–210, at 188–9: 'Consult first primitive utility, and if it be found neuter, *indifferent*, then follow the popular ideas; collect them when they have decided – fix them when they are wavering – supply them when they are wanting; but by one method or another resolve these subtilties; or, what is better, prevent the necessity of recurring to them.'

26 'Equity Dispatch Court Bill', Bowring, iii. 319–431, at 388n. See also 'Principles of the Civil Code', Bowring, i. 297–364, at 304; 'Pannomial Fragments', 266–8 (Bowring, iii. 224–5).

27 'Place and Time', 155 (Bowring, i. 172).

28 Ibid.

29 Of course, in almost every political society there will exist a plurality of shared understandings which vary in origin, in subject matter, and in breadth of support. Just as the community interest

legislator begins with calculation of the abstract pains and pleasures liable to be experienced by human beings as such, that is, independently of their particular beliefs, before accommodating their concrete manifestations in particular contexts, as modified by prevailing beliefs.

Early in his career, Bentham implied that contextual departures from abstract utility would be strictly limited: 'That which is Law, is, in different countries, widely different: while that which ought to be, is in all countries to a great degree the same.'[30] Much later, he distinguished between universally-applying and exclusively-applying circumstances on which the course taken by legislation depended, and again noted that 'In comparison of the *universally-applying*, the extent of the *exclusively-applying circumstances* will be found very inconsiderable'.[31]

At various stages during his career, arguing in the abstract, from the sources of pleasure available to human beings as such, Bentham asserted that since consensual homosexual acts caused no pain and delivered significant pleasure, there could be no utilitarian justification for punishing them.[32] In an abstract utilitarian penal code, such acts would be conspicuous by their absence. However, no such ideal code existed, and, more importantly, human beings did not live in the abstract, but in concrete settings full of non-utilitarian beliefs and attitudes. A legislator's decision to abolish the legal restraint on such acts, in a context wherein such restraint not only existed, but was endorsed by a large majority of the population, would be very likely to inflict significant pains on that majority, of which the legislator should take account.

John Rees, one of the few scholars to investigate Bentham's attitude to this question, argued that, while being much more prepared than J.S. Mill to allow restraint of self-regarding offences by the moral sanction, Bentham subscribed to the position (1) presented earlier – that is, my pain at contemplating your action which I believe wrong, but which causes no other pain, should be disregarded in the calculations of the legislator. Rees is correct in the abstract, but wrong in the concrete. According to abstract

is analyzable into individual interests, so communal beliefs are analyzable into individual beliefs, so that 'culture' is rarely univocal, but rather potentially contested.

30 'A Fragment on Government', in *A Comment on the Commentaries and a Fragment on Government*, eds. J.H. Burns and H.L.A. Hart (London: Athlone, 1977 (*CW*)) (henceforth *Comment/Fragment* (*CW*)), 391–551, at 397–8.

31 'Codification Proposal', 291.

32 For discussion of Bentham's analysis of the pleasures and pains arising from consensual homosexual acts, see P. Schofield, 'Jeremy Bentham on Taste, Sex and Religion', Chapter 5 in this volume, 109–13.

utility, it is true not only that 'antipathies, of themselves, can never be good reasons for applying restraints on conduct',[33] but that pains arising solely from a belief about the wrongness of an harmless action are not properly injuries, because a correct understanding of its harmlessness would eliminate the belief, and thereby the pain associated with it. Rees argues that Bentham, at least implicitly, subscribed to the view that 'the balance of pain is a consequence of (involved in) the action itself, not our personal feelings about the action'.[34] However, given the prevalence of non-utilitarian moral biases, the legislator is bound to take account of the pains dependent on the beliefs of the majority, whether groundless or not. In the abstract, Bentham's position anticipates Mill's very simple principle, but abstract utility, which is utterly universalist and cosmopolitan, is not, finally, the utility that matters, because its conclusions require to be modified in the light of prevailing sensibilities and biases, themselves dependent on beliefs which are specific to particular shared contexts, and which are very often not only parochial, but also anti-utilitarian.

A rational public opinion (and thus a rational popular sanction) would accord with abstract utility. As rendered by Dumont, Bentham described the popular sanction as 'the most active and faithful servant of the principle of utility, the most powerful and least dangerous ally of the political sanction'.[35] Although popular opinion and the dictates of utility were never completely congruent, Bentham sometimes sounded as if simply highlighting their divergence would suffice to eliminate it: 'Still a law conformed to utility may be found opposed to public opinion. But this is only an accidental and transient circumstance: it is only necessary to render this conformity sensible, in order to bring back all minds.'[36] To the extent that that divergence endured, public opinion was a potential source of mischief: 'In the greater part of the field of human action, the rules prescribed [by] public opinion coincide with the rules prescribed by the principle of utility, and so far, *and but so far*, is the influence of it contributory to universal welfare.'[37]

The enemies of utility were prejudice and asceticism. Prejudice was unevidenced assertion, 'a judgment, which being pronounced *before*

33 John Rees, *John Stuart Mill's* On Liberty, ed. G.L. Williams (Oxford: Clarendon Press, 1985), 45.

34 Ibid., 167.

35 'Principles of Penal Law', Part I: 'Political remedies for the evil of offences' (Bowring, i. 367–88, at 380).

36 'Principles of the Civil Code', Bowring, i. 324.

37 'Sextus', in *Of Sexual Irregularities* (*CW*), 51–2 (UC lxxiv. 50) (emphasis added).

evidence, is therefore pronounced without evidence'.[38] Since not all prejudices accorded with utility (although some accidentally did), there was no guarantee that public opinion and utility would coincide:

> To prove that an institution is agreeable to the principle of utility, is to prove, as far as can be proved, that the people *ought* to like it: but whether they *will* like it or no after all, is another question. They would like it if, in their judgments, they suffered themselves to be uniformly and exclusively governed by that principle.[39]

Where popular opinion cleaves to prejudice (that is caprice) or asceticism, 'The clear utility of the law will be *as its abstract utility, deduction made of the dissatisfaction and other inconvenience occasioned by it.*'[40] It is true that Bentham did not mention pain directly here, but dissatisfaction is at the very least a defalcation from pleasure, and elsewhere he criticized common lawyers for making an ill-informed distinction between 'inconvenience' and 'mischief',[41] mischief being understood as simply pain, or loss of pleasure.

Given that widespread prejudices and antipathies exist – often products of religious and cultural beliefs – which are at best supportive of, and at worst directly opposed to, abstract utility – and given that existing prejudicial and antipathetic biases have real effects on the pleasures and pains actually experienced by persons possessing them, there will exist, in effect, widespread variations in the distribution of pleasures and pains consequent on a substantive law which accords with abstract utility. Or, with Bentham:

> [I]t is not a case utterly improbable that the standard of perfection in matters of law may, with regard to certain points, be different in different countries, for a time at least, even where the influence of physical grounds of variation is out of the question. The case may be the same with regard to religion politically considered; but it is more particularly apt to be so with regard to those ordinary and continually repeated points of behaviour which come under the head of manners and way of life.[42]

Bentham wrote that many points in regard to forms of government, to religion and to manners, were 'indifferent',[43] and explained the meaning

38 'The Book of Fallacies', UC ciii. 540 (Bowring, ii. 375–487, at 478).

39 'Principles of Penal Law', Part II: 'Rationale of Punishment', Bowring, i. 390–525, at 411.

40 'Place and Time', 174 (Bowring, i. 181) (emphasis added).

41 *IPML* (*CW*), 24n.

42 'Place and Time', 170 (Bowring, i. 179).

43 Ibid., 169 (Bowring, i. 178).

of *indifferent* thus: 'If there result from an action, an evil, neither of the first nor second order, it belongs to the class of things *indifferent*.'[44] An indifferent action, practice or rule, then, is one that causes no mischief, that is, causes neither pain nor loss of pleasure. The classic examples of indifferent rules provide solutions to co-ordination problems: it makes no difference whether we drive on the right or the left, as long as we all do the one or the other. Elsewhere, Bentham provided a different gloss on indifferent: 'An action indifferent to society (if such there be) is an action that does *neither good nor harm in it*: or if that be not precise enough, that produces in it neither *pain* nor *pleasure*.'[45] Of course, there are two ways in which an act may have no impact on the balance of pains and pleasures. First, it may have no painful or pleasurable consequences at all, and second, it may have consequences of both sorts, which are equal in value and cancel each other out. Since very few, if any, human actions are not explicable in terms of pursuing pleasure or avoiding pain, acts indifferent in the first way will be rare, so that it seems most plausible to interpret indifferent as meaning that, taking account of both pleasant and painful effects, the act has no net impact on the aggregate of pathematic sensations.[46]

To what extent did Bentham allow that laws derived from considerations of abstract utility should be modified in accordance with local sensibilities? And what variations from abstract utility might reasonably be viewed as 'indifferent'?

> It may be better that in Bengal, at least among people of Asiatic race, the husbands should be disposed to expect that their wives should keep confined, and that the women should be disposed to submitt to such confinement: while in England it may be better that the husband should

44 Ibid., 174 (Bowring, i. 181).

45 'A Comment on the Commentaries', in *Comment/Fragment* (*CW*), 1–273, at 33.

46 See, for instance, *IPML* (*CW*), 79: 'So much with regard to acts considered in themselves: we come now to speak of the *circumstances* with which they may have been accompanied. These must necessarily be taken into the account before anything can be determined relative to the consequences. What the consequences of an act may be upon the whole can never otherwise be ascertained: it can never be known whether it is beneficial, or *indifferent*, or mischievous. In some circumstances even to kill a man may be a beneficial act; in others, to set food before him may be a pernicious one.' However, in 'Comment on the Commentaries', in *Comment/Fragment* (*CW*), 67, Bentham seemed to favour the first meaning, even while admitting that indifferent actions will be vanishingly rare: 'actions that are indifferent to pains and pleasures, are actions that produce neither pain or pleasure; Now these, if any such there be, are a sort of actions men, I conceive, are not very apt to do: for my notion of man is, that . . . he aims at happiness . . . in every thing he does.'

> not be disposed to entertain any such expectation, nor the wife to comply with it. If that be the case, there will be no reason why, by any new laws, we should seek to make an alteration in these ancient manners.[47]

Bentham gave a further example of what allegedly happened when a man of low caste accidentally touched the body of a man of superior caste: the upper caste man killed him without compunction, and without any deterrent sanction from either law or opinion. Bentham's comment? 'Such prejudices, should it be possible to avoid giving way to them altogether, would at least require to be attended to.'[48] To be fair, Bentham did not directly argue that casual slaughter, or the incarceration of married women were in fact indifferent, but given the general statement that many issues of religion and manners are indifferent, and the explicit recognition that it might be better to endorse existing cultural practices and beliefs which, for the convenience of men, severely curtailed the options available to women, one might be tempted to ask what it would take to qualify a practice as clearly mischievous rather than indifferent. Many modern liberals would baulk at such an elastic interpretation of the justificatory scope of the argument 'That's how we do things around here'.[49]

Further light is shed on the abstract-versus-concrete dichotomy by a passage in the Civil Code Writings:

> If we could suppose a new people, a generation of children: the legislator, finding no expectations formed which could oppose his views, might fashion them at his pleasure, as the sculptor fashions a block of marble. But as there already exists among all people a multitude of expectations, founded upon ancient laws or ancient usages, the legislator is obliged to employ a system of conciliations and concessions, which constantly restrain him.... *This natural expectation, this expectation produced by early habit, may be founded upon superstition, upon a hurtful prejudice, or upon a sentiment of utility: this is of no importance; the law which is conformed to it maintains its place in the mind without effort*;[50]

Here emerge both the centrality of expectations and the recognition that established expectations often have their roots in irrational prejudice. Consider, for instance, 'condition in life', one of the elements of security. Conditions in life in different societies varied, and they varied

[47] 'Place and Time', 170 (Bowring, i. 178).
[48] Ibid., 160 (Bowring, i. 174).
[49] See, for instance, B. Barry, *Culture and Equality: An Egalitarian Critique of Multiculturalism* (Cambridge: Polity, 2001), 279–92.
[50] 'Principles of the Civil Code', Bowring, i. 323 (emphasis added).

according to law, itself informed by manners and religion. In a rigidly divided society, the pleasures and pains available to the bottom rung of the social order were circumscribed by the rules, and if Bentham was prepared to allow that such rules might be indifferent, which is a possible interpretation of his recommendation that the legislator should maintain whatever distribution of property she finds established,[51] his universalism looks as good as non-existent.

Pitts praises Bentham for resisting, unlike Mill, the siren call of imperialist universalism, and for viewing religious beliefs, traditions and customs as 'parameters within which individuals make choices and as features of a society that must and can "with perfect propriety" be acknowledged by every legislator'. She applauds his conclusion that the designation of offences and extenuating or aggravating circumstances 'will have to vary according to the beliefs prevailing in a society, as will appropriate punishments'.[52] For Pitts, Bentham 'treats such customs as analogous to physical circumstances, such as the frequency of avalanches versus floods or famines'.[53] However, the point of Bentham's analogy was to highlight precisely not similarity, but difference. He drew a basic distinction between underlying physical circumstances, which were 'insurmountable' (i.e., unchangeable by the legislator), and 'the circumstances of government, religion, and manners', which were 'of the opposite cast' (i.e., *not* insurmountable, that is, *not* unchangeable): 'it is not physically impossible, at least for any reason that strikes one at first sight, but that a bad form of government, *a bad set of opinions on matters of religion, or a bad system of manners, may be changed into a better*'.[54] If we ask for the criterion of better or worse, Pitt's conventionalist Bentham would regard the question as meaningless, but the abstract universalist Bentham would simply refer to the balance of pleasures and pains of which human beings as such are susceptible.

It is not the case that Bentham uncritically accepted prevailing opinion, regardless of its content. Although there were large elements of subjectivism in his approach, he would not subscribe to the motto *vox populi, vox dei* without significant qualification. It was always a matter of doing the sum, and setting abstract utility against the affective consequences

51 Ibid., Bowring, i. 311.

52 J. Pitts, '"Great and Distant Crimes": Empire in Bentham's Thought', in *Jeremy Bentham: Selected Writings*, ed. Engelmann, 478–99, at 489.

53 Ibid.

54 'Place and Time', 167 (emphasis added).

of popular opinion. In other words, utility deals in facts, that is, in propositions based on empirical evidence, and capable of truth or falsehood. However, there are two different sorts of propositions involved in the utilitarian calculation. The first, involved in the calculation of abstract utilities, are psychological propositions about human beings as such, which Bentham thinks are true (that is, are supported by the best empirical evidence available, but liable to falsification by new evidence). The second, necessary to complete the calculation of final or net utility, are propositions about prevailing beliefs, and the sensibilities to which they give rise. These beliefs are often also capable of truth or falsehood – though many religious beliefs are capable of neither 3 – but the relevant propositions relate not to the truth or falsehood of the beliefs, which is strictly irrelevant, but to the truth or falsehood of the assertion that they do indeed prevail in particular contexts, and are resistant to alteration. The dictates of abstract utility then follow from psychological truths, but, in cases where prevailing beliefs are false, the dictates of final or net utility are the product of the modification of abstract utility by the affective impact of widely held falsehoods (or, in relation to religion, of neither truths nor falsehoods but of nonsensical propositions – that is, propositions untestable by sense experience).

Kaino places Bentham 'midway between "globalization" and "cultural pluralism"',[55] and his characterization does capture Bentham's sensitivity to both generic commonalities and specific differences, to the importance of both the physiology and psychology which all human beings share, and the conventions which characterize particular communities. Perhaps Armitage, who cautions against 'throwing the universalist baby out with the imperialist bathwater', best sums up Bentham's effort to address all relevant factors: 'The global Bentham who emerges was engaged in a lifelong dialogue between universalism and particularism which neither he nor his followers in the nineteenth century (and beyond) were ever able finally to resolve.'[56]

The Legal and the Moral Sanctions

What is the legislator to do when faced with a public opinion or an existing law which flies in the face of abstract utility? She is to engage in a utilitarian

[55] M. Kaino, 'Bentham's concept of security in a global context: the Pannomion and the Public Opinion Tribunal as a universal plan', *Journal of Bentham Studies* 10 (2008).

[56] D. Armitage, 'Globalizing Jeremy Bentham', *History of Political Thought* 32 (2011), 63–82, at 82, 67.

calculation of the costs and benefits of a reform in the direction of greater utility. Bentham described a set of rules for the calculation,[57] among which should be noted the insistence that some assignable benefit should be likely to issue from the change, the insistence that change simply to bring the law into harmony with the legislator's own 'manners and sentiments' was baseless, and the insistence that in matters of indifference, the law should remain silent, allowing the moral sanction to 'take its course'. The crucial rule has already been cited, and turns on the extent to which the gain in abstract utility of the proposed law is offset by 'the dissatisfaction and other inconvenience occasioned by it'. As Ten notes in criticism of Rees, it is important to distinguish between the fact of antipathy and its ground: 'the fact that non-utilitarians are distressed by conduct they believe to be wrong is as much an "objective" fact about the world, to be settled by empirical observations, as the fact that assault causes physical injury'.[58]

In a society such as Bentham's own, where homosexuality was deeply unpopular, the dissatisfaction arising from the decriminalization of homosexual behaviour might be expected to be extensive, intense and lasting. Whether the legislator would be justified in imposing such a reform depended crucially on its unpopularity, and its unpopularity depended in part on its abstract utility, but in at least as large part on prevailing moral biases. There is a parallel here with Bentham's discussions of the franchise, where he repeatedly argued that the exclusion of women was based on nothing more than deep-seated prejudice.[59] However, in regard to the franchise, Bentham was prepared to surrender to that prejudice, and await the arrival of more enlightened attitudes. Prejudiced or not, existing attitudes determine the utilitarian strategy for reform. As Bentham noted in his sex writings: 'How void so ever of support on any just grounds, popular discontent is not the less an evil.'[60]

The sex writings provide further evidence of the relation between abstract and net utility. Bentham's analysis of the pains and pleasures

[57] 'Place and Time', 173–4 (Bowring, i. 181–2).

[58] C.L. Ten, 'Mill's Defence of Liberty', in *J.S. Mill* On Liberty *in Focus*, ed. J. Gray and G.W. Smith (London: Routledge, 1991), 212–38, at 234.

[59] See, for instance, '*Projet* of a constitutional code for France', in *Rights, Representation, and Reform: Nonsense upon stilts and Other Writings on the French Revolution*, ed. P. Schofield, C. Pease-Watkin, and C. Blamires (Oxford: Clarendon Press, 2002 (*CW*)), 227–61 at 246–8; 'Plan of Parliamentary Reform, in the form of a Catechism', Bowring, iii. 433–538, at 463.

[60] 'General Idea of a Work, having for one of its objects The Defence of the Principle of *Utility*, so far as concerns The Liberty of Taste, against the conjunct hostility of The Principle of *Asceticism* and The Principle of *Antipathy*; and for its proposed title, proposed on the ground of expected popularity, or at least protection against popular rage, – Not Paul, but Jesus', in *Of Sexual Irregularities* (*CW*), 117–44 (henceforth 'General Idea'), at 140 (UC clxi. 18).

arising from sex acts which delivered pleasure to the participants without imposing pains on themselves or others was undertaken in terms of universal generalizations about human capacities, that is, in terms of abstract utility. The result of that analysis was Bentham's advocacy of an 'ultimate liberty – viz. all-comprehensive liberty for all modes of sexual gratification not predominantly noxious'.[61] The reference to 'ultimate' liberty here is ambiguous, but it is plausible that its import is temporal and constitutes a recognition that there was no immediate prospect of establishing such liberty. Thus, in the same text – after a long-sustained and passionate argument to the effect that consensual homosexual sex acts were harmless – Bentham explicitly addressed the probable popular rejection of that argument, and in recognition thereof proposed neither all-comprehensive liberty, nor even decriminalization, but rather that consensual same-sex acts should be punished by banishment instead of hanging. Having sought thus to appease public sentiment, Bentham immediately attempted to recover the ground conceded, and to draw the teeth from his proposed punishment, by adding: 'But, for conviction, except in case of violence, require two witnesses, whereof no person, concerned as principal or accessary in the offence, shall be one.'[62] There is irony that on these two issues Bentham's abstract conclusions are indeed radical: women should have the vote, and consensual gay sex should be free of sanctions. However, precisely in recognition of erroneous popular prejudices, his concrete proposals for reform are, to say the least, rather less radical.

In 1822, Bentham drafted a 'constitutional charter' for Tripoli, a context in which abstract utility might well be expected to make significant concessions to local sympathetic and antipathetic biases. Although sexual behaviour does not feature specifically, the religious sensitivities of Muslims are central to his provisions. What is notable for present purposes is that he can plausibly be interpreted as seeking to balance abstract and concrete utility by providing a succession of 'securities' and 'counter-securities'. Thus freedom of worship is guaranteed by Article 1, as directed by abstract utility, but the counter-security seeks to insulate Muslim sensitivities from potential pain: 'Provided that it be in a chamber enclosed and covered, and that the eyes of the True Believer be not annoyed by

[61] Ibid. This 'ultimate liberty' appears twice in chapter titles for the sex writings, although no extensive discussion was drafted. See 'Sextus', in *Of Sexual Irregularities* (*CW*), 104, and 'General Idea', in ibid., 142 (UC clxi. 18).

[62] 'General Idea', in *Of Sexual Irregularities* (*CW*), 142 (UC clxi. 18).

public ceremonies or processions . . . or his ears by the sound of bells or other noises.'[63]

The two next Articles begin by following the dictates of abstract utility, and guaranteeing free expression on the subject of religion, whether by speech or in writing, 'even although the truth or the goodness of the only true religion be impeached thereby. By the True Believer that which is adverse to the only true religion will either not be read at all, or read with the merited contempt.'[64] However, the corresponding counter-securities again provide protection for Muslim sensitivities, by making the public exposure of writing which would be offensive to the true believer an offence. The counter-security relating to religious speech acts is worth quoting in full:

> Provided that no discourse, whereby either the truth or the goodness of the only true religion is impeached, be uttered in any public place in such manner as to be offensive to the ears of the True Believer as he passes: or in the presence and to the displeasure of any True Believer in any private place. *The utterance of any such discourse in the hearing of the True Believer is an injury to him, and as such may be punished according to law.*[65]

Abstract utility might endorse a more extensive freedom of speech, but the consequences of seeking to establish that freedom would first reduce the chances of adoption of the charter, and second, even were it adopted, would impose pains on true believers which might outweigh the benefits of free speech. Article 4 guarantees to every citizen liberty to express and 'to any extent to make public', 'whatsoever in his judgment it will be contributory to the greatest happiness of the greatest number [for men] to be informed of'.[66] The corresponding counter-security confines itself to protection against defamation, but note that if I act on my judgment that it would contribute to utility for men to be informed of my doubts as to the truth of the only true religion, I immediately transgress Article 2.

In 'Place and Time', Bentham concluded his rules for transplanting laws with the recommendation of a patient, cautious approach, and the avoidance, if possible, of a head-on attack on prejudice: 'As a means of obviating dissatisfaction, indirect legislation should be preferred to direct:

63 *Securities Against Misrule, and Other Constitutional Writings for Tripoli and Greece*, ed. P. Schofield (Oxford: Clarendon Press, 1990 (*CW*)), 79.

64 Ibid., 80.

65 Ibid. (emphasis added).

66 Ibid.

gentle means, to violent: example, instruction, and exhortation should precede, or follow, or, if possible, stand in the place of, law.'[67] Bentham provided only a negative definition of indirect legislation, which consisted in 'whatever . . . can be done in the way of law' which is not direct legislation, which does not, that is to say, prohibit acts identified as sufficiently mischievous to be designated offences.[68] Indirect legislation thus encompassed a vast and disparate range of government action relating to norms. Why prefer indirect legislation to direct? In part precisely because its approach was oblique, and thus offered means of facilitating a change in public opinion without flagrantly contradicting it. By no means all indirect legislation operated by stealth, but part of its attraction to Bentham lay in its capacity to outflank widely held anti-utilitarian prejudices without sharing its intention of so doing: 'There is a secret art of governing opinion, so that it shall not perceive, so to speak, the manner in which it is led.'[69] One strategy was to establish new connections in the public mind. Thus you might try to associate a harmless practice you wish to decriminalize with something else which is highly valued by the public. If you were able to demonstrate that, for instance, widely admired figures in the nation's military or political history had been in the habit of engaging in consensual homosexual sex acts, and successfully disseminated that demonstration, you might hope that hostility to homosexuality would gradually abate.[70]

The Return of Abstract Utility?

In essence, the only way to combat a prejudice is by presenting the evidence in the case. Here, the universalist, objectivist Bentham returns to the fore. If I want to argue that a deeply unpopular activity is, in fact,

[67] 'Place and Time', 174 (Bowring, i. 181–2).

[68] See 'Indirect Legislation', 'Plan', UC lxxxvii. 2–3; 'Principles of Penal Law', Part III: 'Of Indirect Means of Preventing Crimes', Bowring i. 533–80, at 533–4.

[69] 'Of Indirect Means of Preventing Crimes', Bowring i. 563. Admittedly, this quotation comes from Dumont's recension rather than Bentham's English essay 'Indirect Legislation', where it does not appear. However, the following all do appear in the latter: 'In the one case [direct legislation], he aims directly at his mark, he attacks the mischief directly and in front: in indirect legislation he attacks it by oblique and sometimes scarcely perceptible approaches' ('Plan', UC lxxxvii. 3); 'In Indirect [legislation] he nets every thing by imperceptible wires, keeping himself behind the curtain' ('Appendix I', UC xcvi. 257); 'In most systems of law there is a secret history which differs more or less widely from the public one' ('Prefat', UC lxxxvii. 6).

[70] The esoteric nature of some forms of indirect legislation appears to contradict Bentham's deep commitment to transparency and publicity. If the legislator shares her rationale for oblique acts of indirect legislation, she explodes their obliqueness, and thus renders them ineffective. This, however, is a subject for a different paper.

harmless, I have no other recourse than to appeal to the evidence, and to demand of my ipse dixitist opponents that they do the same. In drafting 'Projet Matière', Bentham noted that the legislator might have problems with popular discontent in relation to taxes, whether that discontent was justified or simply prejudiced. To prejudiced discontent, he supplied a single antidote: 'Instruction'.[71]

In instruction, appeal is made directly to the understanding, by advancing propositions capable of truth or falsehood, and capable of demonstration as true or false by appeal to empirical evidence, or, in short, to facts, on the basis of which the utilitarian makes decisions. Bentham's analysis of the alleged evils of consensual homosexual intercourse concluded that there was simply no evidence that they existed. In consequence, British law and British public opinion were both simply wrong in inflicting pain, through the legal and the moral sanction, respectively, on people who did no harm. Law and public opinion both erred in acting on the basis of erroneous, that is false, beliefs. Another case Bentham discussed was that of smuggling, which in Britain was punishable by law, but was indulged by public opinion to the extent that the law was brought into disrepute. What was the legislator to do? She had no recourse but to address the understanding, and to explain the harm, that is the pain, caused by the offence, which was equivalent to stealing from the public revenue:

> In some cases the mischief is the immediate consequence of the conduct to be discountenanced: in others the contingent and remote: in the former cases it lies on the surface of the object and is caught by the first glance: in the latter, being covered up and shrouded by the multitude of intervening links in the chain of causes and effects, it requires the hand of a master to fish it out and lay it open to the eyes of the unreflecting multitude. In former cases then the main object is to warm the affections: in the latter the understanding is to be informed. *In these cases it will be of use to give a concise and familiar demonstration of the mischievousness of the practise: tracing the progress of the evil from the act which is its source to the pain which is its consummation.* The cases of smuggling or to put it more generally of non-payment of taxes, and that of connivance at the escape of criminals, or to put it more generally at the impunity of delinquents, may answer the purpose of examples.[72]

Where the prejudice was strong, as in the case of smuggling, the legislator was obliged to proportion her efforts at instruction to the strength of the

[71] UC xcix. 149.

[72] 'Indirect Legislation', Ch. 15, 'Culture of the moral sanction', UC lxxxvii. 19 (emphasis added).

prejudice, 'or the [degree] of blindness which it has to combat.'[73] Finally, the legislator should beware overstating her case, and recognize the uncertainties inescapably involved in probabilistic judgments of consequences:

> In such, as indeed in most matters, the cautious statesman will avoid the tone of peremptoriness and decision: his conclusions will always, in the first instance, be hypothetical. *If* such and such events are the likeliest to take place: But are they? This is a matter which ought to be stated as accompanied with the degree of uncertainty that belongs to it.[74]

When faced with a strongly opposed public opinion, the pains which the utilitarian legislator wished to impose by the political sanction, and those imposed by the moral sanction operated at loggerheads. The legislator might prefer to create offences on the basis of abstract utility, but public opinion tended to be led by sympathy and antipathy (and, where the Christian religion prevailed, by asceticism). No legislator could simply dictate to public opinion, but she was in a position to guide it:

> The legislator is in an eminent degree possessed of the means of guiding public opinion. The power with which he is invested gives to his instructions . . . far greater weight than would be attributed to them if falling from a private individual. The public, generally speaking, presumes that the Government has at its command . . . the requisite sources of information. It is presumed also, that in the great majority of cases its interest is the same with that of the people, and that it is unbiassed by personal interest, which is so apt to misguide the opinion of individuals. . . .
>
> The legislator is clothed not only with political, but with moral power. It is what is commonly expressed by the words consideration, respect, confidence.[75]

Having just stressed objectivism, it should be noted that Bentham also advised the use of literature and drama, that is, appeal to the emotions:

> History, biography, novels and dramatic compositions are all so many [instruments] by the circulation of which the force of the moral sanction may be encreased, as well as the application of it may be regulated. . . . The burthen of these compositions will turn all along upon the following points: virtue represented as amiable, vice in odious, colours: the former rewarded; the latter punished.[76]

[73] Indirect Legislation', Ch. 4, 'Avoiding to administer incentives to delinquency', UC lxxxvii. 55.
[74] 'Place and Time', 178 (Bowring, i. 183).
[75] 'Rationale of Punishment', Bowring, i. 464.
[76] 'Indirect Legislation', Ch. 15, 'Culture of the Moral Sanction', UC lxxxvii. 18.

Often, individual initiative sufficed to supply countervailing arguments to popular prejudice, but the legislator might sponsor or encourage similar works.

The legislator should always be aware that running too far ahead of public opinion entailed the danger of undermining her capacity to make her will effective. For Bentham, sovereignty depended absolutely on a disposition to obey on the part of subjects: if the legislator fatally weakened that disposition, her sovereignty was at an end. Under Bentham's Constitutional Code, no democratic government could survive a major rejection by public opinion, since its supporters would be ejected at the next election. In Bentham's early writings, the figure of the legislator is, in effect, the embodiment of the principle of utility.[77] The discovery of sinister interest upset this comfortable identification, but the point remains that, regardless of the principles by which the legislator is guided, the popular or moral sanction is typically guided by the principle of sympathy and antipathy.

> Men, private men, punish because they hate. . . . Lawgivers . . . think they see just cause for lawgivers to punish, where they think they see just cause for lawgivers to hate. . . . The more they hate, the more they wish to punish. Crimes, they are told, they ought to hate. Crimes it is made a matter of merit to them to hate. Crimes it is a matter of merit, of more than merit – of necessity, to punish. They are to hate them – they are to punish them. 'Tis their hating makes them wish to punish. How then should they punish but *as* they hate?[78]

For the utilitarian, this approach is completely wrong, since hatred and antipathy have no necessary connection with truth, or with objective harm, demonstrable by evidence. False beliefs produce real pains, but this does not mean that Bentham's legislator should simply surrender to popular prejudice. Instead, she should use every means at her disposal in attempting to substitute for that prejudice the best evidence-based judgment available. 'Every nation is liable to have its prejudices and its caprices, which it is the business of the legislator to look out for, to study, and to cure.'[79] In 'Place and Time', he concluded that if popular prejudices were unremittingly hostile to a reform which promised to deliver a clear gain in human welfare, or were incompatible with 'those obligations by

77 See R. Harrison, *Bentham* (London: Routledge & Kegan Paul, 1983), 206.
78 'Memoirs and Correspondence', Bowring, x. 69.
79 *IPML* (*CW*), 183.

means of which society is kept together', the legislator must be prepared to override them:

> These prejudices have generally some salvo for good government, as the most pernicious tracts in religion have frequently . . . some salvo for good morals. Find out this salvo then. if there is one, and make use of it: and in the mean time, if it be worth while, try what instruction and other gentle means will do, towards getting the better of the prejudice.
>
> But if nothing of this kind will do, and it be found impossible to untie the Gordian knot, do like Alexander and cut it. The welfare of all must not be sacrificed to the obstinacy of a few; nor the happiness of ages to the quiet of the day.[80]

After all, as Bentham noted, the dissatisfaction caused by change was likely to be temporary, but the benefit would be permanent. Elsewhere however, he recognized that if the legislator's efforts at instruction proved unavailing, the balance of utilities might forbid reform:

> A measure is unpopular; but useful, were it not unpopular; should it be put in force? Perhaps it should, perhaps not: one cannot say. Forthwith? By no means. – Should it then be abandoned? Nor that neither. – What then? Thus: – You say it is useful? Yes. – Why is it? For such and such reasons. – But will those reasons be accepted by the people? Who knows? – It may know; it is a matter of experiment; ask them . . . publish your plan, and at the same time publish your intention of adopting it, if they approve of it in a certain time. Is there a violent outcry against it? let it drop. Is there but a faint outcry against it, or no notice taken? carry it into execution. What is to be deemed a violent, what a faint outcry? Ask not things impossible. Rules have here no place; your discretion must direct you; with this one rule only to assist it, *the measure is still to be put into execution, if the good of it to them promises to be greater than the evil of their dissatisfaction at the thought of it.*[81]

What is notable here is the consequence that, on utilitarian grounds, the legal sanction might continue to punish harmless acts even where abstract utility clearly indicated that such punishment was unjustified. So much for cutting the Gordian knot. Further, while Bentham noted that the easiest reform to make was to withhold the endorsement of the legal sanction from prejudiced public sentiment, this reform left full rein to the pains inflicted by the moral sanction.[82] This matters because, as

80 'Place and Time', 175 (Bowring, i. 182).

81 'Memoirs and Correspondence', Bowring, x. 146–7 (emphasis added).

82 See 'Place and Time', 174 (Bowring, i. 181).

Bentham noted, the moral sanction 'is and ever must be an engine of great power in whatever direction it be applied'.[83] Indeed, Bentham recognized that, such was the strength of homophobic prejudice in England, simply refusing to apply the legal sanction to harmless sexual acts would leave those suspected of homosexuality faced with the imposition of huge pains: 'were it even altogether unpunishable by law . . . the consequence of being reputed guilty would be attended with a degree of infamy which can be compared to nothing so properly as that which attends forfeiture of caste among the Hindoos'.[84]

Sidgwick's attitude to popular morality provides an echo here. Orsi's analysis of Sidgwick's treatment of common sense sexual morality concludes that despite finding no consistent and self-evident conceptual basis for that morality, Sidgwick, conscious of the costs involved in changing public attitudes, wished to co-opt some portion of that morality into his utilitarian project.[85] For Orsi, Sidgwick distinguishes between the questions, 'whether a certain kind of behaviour is intrinsically wrong', and 'whether, at a certain point in history, we ought to continue prohibiting that kind of behaviour, even if it is morally permissible'. Centrally, 'A negative answer to the former question does not determine a negative answer to the latter.' Sidgwick may not have used the expression 'abstract utility', but the distinction between the questions, and the possibility that they may demand different responses, provide a striking resonance with the question at issue in this paper. A further echo of Bentham's attitude appears in Sidgwick's comment:

> [I]t has become plain that though two different kinds of conduct cannot both be right under the same circumstances, two contradictory opinions as to the rightness of conduct may possibly both be expedient; it may conduce most to the general happiness that A should do a certain act, and at the same time that B, C, D should blame it.[86]

In circumstances where prevailing opinion remained stubbornly prejudiced, Bentham might have said the same thing. Given his recognition of the harmlessness of many acts punished by English law, and the additional pains imposed by the moral sanction to which public knowledge of such acts would give rise, it is very likely that he would have endorsed the esotericism of the 'don't ask, don't tell' policy entailed by Sidgwick's

[83] UC cxli. 100.
[84] 'Place and Time', 162–3 (Bowring, i. 175).
[85] See F. Orsi, 'Sidgwick and the Morality of Purity', *Revue d'études benthamiennes*, 10 (2012).
[86] Henry Sidgwick, *The Methods of Ethics*, 3rd edn. (London: Macmillan, 1884), 486.

comment that 'it may be conceivably right to do, if it can be done with comparative secrecy, what it would be wrong to do in the face of the world'.[87] The closest Bentham came to an explicit endorsement was in discussion of offences of 'fornication', and more particularly of seduction, when the birth of an illegitimate child ensued. Bentham argued that the evils of this offence arose not from the act itself, but from the public's hostile reaction to it, and commented: 'In general the great object is to bring about detection: here the object is to prevent it: since it is from the detection rather than from the act that the mischief takes its rise.'[88] A major difference between consensual same-sex acts and seduction consisted in the necessarily unprolific nature of the former, which rendered them even more unquestionably harmless than the latter. It is very probable then that both in cases where public opinion precluded the legislator from decriminalizing such acts, and where such acts were punished only by the moral sanction, Bentham would believe that the utilitarian should not disclose her knowledge of them.

Conclusion

It has been argued that in abstract terms, Bentham does indeed appear to have anticipated the very simple principle advocated by J.S. Mill in *On Liberty*. However, Bentham was acutely aware that human beings do not live in the abstract, but in contexts thick with religious and moral beliefs which are often directly opposed to utilitarian reasoning. In seeking to reform prevailing opinions in accordance with abstract utility, the utilitarian legislator is obliged to calculate the costs of reform in the shape of the pains it would inflict on the holders of prevailing beliefs. Identifying the best rule is always and everywhere a matter of calculation, of quantifying abstract utilities and then quantifying the effects of the sensibilities associated with prevailing belief systems. Attacking widely held beliefs head-on is not only likely to be contrary to the dictates of utility – that is to produce a net balance on the side of pain – but also to be unsuccessful, in that public opinion sets limits to the legislator's freedom of action. For this reason, on this issue at least, Sidgwick, rather

[87] Ibid., 485.

[88] 'Indirect Legislation', Ch. 18 'Expedients combating the mischief of the offence', UC lxxxvii. 128. See also Dumont's version of the passage in 'Of Indirect Means of Preventing Crimes', Bowring, i. 578: 'Thus a good citizen, who would esteem it a duty to publish an act of fraud, would take care to conceal a secret fault arising from love.'

than Mill, emerges as the more faithful disciple of Bentham. However, this assertion should be qualified by the recognition that Mill himself was at least as sensitive as Bentham to the impact of historical context, noting notoriously that 'Liberty, as a principle, has no application to any state of things anterior to the time when mankind have become capable of being improved by free and equal discussion'.[89] Perhaps then, *On Liberty* itself is best understood as an attempted exercise in a kind of unofficial and non-deceptive indirect legislation, that is, as an effort to combat the social tyranny of opinion by engaging the understanding of his readers, and modifying their attitudes without modifying their interests. As Mill wrote to Alexander Bain: 'the effect I aim at by the book is . . . to make the many more accessible to all truth by making them more open minded'.[90]

89 Mill, *On Liberty*, 224.

90 *The Later Letters of John Stuart Mill, 1849–73* (*Collected Works of John Stuart Mill*, vol. xv), eds. F.E. Mineka and D.N. Lindley (Toronto and London: University of Toronto Press/Routledge & Kegan Paul, 1972), 631.

5

Jeremy Bentham on Taste, Sex, and Religion

PHILIP SCHOFIELD[1]

Introduction

Bentham addressed the subject of sexual non-conformity when working on his penal code in the 1770s and 1780s. He argued that, since consensual sexual activity did not cause harm to any one, it should not be constituted into a criminal offence, and hence the English penal laws against homosexuality should be repealed.[2] Bentham returned to the subject in the mid-1810s as part of a wide-ranging critique of religion, and this material forms the focus of the present chapter. In 1814, he wrote an essay entitled 'Of Sexual Irregularities'. In 1816, he composed material under the heading 'Sextus',[3] into which he integrated some of the material written for 'Of Sexual Irregularities'.[4] In the autumn and winter of 1817–18, he redrafted 'Sextus' in order to form the third and final volume of 'Not Paul, but Jesus', on which he was working at the time. The first volume was

1 The author wishes to thank the Leverhulme Trust for its support for the editorial work on Bentham's writings on sexual morality which has made this paper possible. He is grateful to colleagues at the Bentham Project, and particularly Catherine Pease-Watkin, Michael Quinn, and Oliver Harris, for their help in transcribing manuscripts and in providing elucidations for many of Bentham's allusions and references.

2 A version of this material was edited by Louis Crompton and published under the title of 'Jeremy Bentham's Essay on Paederasty', *Journal of Homosexuality*, 3 (1978), 383–405, and 4 (1978), 91–107.

In relation to terminology, Bentham did not use the words 'homosexual' or 'heterosexual' (which came into use in the late nineteenth century), and tended to avoid 'sodomy' and 'buggery', which were terms commonly used in his time. He seems to have used 'pæderasty' to refer to sexual relationships where an elder male took the active part in relation to a youthful male.

3 The allusion was to sexual gratification as the sixth sense.

4 A preliminary version has been published in *Jeremy Bentham: Selected Writings*, ed. S.G. Engelmann (New Haven and London: Yale University Press, 2011), 33–100. The authoritative edition of this essay, together with 'Of Sexual Irregularities' and other material, has recently appeared as part of *The Collected Works of Jeremy Bentham* in *Of Sexual Irregularities and Other Writings on Sexual Morality*, eds. P. Schofield, C. Pease-Watkin, and M. Quinn (Oxford: Clarendon Press, 2014 (*CW*)).

eventually published in 1823,[5] but the second and third volumes were not published during Bentham's lifetime.[6] In this substantial text, Bentham aimed to drive a wedge between the religion of Jesus and the religion of Paul – between Christianity and Paulism.[7] He argued that the doctrine of asceticism, the direct opposite of the principle of utility, had not only not been approved but had been condemned by Jesus, whereas Paul had taught and encouraged it. The reason why so many sexual practices were condemned, in some cases criminalized, and in the case of male same-sex relationships, in England at least, punished with death, was the prevalence of a sexual morality that had originated in the Mosaic law but had been incorporated into the Christian tradition by the teachings of Paul. The only sexual practice that was approved was the 'regular' one involving one male and one female, within marriage, for the procreation of children. All other 'modes' of sexual gratification were condemned as unnatural, distasteful, and disgusting, and, therefore, morally wrong. The false standard of 'good taste' was thereby set up against the only true standard, the principle of utility.

Taste in Arts and Sciences

For Bentham, there were two broad meanings of the term *taste* that were perfectly comprehensible and proper. The first meaning was where taste referred to the sensations derived from the palate.[8] The second meaning was where taste referred to the propensity to derive pleasure from an object or, he might have added, an activity: 'Taste for any object is an aptitude or disposition to derive pleasure [from] that object.'[9] There was, however, a third use of the term that was both nonsensical and mischievous, namely where taste purported to refer to an aesthetic sensibility – to

5 *Not Paul, but Jesus* (London: John Hunt), 1823, was published under the pseudonym of Gamaliel Smith.

6 A preliminary version of the third volume is now available for the first time, having been published online by the Bentham Project: see 'Not Paul, but Jesus Vol. III', ed. P. Schofield, M. Quinn, and C. Pease-Watkin, www.ucl.ac.uk/Bentham-Project/publications/npbj/npbj.html (Bentham Project, 2013).

7 See 'Not Paul, but Jesus Vol. III', 10 (UC clxi. 216, (30 December 1817)) for the term 'Paulism'.

8 See 'Table of the Springs of Action', in *Deontology together with a Table of the Springs of Action and Article on Utilitarianism*, ed. A. Goldworth (Oxford: Clarendon Press, 1983 (*CW*)), 79–86, at 79.

9 'Of Sexual Irregularities', in *Of Sexual Irregularities and Other Writings on Sexual Morality* (*CW*), 1–45, at 4 (UC lxxiv. 174 ([18] April 1814)).

an appreciation of 'the sublime and beautiful', in Burke's phrase[10] – which was, at the same time, a quality monopolized by a cultured elite. To speak of 'good taste' and 'bad taste' was to speak nonsense, in the same way that to speak of 'good motives' and 'bad motives' was to speak nonsense. The terms *good* and *bad* could sensibly apply only to the consequences of actions, not to the motives that produced those actions. In the same way, 'taste', or rather the inclination to engage in one activity rather than another, was good only in the sense that the activity produced pleasure, and bad in that it produced pain. In Bentham's view, the notion of 'good taste', or aesthetic appreciation, did not represent a value that stood independently of pleasure and pain, and thus to suggest that some individuals possessed 'good taste', whereas others did not, was to ascribe to them a non-existent quality, and hence to talk nonsense. The point was that pleasures and pains were all that mattered, and that any one person's pleasures and pains, quantity being equal, were of equal value with those of any other person, no matter the activity from which they were derived.

The notion of 'good taste' was supposed to manifest itself in the appreciation of such pursuits as poetry, art, music, and architecture. Bentham placed these pursuits in a wider context in an account of arts and sciences that appeared in *Rationale of Reward*.[11] The distinction that Bentham drew between art and science was not that between the humanities, such as philosophy, literature, and history, on the one hand, and the natural sciences, such as physics, chemistry, and biology, on the other. In Bentham's view, science consisted of abstract knowledge, whereas art consisted of the practical application of that knowledge. Hence, every subject was both an art and a science, although some subjects were more theoretical, and tended to be termed sciences, whereas others were more practical, and tended to be termed arts.[12] Bentham divided the arts and sciences into those of 'amusement and curiosity' on the one hand, and

[10] See Edmund Burke, 'A Philosophical Enquiry into the Origin of Our Ideas of the Sublime and Beautiful', in *The Writings and Speeches of Edmund Burke. Volume I: The Early Writings*, ed. T.O. McLoughlin, J.T. Boulton, and W.B. Todd (Oxford: Clarendon Press, 1997), 185–320.

[11] The text first appeared as the second volume of Étienne Dumont's French recension *Théorie des peines et des récompenses*, 2 vols. (London: Vogel and Schulze, 1811), based primarily on manuscripts written in the 1780s. It was translated into English by Richard Smith, and published as *The Rationale of Reward* (London: John and H.L. Hunt, 1825), and reprinted in Bowring, ii. 189–266.

[12] 'Rationale of Reward', Bowring, ii. 252–3. This particular passage on the distinction between art and science, as Richard Smith acknowledges in an editorial footnote, is copied from a section of *Chrestomathia* that had been printed in 1815 and published in 1816 (see *Chrestomathia*, eds. M.J. Smith and W.H. Burston (Oxford: Clarendon Press, 1983 (*CW*)), 59–60).

those of 'utility, immediate and remote', on the other. This latter category included medicine and legislation, and within this category the distinction between immediate and remote again turned upon whether the subject matter was more practical or more theoretical.[13] As Bentham appreciated, there was no firm line between them, and a subject that appeared highly theoretical at first discovery, such as electricity, could become eminently practical.[14] The arts and sciences of amusement consisted of 'those which are ordinarily called the *fine arts;* such as music, poetry, painting, sculpture, architecture, ornamental gardening, &c. &c.' Bentham was not prepared to enter into 'the metaphysical discussions' that would be necessary to give a complete list, but added: 'Amusements of all sorts would be comprised under this head'. It was not that there was no utility in such amusements, for their utility was 'incontestable', because they gave pleasure to those who engaged in them. Their utility, however, was 'limited to the excitement of pleasure', in that they were unable to 'disperse the clouds of grief or of misfortune'. Bentham's point was that the pursuit of amusements could not produce a diminution in, or avoidance of, pain. Amusements had no benefit beyond 'those who take pleasure in them', and even then the benefit occurred 'only in proportion as they are pleased'. Similarly, the arts and sciences of curiosity were activities that brought pleasure to those who engaged in them. The distinction between the arts and sciences of amusement and those of curiosity lay in the number of persons who pursued them, with the latter restricted to a much smaller number of devotees:

> Of this nature are the sciences of heraldry, of medals, of pure chronology – the knowledge of ancient and barbarous languages, which present only collections of strange words, – and the study of antiquities, inasmuch as they furnish no instruction applicable to morality, or any other branch of useful or agreeable knowledge.[15]

Having said that, no one amusement was any more valuable in itself than another:

> Prejudice apart, the game of push-pin is of equal value with the arts and sciences of music and poetry. If the game of push-pin furnish more

[13] Combining the accounts written for *Rationale of Reward* and for *Chrestomathia*, it would seem that a subject matter of remote utility would tend to be termed a science, and one of immediate utility would tend to be termed an art.

[14] 'Rationale of Reward', Bowring, ii. 255–6.

[15] Ibid., Bowring, ii. 253.

> pleasure, it is more valuable than either. Everybody can play at push-pin: poetry and music are relished only by a few.

Poetry, moreover, could be put to mischievous purposes, since it was often opposed to truth, whereas push-pin was 'always innocent'. Bentham concluded: 'If poetry and music deserve to be preferred before a game of push-pin, it must be because they are calculated to gratify those individuals who are most difficult to be pleased'. Bentham's remark on push-pin and poetry is as well known as any in his corpus, but what is rarely appreciated is that he was making the comparison within the context of the arts and sciences of amusement and curiosity. He did not claim that the pursuit of push-pin had as much value as the arts and sciences of utility.[16] Nevertheless, the crucial point was that the value of an activity was measured by its contribution to happiness, and not by reference to some (non-existent) quality intrinsic to the activity itself.

Arts and sciences of amusement and curiosity had a further value in that 'They compete with, and occupy the place of those mischievous and dangerous passions and employments, to which want of occupation and ennui give birth. They are excellent substitutes for drunkenness, slander, and the love of gaming'. Drawing on Tacitus's account of the Germans, Bentham claimed that in ancient times, because there was little else to do, both men and women had been eager to go to war: 'The chieftain who proposed a martial expedition, at the first sound of his trumpet ranged under his banners a crowd of idlers, to whom peace was a condition of restraint, of languor, and ennui.' In modern times, the 'army of idlers' who would otherwise have amused themselves by playing 'the hazardous and bloody game of war' had devoted themselves to the fine arts, and become opposed to war.[17]

Every art and science, therefore, had its utility, in that it brought pleasure to those who pursued it. Yet there were 'critics' who, 'under pretence of purifying the public taste, endeavour successively to deprive mankind of a larger or smaller part of the sources of their amusement'.

> These modest judges of elegance and taste consider themselves as benefactors to the human race, whilst they are really only the interrupters of their pleasure – a sort of importunate hosts, who place themselves at the table to diminish, by their pretended delicacy, the appetite of their guests.

16 Ibid., Bowring, ii. 253–4; and compare ibid. 255: 'The child who is building houses of cards is happier than was Louis XIV when building Versailles.'

17 Ibid., Bowring, ii. 254.

Bentham went on to criticize Joseph Addison for ridiculing innocent literary pastimes 'by attaching to them the fantastic idea of *bad taste*', and David Hume for praising Buckingham's play *The Rehearsal* on the grounds that it had rendered 'those theatrical pieces which had been most popular, the objects of general distaste'. In both instances, the result had been to deprive people of innocent pleasures, and to expose authors to contempt and to the loss of their source of income.[18]

Bentham reiterated the point that the terms *good taste* and *bad taste* made no sense unless they made reference to pleasure and pain:

> It is only from custom and prejudice that, in matters of taste, we speak of false and true. There is no taste which deserves the epithet *good*, unless it be the taste for such employments which, to the pleasure actually produced by them, conjoin some contingent or future utility: there is no taste which deserves to be characterized as bad, unless it be a taste for some occupation which has a mischievous tendency.

He condemned critics and satirists who reaped pleasure from diminishing the pleasure of others, 'pouring contempt upon everything that employs or interests other men'. The harm they had caused had gone even further, because they had perverted language itself to the extent that it was only with 'great difficulty and long circumlocutions' that it was possible to 'express the motives by which mankind are governed' without implying 'reprobation or approbation'. As a result, language had become 'rich in terms of hatred and reproach', but 'poor and rugged for the purposes of science and reason'.[19] Bentham's irritation here was directed against literary and cultural critics, but in the 1810s, following the emergence of the notion of 'sinister interest' in his thought and his commitment to political radicalism,[20] he drew out the wider democratic implications of his arguments.

In 'Of Sexual Irregularities', for instance, Bentham argued that there were certain practices that 'the man in power' did not find pleasurable: 'On the contrary, the very idea of [any such practice] is a cause of disgust.'

[18] Ibid. For an insightful comparison of Hume, Bentham, and John Stuart Mill on taste, see Malcolm Quinn, *Utilitarianism and the Art School in Nineteenth-Century Britain* (London: Pickering & Chatto, 2012), 24, 59–62, 131–6. Quinn points out that although Bentham misquoted Hume's words, he did not misrepresent the substance of his argument (59).

[19] 'Rationale of Reward', Bowring, ii. 255. For Bentham's listing of neutral, eulogistic, and dyslogistic terms, and the predominance of the latter, under fourteen categories of pains and pleasures, see 'Table of the Springs of Action', in *Deontology* (*CW*), 79–86.

[20] See P. Schofield, *Utility and Democracy: The Political Thought of Jeremy Bentham* (Oxford University Press, 2006), 109–36.

This feeling of disgust towards the idea of the practice extended itself to the persons who engaged in it. The man in power felt antipathy towards these persons, and sought to gratify his antipathy 'in the pleasure of subjecting to pain the person by whose conduct the dissocial affection has been excited'. Such antipathy, 'produced by difference of taste', was analogous to 'antipathy on the ground of difference in opinion'. Where the man in power regarded a religious opinion as 'repugnant' to his own, he termed it *heresy*: 'Analogous to heresy in matters of *religion* is heresy in matters of *taste*.'[21] Bentham's rejection of an aesthetics that existed independently of utility – in other words, that was not a function of pleasure and pain – had radically democratic implications.

In material written for 'Constitutional Code' in the 1820s, for instance, Bentham condemned the use made by rulers of the notion of taste, and the related notion of disgust:

> By substituting the principle of taste to the greatest happiness principle, taste is made the arbiter of excellence and depravity; and thus the great mass of the community is in the very sink of depravity. Witness the use that is made of the words *bad taste* and *disgusting*. Bad taste pours down contempt: disgusting is a superlative above flagitious, – it is a *quasi* conjugate of *taste* and *bad taste*. Those of the democratical section, in so far as they adopt such expressions, act in support of the hostile [i.e. the aristocratical] section against themselves. For the rich and powerful will always be the arbiters of taste: what is an object of disgust to them will, to those who follow this principle, be an object of disgust likewise. But that the poor, labouring and non-labouring, – all those who cannot afford a clean shirt every day, and a suit of clothes every two or three months, – are, to the men of the first circle, objects of disgust, is altogether beyond dispute.[22]

The oppression exercised by the ruling few extended to sexual gratification. Sexual pleasures, which were 'by universal acknowledgment superior in intensity to all other pleasures of sense', were equally within reach of the poorest members of the community as of the most affluent – of the subject many as of the ruling few. Although the member of the subject many could not enjoy the pleasures dependent on wealth to the same extent as a member of the ruling few, he or she could enjoy those of the sexual appetite in equal measure:

> But of the pleasures of this class, to be in a condition to enjoy the greatest quantity that [the] accidental circumstances of his situation throw in his

[21] 'Of Sexual Irregularities', in *Of Sexual Irregularities* (*CW*), 4 (UC lxxiv. 174, 173 (18 April 1814)).
[22] 'Constitutional Code', Bowring, ix. 46.

> way, and that the constitution of his taste has happened to give him a relish for, it will be necessary that all those restraints which have been imposed by blind prejudice be removed: and by the removal of all this mass of prejudice, how prodigious the mass of pleasure that may be, as it were, created – brought into existence – by one single hand![23]

Notions of 'good taste' and 'bad taste' were employed by the ruling few – the aristocracy – in order to delude the subject many – the democracy – into believing that they (the aristocracy) were superior, and hence entitled to rule and to enjoy disproportionate quantities of wealth, power, and esteem. In other words, it was the interest of the ruling few to appeal to 'taste' in order to maintain their dominance over the subject many, and to provide an apparent justification of the oppression which they exercised and from which they benefited. The principle of taste was adopted in order to subvert the principle of utility.

Paul's Asceticism[24]

For Bentham, a critical battle against the proponents of 'good taste' had to be fought on the ground of sexual morality, and hence on the ground of religion. As noted earlier, Bentham argued that the prevalent sexual morality of his own time had originated in the Mosaic law, but had been reinforced by the teaching of Paul. Bentham ranked Paul's condemnation of various sexual practices as follows:

> In the order of vituperation and proscription, first accordingly, under the name of uncleanness, came the gratification when obtained either without the help of any co-operator, or when obtained with a co-operator of the same sex: next comes the gratification in the case when obtained in the more generally preferred mode with the co-operation of a person of the correspondent and opposite sex, but without the sanction of marriage.[25]

According to Paul, noted Bentham, it was best to abstain altogether from sexual activity. Paul had told the Corinthians that 'it is good for a man not to touch a woman'.[26] His proscription extended not merely to fornication,

[23] 'Sextus', in *Of Sexual Irregularities* (*CW*), 47–115, at 112 (UC lxxiv. 217–18 (31 July, 3 August 1816)).

[24] Parts of this and the following section draw on my *Jeremy Bentham: Prophet of Secularism* (London: South Place Ethical Society, 2012), 14–18.

[25] UC cxli. 188 (1 September 1817). Bentham referred to the passages at Romans 1: 26–32 and Ephesians 5: 3.

[26] I Corinthians 7: 1.

but also to 'the union of the sexes under any circumstances'.[27] 'Generally and radically bad, therefore, according to Paul, is all union of the sexes. A thing ever to be desired is, therefore, that every where there shall be as little of it as possible.'[28] It was as much as to say that it was 'Good that no man should be born: better still had none been ever born'.[29] Paul's advice, where individuals had not married or were widowed, was that they should abstain from sex, so long as they could manage to do so. If they could not abstain – 'if they cannot contain' – they would be permitted to marry, on the grounds that it was 'better' (that is 'less bad', glossed Bentham) 'to marry than to burn'. Where married couples were concerned, not content to leave the 'peace of the marriage bed' undisturbed, Paul advised them to abstain from sexual gratification unless one or other of them insisted on it, and to devote themselves to fasting and praying. In order to prevent them from being tempted by Satan, Paul gave them his permission to 'come together again'.[30] One consequence of Paul's doctrine – 'this really unnatural doctrine' – was 'the forced celibacy of the Romish clergy'. Bentham was indignant: 'Behold the spawn of Paul – all these men of chastity, whether real or pretended, with which the Catholic part of the world is infested: in the male votaries behold the instruments and accomplices of his successors, in the females the victims.'[31]

Why had Paul been a proponent of asceticism, and why did he so vehemently object to sexual pleasures in particular? Bentham explained that Paul, like the preacher of any new religion, saw 'in every pursuit in which his wished-for disciples are engaged or liable to be engaged, a source of rivalry, opposition, and competition'. The ferocity of the competition was proportional to the strength of the propensity.[32] There were two main 'rival pursuits' against which Paul had to contend – one spiritual and one carnal. The spiritual consisted in the fulfilment of the duties imposed by the Mosaic law, and the carnal in pleasures of all sorts.[33] The propensity that Paul feared the most, because it was the strongest, was 'the sexual appetite', and it was against this that 'his hostile endeavours' were 'pushed

27 UC cxli. 195 (2 September 1817).
28 UC cxli. 196 (2 September 1817).
29 UC cxli. 192 (2 September 1817).
30 UC cxli. 191 (1 September 1817), 196–7 (2 September 1817). The relevant Bible passage is 1 Corinthians 7: 5–9.
31 UC clxi. 199 (15 September 1817).
32 UC cxli. 187 (1 September 1817).
33 UC clxi. 152 (12 September 1817).

with greatest force and energy'.[34] Paul found no support in the acts or sayings of Jesus for his condemnation of the sexual appetite, but he did find support in a 'counter-propensity' that had been 'established to a certain degree in men's breasts', namely 'the love of distinction'. Bentham had in mind the philosophy of the Stoics, by whom both pleasures and pains had been held in equal contempt. The more valuable the sacrifice made, the greater the distinction bestowed on the individual who had made it. 'For the sake of this brilliant acquisition', remarked Bentham, 'how numerous the instances in which life itself – life the field within which pleasures of all sorts and sizes are included – had been sacrificed!'[35]

A second factor worked in Paul's favour. Jesus had promised, as a reward, a future life full of happiness without end. At the time, in both the Jewish and the Greek mind, the idea of sacrifice was associated with the Almighty, and hence it was assumed that, without sacrifice, such a benefit could not be obtained. It was further assumed that the greater the sacrifice, the greater the chance of obtaining the benefit, and so, for even the smallest chance of obtaining such a benefit, no sacrifice could be too great. There could be no greater sacrifice than '[t]he gratification belonging to the sexual appetite'. Total abstinence from food or drink would be suicide, and so there was no plausible rival to the sacrifice of sexual gratification. Hence, sexual gratification was prohibited, and the prohibition sanctioned 'by a punishment the magnitude of which was to be proportioned to the value of the sacrifice'.[36]

Jesus' Sexuality

Bentham claimed that, unlike Paul, Jesus did not, according to any account that appeared in the four Gospels, condemn either the pleasures of the table or the pleasures of the bed.[37] On the contrary, Jesus' opposition to asceticism was shown in his condemnation of the Mosaic law. Disciples of John the Baptist came to Jesus, and asked: 'Why do we and the Pharisees fast oft, but thy disciples fast not?' Jesus replied with two parables: first, that no one put a piece of new cloth into an old garment; and second, that no one should put new wine into old bottles, because the bottles

[34] UC clxi. 187 (1 September 1817).
[35] UC cxli. 189 (1 September 1817).
[36] UC clxi. 190 (1 September 1817).
[37] 'Not Paul, but Jesus Vol. III', 79 (UC cxli. 342 (19 November 1817)).

break and the wine runs out.[38] In the first parable, argued Bentham, Jesus drew attention to the badness of the Mosaic law, which was represented by the old garment. John the Baptist's attempt to perfect the Mosaic law by abstaining from food was to put a patch on the old garment, but this only made it worse. In the second parable, Jesus introduced what he regarded as the true doctrine. The Mosaic law was represented by the old bottle. By adding more asceticism to the Mosaic law – by putting new wine into old bottles (or rather skins, as Bentham pointed out, because the 'bottles' in question were not made of glass), the old bottles would burst. In other words, the whole system would be 'blown to pieces', and any good that it contained would be 'scattered and lost'. Put new wine into new bottles, and nothing was lost. The new bottle represented the religion of Jesus. The new doctrine, represented by the new wine, was the abolition of asceticism, and so, while John the Baptist had attempted to strain the old asceticism 'still tighter than before', Jesus had condemned it. Yet in Bentham's own day, he complained, the 'hypocrisy of the Pharisees', despite the condemnation of Jesus, was 'held in honour, . . . pursued and imitated'.[39]

Bentham continued with what he described as a matter of 'extreme delicacy', namely the sexuality of Jesus himself.[40] Whereas Paul's most forceful condemnation was directed towards homosexuality, noted Bentham, not only had Jesus never condemned homosexuality, but he had quite possibly engaged in same-sex relationships himself. There were, moreover, many females in Jesus' immediate circle, and again Bentham saw no reason why Jesus might not have engaged in heterosexual activity as well. Not accepting that there was any sense in the proposition that Jesus was God, or part of God, Bentham saw Jesus as a man of his time.[41] Given that, in the Greco-Roman classical world, sex between males was not condemned as such, but rather, under certain circumstances, was accepted as normal, Bentham saw no reason why Jesus might not have taken the same view. To the objection that the destruction of Sodom and Gomorrah showed that God condemned all homosexual activity without exception, Bentham responded that what the story actually condemned

38 See Matthew 9: 9–17.

39 'Not Paul, but Jesus Vol. III', 94–7 (UC clxi. 348–50 (29 December 1817)).

40 Ibid., 177 (UC clxi. 475 (20 November 1817)).

41 See UC cxxxix. 219 (10 September 1817): 'Throughout the whole course of this examination, the men in question will, all of them, be alike considered as actuated by human interests, human desires [and] human motives – actuated by such interests, desires and motives as all men in general are actuated by.'

was the force that was used and the number of people involved – it was not homosexuality that was condemned, but gang rape.[42] There were, moreover, positive, or at least non-condemnatory, accounts of homosexuals in the Old Testament, the most pertinent and prominent example being the relationship between David and Jonathan.[43]

In relation to Jesus' homosexuality, in the first place, there was, amongst Jesus' followers, the youth with the 'linen cloth cast around his naked body' in Mark's account of Jesus' arrest in the Garden of Gethsemane.[44] According to Bentham, the youth was a male prostitute, and given his loyalty to Jesus when all his other followers had fled, there must have existed a particularly strong bond of attachment between Jesus and the youth.[45] In the second place, there was Jesus' relationship with his disciple John, as portrayed in John's Gospel:

> If in the love which, in and by these passages, Jesus was intended to be represented as bearing towards this John was not the same sort of love as that which appears to have had place between King David and Jonathan, the son of Saul, it seems not easy to conceive what can have been the object in bringing it to view in so pointed a manner, accompanied with such circumstances of fondness. That the sort of love of which, in the bosom of Jesus, Saint John is here meant to be represented as the object was of a different sort from any of which any other of the Apostles was the object is altogether incontestable: for of this sort of love, whatsoever it was, he and he alone is, in these so frequently recurring terms, mentioned as being the object.[46]

It might be objected that an attachment of this sort would not have been tolerated in Jesus' time when it was ranked among capital crimes by the law of the land, and more especially by the law of God, and, moreover, had produced the destruction of Sodom and Gomorrah by supernatural means. In relation to the law of Moses, Bentham's view, as noted earlier, was that Jesus held the law of Moses in contempt, thinking it merely a human law and ill adapted to the welfare of society:

42 'Not Paul, but Jesus Vol. III', 177–83 (UC clxi. 475–82 (20, 28 November 1817)).

43 Bentham picked out passages at I Samuel 17: 56–8, 18: 1–4; I Samuel 20: 17; and II Samuel 1: 17, 19, 26, as evidence that their relationship was homosexual. See 'Not Paul, but Jesus Vol. III', 163–7 (UC clxi. 457–60 (21, 24 December 1817)).

44 Mark 14: 51–2.

45 British Library, Grote Papers, Add. MS 29,808, fols. 6–11 (3 October 1811). For a more detailed account, see P. Schofield, *Bentham: A Guide for the Perplexed* (London: Continuum, 2009), 132–3.

46 'Not Paul, but Jesus Vol. III', 178 (UC clxi. 476 (28 November 1817)).

> On this whole field, on which Moses legislates with such diversified minuteness, such impassioned asperity and such unrelenting rigour, Jesus is altogether silent. Jesus, from whose lips not a syllable favourable to ascetic self-denial is, by any one of his biographers,[47] represented as having ever issued. Jesus who, among his disciples, had one to whom he imparted his authority and another in whose bosom his head reclined, and for whom he avowed his love:[48] Jesus who, in the stripling clad in loose attire, found a still faithful adherent, after the rest of them had fled:[49] Jesus in whom the woman taken in adultery found a successful advocate:[50] Jesus, on the whole field of sexual irregularity, preserved an uninterrupted silence.[51]

The Modern Ascetics

The modern ascetics had directed their keenest hostility against the pleasures of the table and the pleasures of the bed, but more particularly against the latter. Even though pleasure always accompanied eating and drinking, the pleasures of the table could not be 'altogether excluded', because to banish eating and drinking would lead to the extinction of the species, and there would be no one to suffer pain: 'to the votary of asceticism, life is indispensable, as being the only receptacle into which pains can be inserted'. In contrast, it was possible to take away all the pleasures of the bed from an individual, because he or she would remain alive and hence capable of suffering pain: 'Therefore, to keep on foot so many receptacles of pain, human beings must be kept alive – the population must be kept up: and to the number of those in whose instance life is purified of all pleasure in this shape, limits must somehow or other be set.' The ascetic needed to calculate the optimum proportion of breeders to non-breeders, so that both as many individuals as possible could be denied sexual pleasure, while at the same time the total number of the species was maintained. In order to achieve the former objective, individuals might be castrated, but this 'physical cause of exclusion' was

47 That is, by the authors of the four Gospels.

48 For Jesus' conferral of authority on Peter, see Matthew 16: 18–19, and for the disciple 'whom Jesus loved', traditionally taken to be John, see John 13: 23, 25.

49 See Mark 14: 51–2, recounting an incident in the Garden of Gethsemane at the time of Jesus' arrest by the Jewish authorities.

50 See John 8: 1–11.

51 'Of Sexual Irregularities', in *Of Sexual Irregularities* (*CW*), 14–15 (UC lxxiv. 104 (21 April 1814)).

rejected by ascetics on the grounds that this would also exclude 'the pains of unsatisfied desire'.[52]

The religious ascetic believed that he was reflecting the will of God in his antipathy to irregular sexual practices:

> It is easy to see that in imputing to the Almighty a desire to see a man forego pleasure, accompanied moreover (for such is the notion of ascetics of the religious cast) with an eventual determination to render [him][53] everlastingly miserable in case of his ever omitting to forego it, the persuasion of the religious ascetic that such is the determination taken by the Almighty will be stronger – and indeed much stronger – in the case where the pleasure in question is attached to any more irregular gratification of the sexual appetite than to any less irregular gratification of that same appetite.

If God had wanted the human race to be extinct, such an outcome would have occurred already. But such a desire would be inconsistent with another desire attributed by religionists to God, namely that 'of consigning in an appropriate receptacle a great majority of the human race to infinitely intense and infinitely lasting torture'. Hence, God tolerated the regular mode of sexual gratification:

> But, in the instance of those modes of gratification of which a contribution to the continuance of the species can not, in any case, be the accompaniment, in this case the cause of toleration has no place: in this case, therefore, the thus impure and inexcusable pleasure remains a just object of the unbridled and insatiable vengeance of the being in whose composition an infinity of power has for its accompaniment an infinity of benevolence.

The religious ascetic, argued Bentham, should simply abstain from the practice that he found distasteful, and not extend his antipathy to those who practised it because they did not find it distasteful. However, the point of the ascetic's behaviour was to recommend himself to God, and there was no better means of doing so than to take God's enemies for his own:

> Where the person whose enemies are to be dealt with as our own is no more than a human being such as ourselves, Charity may interpose, and, to the disposition by which we are led thus to deal with them, apply a sort of bridle: but where that person is the Almighty himself, no such bridle is

[52] 'Not Paul, but Jesus Vol. III', 25–6 (UC clxi. 266–7 (1 January 1818)).
[53] MS 'them'.

> necessary or so much as proper and admissible. The being infinite, such ought to be our love, such consequently our hatred for his enemies – such consequently, in determination and efficiency, the acts in and by which that hatred is exercised, manifested, gratified, demonstrated.[54]

Religious belief both justified and intensified the antipathetic passion of the ascetic.

Utility versus Asceticism

Bentham presented a detailed comparison of the principle of utility and the principle of asceticism, in order to show how the one was 'directly opposite' to the other. The term 'the principle of utility . . . designated that doctrine by which endeavours are used to engage men on every occasion to pursue that course of action by which, in so far as happiness is concerned, the greatest quantity of happiness, say or *well-being*, will be produced'. Hence, 'an action of which utility is a quality' was 'an action which has for its effect, or at any rate for its tendency, the augmentation of the stock of pleasures or, what is correspondent and may be equivalent, the diminution in the stock of pains'. In contrast, the principle of asceticism recommended the sacrifice of pleasure and the seeking of pain.[55] Bentham expressed reservations about the term *utility* on the grounds that it did not give 'any immediate or certain indication' of its relationship to the notions of happiness and of pain and pleasure. The problem was that there was no better term.[56] A further problem was that ordinary usage obscured the relationship between happiness on the one hand, and

[54] 'Of Sexual Irregularities', in *Of Sexual Irregularities* (*CW*), 17–19 (UC lxxiv. 108–10 (22 April 1814)).

[55] Compare *An Introduction to the Principles of Morals and Legislation* (henceforth *IPML* (*CW*)), ed. J.H. Burns and H.L.A. Hart, with a new introduction by F. Rosen (Oxford: Clarendon Press, 1996 (*CW*)), 17–21, where Bentham noted that, in contrast to an adherent of the principle of utility, an adherent of the principle of asceticism approved of those actions that increased pain and diminished pleasure. If one-tenth of the inhabitants of the world pursued the principle of asceticism consistently, 'in a day's time they will have turned it into a hell'. It had nevertheless been pursued by two classes of people. The first were the Stoic philosophers, who had pursued the principle in the hope of furthering their reputation, which was in fact a source of pleasure. The second were religionists, who had 'frequently gone so far as to make it a matter of merit and of duty to court pain', and who had been motivated by 'the fear of future punishment at the hands of a splenetic and revengeful Deity'.

[56] 'Not Paul, but Jesus Vol. III', 10–11 (UC clxi. 216–19 (30 December 1817)). Within five or six years he had come to adopt 'the greatest happiness principle' as a better alternative: see *IPML* (*CW*), 11n, and J.H. Burns, 'Happiness and Utility: Jeremy Bentham's Equation', *Utilitas*, 17 (2005), 46–61.

pain and pleasure on the other. Bentham was critical of the grammarian James Harris who, in dealing with the topic of happiness, had failed to understand its relationship to pleasure: 'The consequence is that with him *happiness* is a mere empty name – a word with which no determinate idea stands associated: a sign by which nothing whatsoever is signified: a straw would be too much to give for all that in his work is presented to view by the word *happiness*.'[57] Moreover, the term *happiness*, complained Bentham, tended to be used to describe a large quantity of pleasure, but seemed to exclude a small quantity. When a hungry man sat down to his dinner, and took his first bite of food, no one would deny that he experienced pleasure, but this particular sensation would not ordinarily be described as happiness. Hence, it was assumed that '*pleasure is not happiness*', that pleasures had nothing to do with happiness, that happiness was not composed of pleasures, and that no quantity of pleasure could constitute happiness. The term *wealth* suffered from the same 'inconvenience'. No one would describe a rag dropped by a beggar as 'wealth'. 'But', asked Bentham,

> this rag, whence comes it that it is not wealth? Only because there is not enough of it. Add to it as many more such as will make it fill a waggon, it shall be worth £20 or £30. Of these rags are there not as yet enough in quantity to constitute wealth? Well, then, add to it as many more as are imported into England in the course of a twelve months for the use of the paper-makers: then, instead of pounds, you will have thousands of pounds.

Bentham recommended the adoption of the term *matter*. The chemist, for instance, spoke about the 'matter of heat', without regard to the quantity of heat involved. By analogy, it might be said that, in the rag, there was 'the matter of wealth', and similarly, in pleasure, 'be it in what shape it may and in whatsoever small quantity it may', there was 'the matter of happiness'. The matter of happiness had 'two species or ideal parcels', a positive one, namely pleasure, and a negative one, namely exemption from pain: 'In one or other of these shapes will every thing, for the designation of which the compound term matter of happiness can be employed, be found.'[58]

[57] 'Not Paul, but Jesus Vol. III', 12 (UC clxi. 220 (30 December 1817)). See James Harris, *Three Treatises: The First concerning Art: The Second concerning Music, Painting and Poetry: The Third Concerning Happiness*, 2nd edn. (London: J. Nourse and P. Vaillant, 1765), 107–247, particularly 131–5, where Harris argues against the equation of pleasure with happiness.

[58] 'Not Paul, but Jesus Vol. III', 12–14 (UC clxi. 221–3 (30 December 1817)).

According to the principle of utility, the proper course of action for all sensitive beings was to pursue pleasure and to avoid pain. 'Virtue' consisted in the pursuit of pleasure according to two rules: first, do not exclude a greater pleasure; second, do not produce more than equivalent pain.[59] Virtue was divided into two branches: the first was 'self-regarding prudence', where the pleasure gained or pain avoided concerned the actor alone; and the second was benevolence or beneficence (depending respectively upon whether the intention or the action was being considered), where the pleasure gained or pain avoided concerned other persons as well as the actor.[60] Where benevolence or beneficence was obligatory, the virtue was known as probity. If the obligation was imposed by law – in other words, a 'perfect' obligation – it was 'legal justice', and if it was imposed by morality, in other words an 'imperfect' obligation, it was 'natural justice'.[61] Like the principle of utility, the principle of asceticism had two branches: first, the negative branch called for the avoidance of pleasure, and second, the positive branch called for the 'voluntary susception' of pain.[62] According to the principle of utility, however, to forego pleasure for any other reason than the production of greater pleasure (the first rule of 'virtue') was imprudence, while to wish that others forego pleasure was malevolence (the opposite of benevolence), and to force them to do so was maleficence (the opposite of beneficence). Asceticism was, therefore, a vicious and mischievous doctrine. There was no other justification for condemning an action as vicious, and subjecting criminality to punishment, than the fact that it resulted in the loss of pleasure or the infliction of pain:

> If the causing or seeking to cause a man to forego any the least particle of pleasure otherwise than as above be not vice, be not maleficence, be not malevolence respectively, then neither is the inflicting or seek[ing] to inflict on him any injury whatever, whether to person, reputation, property or condition in life, vice, maleficence or malevolence respectively: then neither for the subjecting to punishment or reproach the crimes of rape, robbery or murder, for example, can there be any reasonable cause. The money which a man is robbed of, of what use, had he not [been] robbed of it, would it have been to himself or any one, unless it be by adding in some shape or other to the sum of his or some one else's pleasures, or substracting in some shape or other from his or some one else's pains?[63]

59 Ibid., 14–15 (UC clxi. 224 (30 December 1817)).
60 Ibid., 15 (UC clxi. 239 (30 December 1817)).
61 Ibid., 16 (UC clxi. 240 (30 December 1817)).
62 Ibid. (UC clxi. 242 (30 December 1817)).
63 Ibid., 18 (UC clxi. 244 (31 December 1817)).

Bentham wished to emphasize not only that to be an adherent of the doctrine of asceticism was to promote evil, but also that to prevent an individual from enjoying an innocent pleasure was just as much to do evil as it was to inflict a pain on him or her.

The next point that Bentham wished to establish was that the notion that certain, if not all, forms of pleasure were morally reprehensible was nonsense. The argument here was in effect the same as that which justified his comment about push-pin and poetry. Bentham argued that there was no morally relevant distinction between one pleasure and another, except for their respective quantities. Hence, the '*shape* and *source*' of a pain or pleasure were 'matters of indifference'. Once the elements of propinquity and certainty, that is respectively the nearness in time and the probability of experiencing a pleasure or pain, had either been 'given' or taken 'out of the question', 'quantity is the sole measure of *value*' – and quantity consisted of intensity multiplied by duration.[64] Shape and source were relevant considerations to the extent that a pleasure of the same sort experienced in one shape or from one source might result in some pain which would not result if the pleasure were experienced in another shape or from another source. Even in this case, it was not the shape and source that actually mattered, but 'the purity or impurity of the pleasure'. When the act that produced pleasure also produced pain, the pleasure was impure; when the act also produced a subsequent pleasure, the pleasure was said to be fruitful or fecund. Still, this amounted to nothing more nor less than the 'magnitude' of the pleasure. Although, in strictness, it was the act that produced the subsequent pleasure, and not the pleasure itself, it was appropriate to ascribe this subsequent pleasure to the initial pleasure, because the reason or motive for performing the act was the prospect of experiencing the pleasure. Hence,

> The value of the pleasure may be said to be augmented by and in proportion to its fecundity, diminished by and in proportion to its impurity: in the first case the reason for pursuing it, encreased and strengthened; in the other case, done away or lessened. Thus may be seen the practical uses of these locutions in and by which, by a sort of fiction of language, the effects of the act are ascribed to the pleasure as their cause.[65]

[64] For the seven elements that together constituted the value of a pleasure – namely intensity, duration, certainty, propinquity, fecundity, purity, and extent – see *IPML* (*CW*), 38–41.

[65] 'Not Paul, but Jesus Vol. III', 19 (UC clxi. 245 (31[?] December 1817)). The same propositions were true for pain.

The only thing that mattered, then, was the quantity of pleasure and pain – and whether it was derived from push-pin or poetry – or from the regular or irregular modes of sexual gratification – was irrelevant.

Since the time of Paul, not to go back any further, noted Bentham, there had always been men who had claimed that asceticism was virtue, and hence had made 'war upon pleasure: upon pleasure in every shape, or at any rate upon pleasure in general without any determinate exception'.[66] They had brought forward various 'pretences' in order to carry on 'this war against every thing that is good'.

> Among the most common is that which bears relation to the *shape* in which the pleasure is enjoyed, or in other words (for it comes to much the same thing) the *source* from whence it is derived, or the *seat* in which it has place.

Pleasures had their 'seat' in the body, or in the mind, or in both. The ascetics had made 'unceasing war' against the bodily pleasures, on the grounds that that 'the pleasures of the mind [were] more *noble* than the pleasures of the body'. 'But', asked Bentham, 'by this word *noble* what is meant'? He answered: 'either it means *greater*, viz. in respect either of intensity or duration, or it means nothing and is so much nonsense'. If a pleasure of the mind were greater than a pleasure of the body, and if the former could not be enjoyed without foregoing the latter, it would be right to prefer the pleasure of the mind, but conversely, if the pleasure of the body were greater, it would be right to prefer it instead. Bentham did not accept, however, that there was any real competition between the two sorts of pleasures – insofar as there was competition, it was between all pleasures, and not pleasures of the body on the one hand, and pleasures of the mind on the other.[67] An adherent of the principle of utility would investigate whether there was any real incompatibility between a pleasure of the body and a pleasure of the mind, and if there was, come to a determination as to which pleasure should be foregone. An adherent of the principle of asceticism, on the other hand, condemned the pleasures of the body 'without enquiry'.

> Under the principle of utility, nothing is lost, unless in so far as, according to the estimate formed by the only competent judge, something better worth is gained: whereas under the principle of asceticism, good things by

66 Ibid. (UC clxi. 258 (31 December 1817)).
67 Ibid., 19–20 (UC clxi. 259–60 (31 December 1817)).

> wholesale are thrown away, and in the room of them nothing is so much as attempted to be gained.[68]

The principle of asceticism relied on a linguistic sleight of hand to condemn the pleasures of the body. It lay in the word *impure*. A pleasure of the body was said to be 'impure' in the physical sense, and was, therefore, 'impure' in the moral sense; such a pleasure ought not to be experienced; the experiencing of it was a vicious act, and ought to be prohibited and punished; and hence it became a crime.[69] Bentham concluded:

> No condemnation can justly be passed on any pleasure on any such ground as that of its *shape*, *seat*, *source*, or *inlet*: the *shape* in which it exists, the *seat* in which it resides, the *source* from whence it is derived, or the *inlet* through which it is derived.

Indeed, to regard the mind as distinct from the body was itself fallacious. The pleasures of the mind, including the fine arts such as music and painting, were to a large degree derived from hearing and reading, and hence found their 'necessary inlet' in the body – through the ears and eyes.[70] More generally, without sense perception, there would be no knowledge anyway: 'if sensation were taken away, understanding would go along with it: if all pleasures of the body were taken away, along with them would go the pleasures of the mind'.[71]

Bentham's Response to the Ascetics

In 'Sextus', Bentham noted that the 'regular mode' of sexual gratification involved one male and one female, within marriage, for the purpose of procreation. He went on to draw up a list of the various 'irregular modes'. As well as the 'solitary' mode, the irregular modes included sexual activity involving a male and a female who were not married; a male and a female, one or both of whom might be married, but not to each other; a male and a male; a female and a female; more than two persons; minors; the use of parts of the body that would not result in impregnation ('Cunilinction, Fellation or Irrumation'); humans and animals of other species (with the

68 Ibid., 21 (UC clxi. 261 (31 December 1817)). Bentham did allow that pleasures of the mind did tend to be underestimated in comparison with pleasures of the body, due to the more immediate gratification characteristic of the latter, and 'the long and painful course of preparation' often required in order to experience the former.

69 Ibid., 21–2 (UC clxi. 262–3 (31 December 1817)).

70 Ibid., 23n (UC clxii. 265a (31 December 1817)).

71 Ibid., 24 (UC clxi. 265b (1 January 1818)).

human taking an active or a passive role, and either one human and one animal or more than 1); a human and an inanimate object; and a living and a dead human.[72] There was an almost endless variety of forms that sexual activity could take, and therefore pleasures to be reaped, beyond the 'regular mode'. Bentham pointed out that 'regular' meant conformity to 'the rule prescribed by public opinion', and that this simply reflected the prevailing attitudes in the society in question. Bentham's purpose was to show that to apply the terms 'regular' or 'irregular', or 'natural' or 'unnatural', to any mode of sexual activity – and in particular the legal description of homosexuality as 'the crime against nature'[73] – expressed nothing beyond the opinion that any particular person or group of persons held in relation to that activity. To condemn an action as 'irregular' or 'unnatural' was equivalent to condemning it on the grounds of 'bad taste'.

Hence, rulers had justified the imposition of punishment on such practices as they disliked by terming them 'unnatural'. All that this proved was that they desired 'to bring down the hatred of mankind upon the individual or individuals to whom the species of irregularity in question is attributed'. The only sensible meaning that could be given to the epithet 'unnatural' when applied to a practice was that it was a 'rare occurrence'. Otherwise, to condemn a practice as 'unnatural' said little, if anything, about the practice itself, but indicated the existence of 'dissocial passion' in the person who employed the term, but 'without staying to enquire or to consider with himself whether the practice, and thence the conduct and character of him whose practice it is, be or be not in any way, and if in any way in what degree, noxious to society'. Moreover, the point was to engender the same ill-will in other persons, in order to inflict suffering on those against whom it was directed.[74]

Ascetics had directed their strongest condemnation against male same-sex relationships. The fact that they had tended to ignore female same-sex relationships merely revealed their inconsistency. The reason, Bentham suggested, lay in the notion of 'impurity'. Because male sexual activity led to emission, the 'dæmon of asceticism' regarded such activity as physically, and hence morally, impure: 'Thus it is that in which the sex concerned is

[72] 'Sextus', in *Of Sexual Irregularities* (*CW*), 56–7 (UC lxxiv. 46–8 (28 July 1816)).

[73] See, for instance, William Blackstone, *Commentaries on the Laws of England*, 4 vols., Oxford, 1765–9, iv. 215, referring to 'the infamous *crime against nature*, committed with either man or beast' as a crime 'of a still deeper malignity' than rape.

[74] 'Of Sexual Irregularities', in *Of Sexual Irregularities* (*CW*), 6 (UC lxxiv. 89–90 (18 April 1814)).

on both sides the male, is the case of aberration by which the attention of the religionist, the moralist and the legislator have nearly been engrossed.' There were, however, two arguments employed against homosexual relationships that apparently appealed to the principle of utility: the first was that such relationships constituted an 'injury to population'; and the second that they injured 'the useful and desirable influence of the female sex'. Both charges, argued Bentham, were groundless.[75] First, to the claim that homosexuality would lead to a reduction in population, Bentham responded by pointing out that since Malthus had published his 'great work . . . on this subject',[76] every one now agreed that the problem lay in an 'excess' of population, rather than in a 'deficiency'. Even so, the argument that homosexuality could affect population was absurd. A married male, for instance, could, on average, allowing for absence and sickness, perform 300 acts of impregnation per year, yet only one such act might be enough to increase the population to the maximum extent possible.

> According to this estimate, ere it could have any effect capable of making any defalcation not only from the actual, but also from the greatest possible degree of population, the propensity of this appetite to the same sex would have to be 300 times as great as towards the correspondent and opposite sex.[77]

In order to make any reduction from the maximum increase possible in population, the appetite in the male for same-sex relationships would have to be 300 times greater than the appetite for heterosexual relationships. In that case, remarked Bentham, the epithets 'eccentric' and 'unnatural' would be properly applied to the heterosexual, and not to the homosexual, appetite.[78]

If any check to population did result, then it would not be 'an evil', but rather 'a remedy'. Wherever there was a 'tolerable' degree of security provided by government, population tended to increase beyond the capacity to provide subsistence. This led, in the indigent, to 'premature death preceded by lingering disease', and in the affluent, to the 'pain of privation' to the extent that they were obliged to provide relief to the

[75] 'Not Paul, but Jesus Vol. III', 28–30 (UC clxi. 273–5 (2 January 1818)).

[76] (Thomas) Robert Malthus (1766–1834), political economist, was the anonymous author of *An Essay on the Principle of Population, as it affects the future improvement of society. With remarks on the speculations of Mr. Godwin, M. Condorcet, and other writers* (London: J. Johnson, 1798), where he argued that population growth tended to outstrip food supply. Subsequent editions in 1803, 1806, 1807, 1817, and 1826 carried the author's name.

[77] 'Not Paul, but Jesus Vol. III', 33 (UC clxi. 279 (2 January 1818).

[78] Ibid., 30–3 (UC clxi. 276–9 (2 January 1818)).

indigent. By providing relief, moreover, an encouragement was given to 'that union by which an addition is made to the mass of the population, and thence to the mass of indigence. Be the encrease in the magnitude of the remedy ever so great, the encrease in the mass of the evil is constantly outstripping it'. Malthus had identified three checks to population growth: the first was misery, that is premature death caused by the lack of the means of subsistence; the second was vice, that is non-prolific sexual activity; and the third was moral restraint, that is the non-satisfaction of the sexual appetite. Malthus himself, noted Bentham, recommended the third alternative. Under both the principles of asceticism and utility, the first alternative, premature death, was regarded as an evil, since the dead could feel neither pleasure nor pain. The principle of asceticism regarded 'vice' as not only an evil, but an evil which, 'if it be a remedy, is still worse than the disease'. In contrast, the principle of utility regarded 'vice' as 'a good, in whatsoever degree it may operate . . . in the character of a remedy in relation to the evil of indigence'. Under the principle of utility, to whatever degree moral restraint mitigated the growth of population and to that extent proved beneficial, it would still produce two evil effects:

> these are 1. loss of pleasure, by the amount of the capacity of gratification thus prevented from coming into act. 2. actual pain, viz. pain of unsatisfied desire, as measured by [1.] the number of individuals in whose instance the desire, having existence, remains unsatisfied: 2. its intensity: and 3. its duration in the instance of each of them.[79]

For the utilitarian, non-prolific sex was not only good in itself, but, in conditions of scarcity or potential scarcity, it also operated as a remedy to the evil of overpopulation.

The second argument against homosexual relationships that apparently appealed to the principle of utility was the negative impact that such relationships had on the position of the female sex. In order for this argument to be tenable, noted Bentham, it would need to be shown that the appetite amongst males for same-sex relationships predominated to an extravagant extent above the appetite for heterosexual relationships. 'No where either in geography or history', he retorted, 'will any such apprehension find any the slightest countenance.' In Eastern countries, where 'the eccentric propensity' was not condemned, the importance attached to the possession of 'the charms of the female sex' exceeded

[79] Ibid., 33–6 (UC clxi. 280–3 (2–3 January 1818)).

anything found in Europe: 'In an European, jealousy is as ice to fire in comparison of what it is in an oriental breast.' In the East, insofar as the condition of females was 'wretched', and population was 'in decline', it was due to the lack of security provided by government. On the other hand, in Italy, where 'the eccentric propensity prevails to such a degree as to be gratified not only without danger but without shame', not only did the female sex govern 'with a degree of ascendancy beyond any thing exemplified in Britain where the propensity is so rare', but 'the misery produced by overpopulation rages at the same time to a degree of excess unknown to any other European country'. In fact, the female sex had 'more to gain than to lose' from the eccentric propensity, because a female rival was 'much more formidable to the wedded female' than a male rival. In ancient Rome, Bentham noted, once a male reached the age of about 20, he lost his attraction to another male: in other words, a male rival had a limited shelf life. It was the prostitute, and not the wife, who had most to fear from sexual liberty.[80]

The Benefits of Sexual Liberty

Bentham identified three main benefits from the sexual liberty that he advocated. The first was the simple 'Addition to the mass of pleasure'. To the objection that there could be no enjoyment derived from such a disgusting source, he responded that the logic of such an argument was the same as that employed by the man who stated, 'Beholden in the character of an object of sexual appetite, that sow is to me an object of abhorrence: therefore so she is and always has been, and always will be, to the father of her pigs'. Each individual should be left free to decide whether or not a particular activity was a source of enjoyment to him or her and thus whether to engage in it: 'Whether he be or be not the *proper* judge, every man is in fact the judge, and, to the purpose of his own conduct, the sole effectual judge, of what is agreable or disagreable to himself.'[81] Bentham reiterated the point that, once the quantity of happiness during a given period had been given, then 'what the shape is in which it has been enjoyed, is . . . a matter of indifference'. Assuming that, in the enjoyment of a particular pleasure, there was no evil from, for instance, loss of health or strength,

[80] Ibid., 36–9 (UC clxi. 284–7 (3 January 1818)).

[81] 'Of Sexual Irregularities', in *Of Sexual Irregularities (CW)*, 43 (UC lxxiv. 202 (1 May 1814)).

> then how *impure* so ever, in the physical sense of the word *impure*, the pleasure from that source be deemed – deemed, viz. by those to whom it would not be a pleasure in the psychological and moral sense of the same word, there is no impurity in the case, but quantity for quantity, it is no less pure in this shape than in any other.[82]

The second beneficial effect was to divert individuals from the 'solitary gratification', and hence avoid damaging their health.[83] Bentham compared the impact on health of heterosexual activity (the 'regular mode'), homosexual activity (the 'irregular mode'), and masturbation (the 'solitary mode'). Based on 'medical observation', Bentham claimed that there was no difference in the 'physiological and pathological effects' of the two 'social' modes. Indeed, there was less 'danger of a carnal disease' from the irregular mode, although, contrary to popular opinion, his own 'enquiry into the state of medical practice in countries in which the irregularity in question receives a sort of tacit and virtual toleration' had shown that 'the exemption' was 'comparative only, and not altogether absolute'. Bentham noted that, according to medical opinion, the solitary mode did, however, have severe consequences if the indulgence became excessive. The problem was that it was constantly available to the individual, whereas the social mode depended on 'contingencies' which might occur infrequently. It would be better for health if individuals were encouraged to practise one or other of the social modes.[84] It might be objected, continued Bentham, that the decriminalization of pederasty would lead to the seduction of pupils by their teachers. In his view, it was better that pupils engage in sex in the social rather than the solitary mode; they would anyway be more likely to be attracted to children of their own age than to their teacher; and, if they did have such a relationship, it might produce greater relish for their studies.[85] The third beneficial effect was 'Diminution of the amount of female prostitution'. The assumption here, admitted Bentham, was 'that female prostitution contains a net balance on the side of evil – i.e. is productive of pain and loss of pleasure to a greater value than any pleasure of which, on both sides taken together, it is productive'.[86]

82 Ibid., 44 (UC lxxiv. 202–3 (1 May 1814)).

83 Ibid., 45 (UC lxxiv. 195 (4 May 1814)).

84 Ibid., 30–1 (UC lxxiv. 140–2 (1 May 1814)).

85 'Sextus', in *Of Sexual Irregularities (CW)*, 105–8 (UC lxxiv. 206–11 (31 July, 2 August 1816)).

86 'Of Sexual Irregularities', in *Of Sexual Irregularities (CW)*, 45 (UC lxxiv. 196 (4 May 1814)). For Bentham's attitude towards prostitution more generally, see M. Sokol, *Bentham, Law and Marriage: A Utilitarian Code of Law in Historical Context* (London: Bloomsbury, 2011), 24–6.

Bentham did not argue for complete sexual licentiousness. There were instances when the practice of one or other of the irregular modes should be subject to legal punishment. These included 'simple lascivious injuries', rape, seduction, defilement of infants under the age of consent, indecent deportment and discourse by males in the presence and without the consent of females, adultery, and polygamy (where this had been legally prohibited).[87] Having said that, in the cases where no mischief resulted, there were no grounds for condemnation, still less for legal punishment.[88] There were, moreover, several legitimate grounds for abstaining from sexual activity. The first was where such activity was detrimental to health. This was a matter for medical science, and was not an appropriate area for legislative interference. The second was where the activity would be detrimental to a person's reputation, but that should be left to the individual to determine. The third was where there was lack of, or incapacity to give, consent. Here, the legislator was justified in interfering.[89] Given that sexual activity was pleasurable, and that an agent would not consent to engage in it unless he or she expected it to be pleasurable, there were no grounds for prohibiting and punishing it, providing it was consensual, in whatever form it took.

Bentham versus Mill on Higher and Lower Pleasures

Bentham's arguments are pertinent not only in response to asceticism, but as a riposte to the distinction that John Stuart Mill later drew between

[87] Ibid., 3 (UC lxxiv. 35–6 (18 April 1814)).

[88] In a summary of the third volume of 'Not Paul, but Jesus', Bentham suggested that, due to the need to assuage popular antipathy towards certain of the 'modes' of irregular sexual activity, the punishment of banishment should be attached to them, with the proviso that, 'for conviction, except in the case of violence, require two witnesses, whereof no person, concerned as principal or accessary to the offence, shall be one'. See 'General Idea of a Work, having for one of its objects The Defence of the Principle of *Utility*, so far as concerns The Liberty of Taste, against the conjunct hostility of The Principle of *Asceticism* and The Principle of *Antipathy*; and for its proposed title, proposed on the ground of expected popularity, or at least protection against popular rage, – Not Paul, but Jesus', in *Of Sexual Irregularities* (*CW*), 117–44, at 140 (UC cxli. 18 [August 1817]). Bentham did not state to which of the 'modes' this punishment would apply, but even if it applied to all of them, then consensual sexual activity that took place in private would in effect have been decriminalized. Moreover, Bentham's proposal would have ended the possibility of false accusations of homosexuality, which was a common practice of blackmailers. For a prominent example, involving Edward Walpole, the son of Robert Walpole, see N.M. Goldsmith, *The Worst of Crimes: Homosexuality and the Law in Eighteenth-Century London* (Aldershot: Ashgate, 1998), 107–87.

[89] 'Of Sexual Irregularities', in *Of Sexual Irregularities (CW)*, 58–9 (UC lxxiv. 63–5 (28 July 1816)).

the higher and lower pleasures in his essay *Utilitarianism*, published in 1861. In his earlier essay on 'Bentham' of 1838, Mill had complained that Bentham 'could not bear to hear pronounced in his presence' the phrases '*good* and *bad* taste', since he regarded it as 'an insolent piece of dogmatism in one person to praise or condemn another in a matter of taste'. Mill continued in a critical tone:

> as if men's likings and dislikings, on things in themselves indifferent, were not full of the most important inferences as to every point of their character; as if a person's tastes did not show him to be wise or a fool, cultivated or ignorant, gentle or rough, sensitive or callous, generous or sordid, benevolent or selfish, conscientious or depraved.[90]

Mill disagreed with Bentham's view of taste, and his distinction between higher and lower pleasures is intimately related to that disagreement. In *Utilitarianism*, Mill argued that there were qualitative differences between pleasures, with 'some *kinds* of pleasures' being 'more desirable and more valuable than others. It would be absurd that while, in estimating all other things, quality is considered as well as quantity, the estimation of pleasures should be supposed to depend on quantity alone'. The pleasures of the 'intellect' – Bentham's pleasures of the mind – were the higher pleasures, while the pleasures of 'mere sensation' – Bentham's pleasures of the body – were the lower. The test, however, for Mill, as to whether a particular pleasure was more valuable, and hence a higher pleasure, than another, was not whether it had its 'seat' in the mind or in the body, but whether 'those who are competently acquainted with both' – 'those who were equally acquainted with, and equally capable of appreciating and enjoying both' – 'the only competent judges' – gave it 'a decided preference'. Such people, noted Mill, 'do give a most marked preference to the manner of existence which employs their higher faculties', and so the dissatisfied Socrates would not exchange his position with the satisfied fool, or the dissatisfied human being with the satisfied pig. Mill's

[90] See 'Bentham', in *Essays on Ethics, Religion and Society* (*Collected Works of John Stuart Mill*, vol. x), ed. J.M. Robson in *Collected Works of John Stuart Mill* (Toronto and London: University of Toronto Press/Routlege & Kegan Paul, 1969), 75–115, at 113. Mill no doubt perceived that Bentham's rejection of taste as an independent principle was problematic for his own 'art of life', which assigned separate spheres and value systems to morality, prudence, and aesthetics; see *A System of Logic Ratiocinative and Inductive: Being a Connected View of the Principles of Evidence and the Methods of Scientific Investigation – Books IV–VI and Appendices* (*Collected Works of John Stuart Mill*, vol. viii), ed. J.M. Robson (Toronto and London: University of Toronto Press/Routledge & Kegan Paul, 1974), 949.

argument here relies on a further distinction that Bentham rejected – namely between happiness and contentment. For Bentham, contentment was just another word for describing happiness, that is a state in which a sentient being enjoyed a balance on the side of pleasure over pain. According to Mill, the satisfied fool was contented, but not capable of achieving the happiness that made Socrates' life superior, even if Socrates' happiness was mixed with 'acute suffering'. For Bentham, this would have been as much as to say that happiness without suffering was worse than happiness with suffering, which was nonsensical. Mill's explanation was that the difference between contentment and happiness lay in the 'sense of dignity' that Socrates possessed, but the fool did not. Bentham would not have accepted that dignity could play such a role in human psychology, because dignity was nothing more than being held in esteem or respected by others, and so valuable to the extent that being the object of such respect produced pleasure. Finally, Mill referred to 'the nobler feelings' and commended 'youthful enthusiasm for everything noble'.[91] Again, we have seen that Bentham thought that the term *noble* meant nothing in this context unless it meant greater in quantity of pleasure. It is intriguing, moreover, that, as well as following Bentham in referring to the pleasures of the mind as 'noble', Mill also used Bentham's phrase 'the only competent judge', albeit in plural form, in his discussion of the higher and lower pleasures. This suggests the possibility that Mill had read Bentham's passage on the quantity of pleasure, and was attempting to respond to it. There is no direct evidence that this was the case, although Bentham wrote the passage while at Ford Abbey, when the Mill family was staying there.[92] John Stuart Mill would, presumably, have at the time been regarded as too young to have been given access to the material, or to be present at possible discussions between his father and Bentham on the subject. Nevertheless, given that Mill was aware of Bentham's condemnation of the use of the terms *good taste* and *bad taste*, and thought it important enough to refer to it and to express his disapproval in his essay on 'Bentham', it is not too great a presumption to think that he was fully aware of Bentham's reasons for his condemnation. For his part, Bentham would have taken the view that Mill's distinction between higher and lower pleasures had compromised his utilitarianism in order to accommodate the sensibilities of persons

91 See 'Utilitarianism', in *Essays on Ethics, Religion and Society* (*Collected Works of John Stuart Mill*, vol. x), 203–59, at 211–13.

92 See Alexander Bain, *James Mill: A Biography* (London: Longman, Green & Co, 1882), 162.

who believed themselves to be superior in culture and civilization, but whose sensibilities it was anti-democratic, and hence wrong, to try to conciliate.

Conclusion

In terms of sexual morality, the distinction between good and bad taste was enforced, according to Bentham, by Paul's promotion of the principle of asceticism. Paul had condemned sexual pleasure in general, and in particular homosexual relationships. Even though Jesus himself had never condemned homosexuality, Paul's views had been adopted as part of the Christian tradition, because they had been found conducive to maintaining the authority of rulers. The privileged elite – the aristocracy who dominated Britain's political, ecclesiastical, legal, and military establishments – employed the notion of 'good taste' to assert their cultural and hence moral superiority, and thereby maintain their social status, power, and wealth. In other words, rulers imposed on their social inferiors the delusion that they were the guardians of an entity called 'good taste' in order to justify the privileges they enjoyed, and the oppression that maintaining those privileges occasioned. In contrast, in a political state governed by adherents of the principle of utility, the standard of right and wrong would be a function of the quantity of pleasure and pain produced. Hence, if the game of push-pin furnished more pleasure, it was more valuable than the fine arts. If a person preferred to indulge in 'irregular' modes of sexual gratification, it was because he or she found them more valuable than the 'regular' mode. The reason that a person preferred to pursue the fine arts was no different from the reason that a person preferred to engage in a homosexual rather than a heterosexual relationship, or preferred to have sexual intercourse with an animal of a different species. Bentham did not by any means condemn the practice of the arts and sciences of entertainment and curiosity, but he opposed claims that they were intrinsically superior to those forms of gratification that had their 'seat' in the body. Moreover, to prevent an individual from engaging in a pleasurable pursuit that did not cause harm to others was to do evil in the same way that to inflict a needless pain on an individual was to do evil. In short, Bentham's arguments constituted a systematic defence of sexual liberty.[93]

[93] See F. Dabhoiwala, 'Lust and Liberty', *Past and Present*, 207 (2010), 89–179, at 168–74.

6

Bentham's Jurisprudence and Democratic Theory

An Alternative to Hart's Approach

DAVID LIEBERMAN[1]

Jeremy Bentham's democratic theory, as ultimately embodied in a proposed *Constitutional Code* designed for 'all governments professing liberal opinions',[2] was a late development in his programme of reform, occupying his attention most intensely in the twenty-year period before his death in 1832. In contrast, the more general project of legislative codification, along with the jurisprudence developed in its support, had engaged Bentham from the very start of his career in the late 1760s. The process by which Bentham became committed to democratic radicalism has long served as a major theme of his intellectual biography, and a major area of disagreement among scholars of his thought.[3] Less concentrated attention has been devoted the thematic relationship between his jurisprudence (on the one hand) and his democratic theory (on the other). This chapter seeks to explore this relationship.

I begin with the approach to this question developed by H.L.A. Hart in his deservedly influential studies of Bentham. More than any other modern scholar, Hart brought Bentham's legal theory to the attention of modern jurists, and established the value of his contributions for current debates in the philosophy of law. He also discussed Bentham's democratic theory and his *Constitutional Code*, although these were not leading topics for him. Nonetheless, he gave his 1982 collection of *Essays on Bentham* the

[1] I am grateful to Professor Xiaobo Zhai for his welcome invitation to participate at the international symposium at the Law School of Zhengzhou University for which this chapter was first composed. I am further indebted to him, as well as to the other symposium participants, for their many questions and suggestions. In revising the paper, I benefited greatly from the detailed and probing comments furnished by Peter Niesen.

[2] Jeremy Bentham, *Constitutional Code: Volume I* (CW), eds. F. Rosen and J.H. Burns (Oxford: Clarendon Press, 1983 (*CW*)), title page.

[3] For a brief review of this scholarship, see my 'Bentham's Democracy', *Oxford Journal of Legal Studies* 28 (2008), 605–26, at 608–14.

subtitle, 'Jurisprudence and Political Theory', and the thirtieth anniversary of this publication provides an apt moment to consider the manner in which Hart drew a connection between his two subject matters. For Hart, Bentham's discussion of sovereignty earned special prominence and functioned as a shared foundational concept for both jurisprudence and political theory. As we shall see, Hart's handling of this topic was expressly shaped by his own celebrated revision of the tradition of jurisprudence he associated with Bentham and his successor, John Austin. As an interpreter of Bentham, Hart probed deeply and powerfully by focusing his analysis on a discrete set of central and contested questions in the philosophy of law. The approach, however, introduced an unfortunate and distorting narrowness into Hart's interpretation. I emphasize other important and alternative lines of continuity between Bentham's jurisprudence and his democratic politics. Much less weight should be placed on the concept of sovereignty, and much more attention devoted to Bentham's codification ideal.

Hart and Bentham

Essays on Bentham focused on those features of Bentham's thought that Hart judged of greatest philosophical significance, and his standard of significance was unabashedly set by then contemporary debates in Anglo-American analytical philosophy and jurisprudence. Numerous references appear regarding the manner in which Bentham's ideas anticipated later developments, as made by such luminaries as Wittgenstein and Russell, or provided better treatments of classical issues than those offered by better-known theorists.[4] In the case of jurisprudence, the last six of the ten chapters comprising *Essays on Bentham* – which form the intellectual core of the collection – share a common intellectual strategy, best exemplified in the papers on 'Legal Duty and Obligation' and 'Legal Powers'. Hart began with an illuminating explication of Bentham's contributions, drawn from the material Hart edited as Bentham's *Of Laws in General* (and since re-edited as *Of the Limits of the Penal Branch of Jurisprudence*),[5] emphasizing the originality and richness of the discussion. He then proceeded

[4] H.L.A. Hart, *Essays on Bentham: Studies in Jurisprudence and Political Theory* (Oxford: Clarendon Press, 1982), 10–11, 43, 130.

[5] Bentham, *Of Laws in General*, ed. H.L.A. Hart (London: Athlone, 1970 (*CW*)); *Of the Limits of the Penal Branch of Jurisprudence*, ed. P. Schofield (Oxford: Clarendon Press, 2010 (*CW*)) (henceforth *Limits* (*CW*)).

to identify problems and omissions, bringing to bear the insights and arguments found in the work of contemporary legal philosophers, such as Raz, Dworkin, and especially Hart himself. The interpretative strategy placed Bentham squarely in the setting of the modern jurisprudence seminar, where Hart clearly believed he fully belonged. The 'originality and power' of *Of Laws in General*, Hart maintained,

> certainly make it the greatest of Bentham's contributions to analytical jurisprudence, and I think it is clear that, had it been published in his lifetime, it, rather than John Austin's later and obviously derivative work, would have dominated English jurisprudence, and that analytical jurisprudence, not only in England, would have advanced far more rapidly and branched out in more fertile ways than it has since Bentham's days.[6]

Hart's approach always involved the risk of distorting Bentham's philosophy by making it speak to an audience that was not his own. In a recent article, Philip Schofield has directly engaged with this issue and offered a sweeping critique of Hart's interpretation, based on the argument that Hart's efforts to reclaim Bentham for modern discussions generated major misrepresentations at the foundational level. Whatever the valuable stimulation Hart found in Bentham's legal theory, Bentham – on Schofield's reading – did not embrace the version of jurisprudence which Hart attributed to him.[7] For my purposes here, of equal significance is another shaping feature of Hart's approach. This concerns the particular path of discovery and exposition that attended Hart's own renowned reshaping of what he frequently termed the 'utilitarian tradition in jurisprudence'. Hart identified Bentham and John Austin as his two most important predecessors within that tradition.[8] In his 1961 *The Concept of Law*, the contribution which so powerfully shaped decades-long debates within and beyond analytical jurisprudence, Hart elaborated his theory of law through a critique of, and constructive response to, John Austin's *Philosophy of Positive Law*.[9] Like so many others, Hart began with the 'derivative' Austin, rather than the superior Bentham, as his

6 Hart, *Essays on Bentham*, 108.

7 P. Schofield, 'Jeremy Bentham and H.L.A. Hart's "Utilitarian Tradition in Jurisprudence"', *Jurisprudence* 1 (2010), 147–67.

8 See H.L.A. Hart, 'Positivism and the Separation of Law and Morals', in *Essays in Jurisprudence and Philosophy* (Oxford: Clarendon Press, 1983), 49–87.

9 John Austin's *Lectures on Jurisprudence or The Philosophy of Positive Law* first appeared in 1861–3. The first part of Austin's jurisprudence had appeared in 1832 as *The Province of Jurisprudence Determined* (London: John Murray). This is the section of the work most relevant to Hart's discussion.

chief interlocutor. Later, when he came to examine Bentham, he valued and concentrated on those elements of Bentham's jurisprudence which seemed significantly stronger than the better-known treatments by Austin. His critical response to Austin thus provided a standard and a principle of selection for the discussion of Bentham, and this framework served to elevate the concept of sovereignty in the interpretation of Bentham's jurisprudence and political theory.

Hart characterized the 'utilitarian tradition in jurisprudence' in terms of three defining positions: the definition of law as a species of command; the distinction between law and morals; and the emphasis for jurisprudence on the conceptual clarification of basic legal terms and relationships.[10] *The Concept of Law* retained the latter two positions: the 'separation thesis' (whereby the morality of a legal provision was differentiated from the question of its status as law); and the use of analytical and especially linguistic techniques to clarify the concept of law. Hart's most influential revisions concerned the command theory of law.[11] Austin dedicated his jurisprudence to the study of 'positive law', and he identified 'positive law' with a command issued by a sovereign in an independent political community. Hart endorsed the legal positivist understanding of law as a human artefact, whose identity and nature were to be explained in terms of human sources. But he rejected Austin's account of law as a species of sovereign commands. The command theory failed to capture the complexity and full normative dimensions of law as a social institution. The paradigmatic form of law as a command – a criminal law prohibition – scarcely exhausted the distinctive forms and functions of law in a modern legal system. The legal subjects' understanding of the manner by which law guided social conduct went well beyond the Austinian discussion of obedience derived from threatened legal sanctions. And Austin's treatment of sovereignty – a legally unlimited source of those commands which constituted law in a given political community – failed to acknowledge the complex institutional reality in virtue of which specific rules and practices were recognized as law.

Having begun *Concept of Law* with a careful review and critique of Austin's version of the command theory, Hart next urged a 'fresh start'

10 See Hart, 'Positivism and the Separation of Law and Morals', 57.

11 Among Hart's first publications in jurisprudence was an introduction to an edition of Austin's *Province of Jurisprudence Determined*, ed. Hart (London: Weidenfield and Nicholson, 1954), vii–xviii) that presented several of the major critical themes later elaborated in *The Concept of Law* (Oxford University Press, 1961).

and elaborated the famous revisionist thesis that law comprised 'the union of primary and secondary rules'.[12] On this formulation, the idea of 'following a rule' replaced the idea of 'obeying a command' as the general phenomenon in terms of which the nature of law was elucidated. In a developed legal system, law involved the combination of two distinctive kinds of legal rules: primary rules directly guiding social conduct, and secondary rules that specified the ways in which the primary rules were introduced, modified, implemented, and confirmed. Among other functions, the secondary rules provided a 'rule of recognition', by which other rules and norms were validated as law for the community. This alternative formulation, for Hart, readily accommodated as law the various kinds of facilitative and regulative rules which did not take the form of commands backed by threatened sanctions. It better captured the normative dimensions of legal ordering by explaining the law's function in creating particular kinds of obligations, and in providing authoritative reasons for particular decisions and behaviour. Critically for Hart, the account of rules of recognition also explicated the institutional practices of judges and courts, as well as the operation of such constitutional restraints on public authority as judicial review, which typically involved procedures and methods for determining the validity and valid interpretation of legal rules.

Hart's critical engagement with Austin's jurisprudence fashioned the script for his later appreciation of Bentham. He treated the definition of law presented in Bentham's *Limits* – 'an assemblage of signs *declarative* of volition conceived or adopted by the *sovereign* in a state'[13] – as a version of the 'command theory', and focused on those elements of Bentham's theory which departed from the Austinian model. Bentham's jurisprudence valuably addressed features of law or conceptual challenges that Austin neglected. Among the leading examples for Hart was Bentham's 'logic of the will' (deontic logic), which elucidated the idea of 'command' by delineating the four basic modes by which law could attempt to order lines of conduct (command; prohibition; permission to act; permission to forbear). His treatment of 'legal duty' pushed beyond the Austinian simplification that reduced the idea of 'obligation' to a prediction relating future conduct to threatened sanctions. And in exploring at length the nature of 'legal powers', Bentham treated a central topic that had been largely and unwisely ignored by other jurists.[14] In these discussions, Bentham could

[12] See Hart, *Concept of Law*, Chs. 5 and 6, which set out the core elements of Hart's 'fresh start'.
[13] *Limits* (*CW*), 24.
[14] See Hart, *Essays on Bentham*, Chs. 5, 6, and 8.

be thought to travel a path similar to Hart's own, correctly identifying and addressing conceptual problems that proved especially vexing to any command theory of law. Ultimately for Hart, Bentham's adherence to the command theory left him without the conceptual resources required fully to resolve these problems. Instead, one needed to abandon the command theory for the alternative model of *Concept of Law* and Hart's later elaboration of its major themes.[15]

The same pattern held when Hart turned to the discussion of sovereignty. The attention he devoted to the concept was scarcely surprising. In Austin's jurisprudence – and, for Hart, in the command theory more generally – the concept of sovereignty performed crucial double duty. Sovereignty was central to the definition of law, and it denoted the core relationship that constituted political society. 'Every positive law, or every law simply and strictly so called', Austin maintained, 'is set by a sovereign person, or a sovereign body of persons, to a member or members of the independent political society wherein that person or body of persons is sovereign or supreme'.[16] Political society itself existed in virtue of a stable structure of sovereign command and subject obedience; and law – 'simply and strictly so called' – was the institutional embodiment of sovereign command. It followed, for Austin, that as the ultimate source of law in an independent political society, sovereignty was necessarily without legal limit. 'Supreme power limited by positive law', Austin reported, 'is a flat contradiction in terms'.[17]

Hart's *Concept of Law* contained a full chapter analyzing the inadequacies of Austin's account. Though this was not something to which Hart drew attention, such criticisms of Austin on sovereignty had been common in the scholarship and pedagogy of Anglophone jurisprudence,

[15] Hart offered the following summary at ibid., 243: 'A pervasive theme of the later essays in this book is that the central concepts of Bentham's imperative theory of law, viz. command and permission, habits of obedience, legality and illegality, are inadequate in the sense that there are important features of law which cannot be successfully analyzed in these terms and are distorted by Bentham's attempted analysis of them. These features include legal obligation and duty, legislative power, legally limited government, and the existence of the Constitution conferring legislative power and legally limiting its scope, and also the notions of legal validity and invalidity as distinct from what is legally permitted and prohibited. I have argued that to understand these features of law there must be introduced the idea of an authoritative legal reason: that is a consideration . . . which is recognized by at least the Courts of an effective legal system as constituting a reason for action of a special kind.'

[16] Austin, *Lectures on Jurisprudence*, 5th edn, ed. Robert Campbell, 2 vols. (London: John Murray, 1885), i. 220.

[17] Ibid., i. 263.

and much of Hart's critique echoed these established lines of criticism.[18] Not every act of sovereign law-making could be reduced to the form of a command. The presence and importance to the legal system of rules of recognition rendered the idea of legally limited sovereign power fully coherent. Indeed, in the standard practices of modern constitutional government, legally limited law-making power comprised a familiar and valued norm.[19]

Against this background, Bentham's discussion proved something of a revelation. Bentham first discussed sovereignty in his earliest major publication, the anonymous *Fragment on Government* of 1776,[20] where he criticized Blackstone's definition of sovereignty as the legally unlimited power to make and alter law. In the series of immediately following compositions – *An Introduction to the Principles of Morals and Legislation*[21]; *Limits* (*Of Laws in General*, in Hart's edition); *Projet d'un corps complet de droit*[22] – he returned to the concept of sovereignty, refining and expanding his analysis in significant ways.[23] Bentham defined political society in terms of settled social experience: a political society existed on account of a general 'habit of obedience' within a given community towards a structure of authority. Given variation across communities, habitual obedience could differ in degree (how stable and thorough was the obedience) and in extent (the range of practices for which the obedience held). When Bentham turned to sovereignty, he elaborated the implications of this variation. The bounds of sovereign authority in a particular

[18] See Postema, *Legal Philosophy in the Twentieth Century: The Common Law World* (Dordrecht: Springer, 2011), 7–13. These criticisms emerged in the earliest reception of Austin's jurisprudence; see, for a particularly influential example, H.S. Maine, *Lectures on the Early History of Institutions* (first published 1875), 7th edn. (London: John Murray, 1905), 345–70.

[19] See Hart, *Concept of Law*, 64–76.

[20] Bentham, *A Fragment on Government; Being an Examination of What Is delivered, on the Subject of Government in General, in the Introduction to Sir William Blackstone's Commentaries* (London: T. Payne, 1776), published in the critical edition of Bentham's collected works in *A Comment on the Commentaries and a Fragment on Government*, eds. J.H. Burns and H.L.A. Hart (London: Athlone, 1977 (*CW*)), 391–551 (henceforth 'Fragment', in *Comment/Fragment* (*CW*)).

[21] *An Introduction to the Principles of Morals and Legislation*, eds. J.H. Burns and H.L.A. Hart, with a new introduction by F. Rosen (Oxford: Clarendon Press, 1996 (*CW*)) (henceforth *IPML* (*CW*)).

[22] For discussion of the composition of this unfinished and as yet unpublished work, see E. de Champs, 'Utility, Morality, and Reform: Bentham and Eighteenth-Century Continental Jurisprudence', Chapter 8 in this volume.

[23] For a detailed discussion of the relevant Bentham texts and the development of his analysis, see J.H. Burns, 'Bentham on Sovereignty: An Exploration', *Northern Ireland Legal Quarterly* 24 (1973), 399–416.

political community would often be difficult to specify with precision. The same authority could be 'supreme' with regard to some groups, but subordinate to others. Commands concerning particular areas of conduct (such as religious observance) might fall outside the structures of habitual obedience even under very stable conditions of political authority. The counter-position adopted by Blackstone (and later by Austin) – that sovereignty was by definition without legal limit – was flatly contradicted by the political experience of many states, ancient and modern, where such limitations clearly and routinely functioned. Bentham's favoured illustrations were cases of federal political systems (the German empire; the Dutch Provinces; the Swiss Cantons; the Achaean league) and states where an 'express convention' served publicly to specify boundaries on the operation of sovereign power.[24]

In *Limits*, Bentham considered other practices that served to limit sovereignty. Among these were what he termed laws '*in principem*'. Unlike 'express conventions', which typically were addressed to the entire community, laws '*in principem*' were legal limits on power which the sovereign law-maker imposed upon him- or herself. Bentham conceded the oddity of a form of law in which the commander commanded him- or herself. But he made sense of the paradox by explaining that these kinds of law obtained their efficacy not through the threat of a legal sanction (the sovereign punishing him- or herself), but through the operation of the religious and moral sanctions.[25]

Hart devoted an entire essay to Bentham on 'Sovereignty and Legally Limited Government'. As in other areas of his jurisprudence, Bentham was praised for addressing issues that Austin and other versions of the command theory of law failed to resolve. At the same time, however, Bentham's own adherence to the command theory again left him unable properly to explain the nature of legally limited government. The key problem was the failure to distinguish the question of the validity or invalidity of law from the question of the effectiveness or ineffectiveness of law in securing obedience. In the modern constitutional system of legally limited government, courts routinely recognized constitutional provisions 'as constituting authoritative reasons for judicial decision and action', and the practice of judicial review revealed the legal system's distinctive concern with establishing the authoritativeness and validity of

[24] See Bentham, 'Fragment', in *Comment/Fragment* (*CW*), 428–34, 485–90.

[25] See Bentham, *Limits* (*CW*), 86–93.

legal sources.[26] Bentham failed to recognize the distinctiveness of these features of law. In a final chapter, Hart further explored this critical theme through an account of 'the idea of an authoritative legal reason' which, among other 'important features of law', included 'the existence of the Constitution conferring legislative power and legally limiting its scope'.[27]

Hart's perspective – for all its striking insights and precision – generated several strained readings of Bentham's position, particularly as attention shifted from jurisprudence to political theory. The experience of modern constitutional practice and judicial review of legislation unsurprisingly loomed large in Hart's own jurisprudence, but distortions resulted from the decision to frame so much of the analysis of Bentham in terms of the conceptual challenges posed for the command theory of law by the modern experience of 'legally limited government'. Hart was absolutely correct to emphasize the differences between Bentham and Austin, and Bentham's express concern to acknowledge and explain the political reality of limits to sovereign authority. Hart's discussion, in turn, stimulated further valuable commentary from other Bentham scholars.[28] Still, the phenomenon of 'legally limited government' was never an organizing issue for Bentham in the early writings that occupied Hart. Hart's chosen focus imposed a quite narrow frame on these materials and excluded from view other prominent and relevant components of Bentham's jurisprudence, as well as his political theory.

A good example of the difficulty appears in the context of Hart's repeated emphasis on the need in jurisprudence to explicate the distinctive and established role of courts in determining the validity of legislation. He was particularly struck by a brief discussion in 'Fragment' in which Bentham, as part of the repudiation of Blackstone's claim that sovereign power was necessarily without legal limits, considered the situation in which 'the judicial power' might enjoy 'a controlling power over the acts of the legislature' by treating certain laws as 'being void'.[29] Hart observed of the passage 'that Bentham contemplated the possibility that legal limitation on supreme legislative power might be secured by something like a system of judicial review'.[30] Hart's gloss likely pushed the material too far

[26] See Hart, *Essays on Bentham*, 234–42, and 58–60.

[27] Ibid., 243.

[28] See the discussion at notes 39–41 in this chapter.

[29] 'Fragment', in *Comment/Fragment* (*CW*), 487–8 (paras. 30–3).

[30] Hart, *Essays on Bentham*, 231–2; and see ibid., 60, where Hart noted that Bentham wrote 'twenty-seven years before *Marbury* v. *Madison* was decided by the U.S. Supreme Court'.

towards this specific constitutional destination. The burden of Bentham's comments was to suggest that it would be less politically dangerous to assign a power to 'void' legislation to judges rather than to the community at large, though overall he also believed it unwise for the courts to exercise this power. Whether he contemplated 'something like a system of judicial review' is less clear. His examples and language in these paragraphs echo a somewhat different institutional context: the established rules adopted by the common law for the 'construction' of acts of parliament. Blackstone, in the *Commentaries*, presented ten such rules, which included those discrete situations in which the courts treated statutes as 'of no validity' because the law was 'impossible to be performed', or as 'void' with regard to 'any absurd consequences'. Bentham, in his 'Comment on the Commentaries' (the unfinished parent-work from which 'Fragment' was extracted), undertook a sustained critique of Blackstone's treatment, and the passages in 'Fragment' that drew Hart's attention recall elements of this longer discussion. In both places, Bentham was especially concerned to establish the unhelpfulness of Blackstone's traditional reliance in these settings on appeals to 'reason' and 'reasonableness', as opposed to Bentham's own insistence on the standard set by demonstrations of utility.[31] Even if we follow Hart in recognizing that in these passages Bentham delineated the space for 'something like a system of judicial review', to leave the topic there omits too much, given how extensively and deeply in his jurisprudence and political theory Bentham examined the relationship between legislation and judicial capacity. This was an issue that preoccupied Bentham throughout his career. But it was never an issue he principally pursued in terms either of 'sovereignty' or of 'legally limited government'.

During the first phase of his career – roughly in the period preceding the belated 1789 publication of *IPML* – Bentham's leading project was the composition of a comprehensive theory and plan of legislation. What he described as a *Pannomion* – 'a complete body of law'[32] – served as the foremost institutional vehicle for his plans for systematic law reform and the promotion of human happiness. The setting in which he devoted most sustained attention to judges and courts was his critique of customary law (in England, common law), where his remorseless demonstration of the failures of judge-made common law always featured as a basic

[31] See 'A Comment on the Commentaries', in *Comment/Fragment* (*CW*), 1–273, at 137–61, esp. 157–61.

[32] *IPML*, 305.

part of his positive case for legislative codification.[33] Among the signal merits of his codification plan was its capacity 'to check the license of interpretation', and a major challenge for Bentham was to identify the institutional arrangements that would prevent adjudication under the *Pannomion* from becoming a separate source of rival customary law. An organizing goal was to preserve the legal certainty and resulting utility he ascribed to codification from the mystery, obscurity and abuses he treated as necessary features of judge-made law.[34]

With his conversion to democratic radicalism, Bentham's approach to judicial power acquired further urgency as he came to perceive 'judge and company' as a paradigmatic instantiation of an organized corporate elite that functioned to prevent government and law from advancing the greatest happiness of the entire community. In addition to being a potential source of legal uncertainty and confusion, lawyers and judges functioned as a powerful 'sinister interest' and source of political 'misrule'.[35] The plan for democratic government in his Constitutional Code contained elaborate provisions for the organization of courts and judicial procedure, designed to insure both the faithful implementation of the legislative code and effective security against the abuse of judicial power. These included a novel system of procedures that would enable the legislature to benefit from regular recommendations for the improvement of the law generated by the experience of the courts, while at the same time preventing the judiciary from operating as a rival to legislative power.[36] Whatever the merits of these elaborate institutional designs, the lavish detail at least makes plain how much of the analysis of 'judicial power' for Bentham was not a question that turned on the nature of sovereignty and its potential forms of legal limits.

Other problems arise in relation to Hart's abrupt characterization of Bentham's position in his mature democratic theory. In *Constitutional Code*, Bentham identified sovereignty with what he termed the 'the Constitutive Authority' of the community. The community was sovereign in virtue of its power to elect legislative representatives and remove from

[33] See my 'Bentham on Codification', in *Jeremy Bentham: Selected Writings*, ed. S.G. Engelmann (New Haven and London: Yale University Press, 2011), 460–77, at 464–70.

[34] See *Limits* (*CW*), 227–9.

[35] The theme of 'sinister interest' and the importance of its emergence in Bentham's political theory receives valuable analysis and emphasis in P. Schofield, *Utility and Democracy: The Political Thought of Jeremy Bentham* (Oxford University Press, 2006), 109–36.

[36] See Bentham, 'Constitutional Code', Bowring ix. 1–647, at 504–14. (This was material assembled by Richard Doane, who edited 'Constitutional Code' for the Bowring edition.)

office those who failed to fulfil their political responsibilities. Bentham distinguished this form of popular sovereignty from the 'Operative' authority of the state, which comprised the Legislative, Administrative, and Judicial bodies.[37] Hart chose to exclude this material in his treatment of Bentham on sovereignty because he believed it marked such a clear departure from the approach Bentham adopted elsewhere. 'The concept of popular sovereignty as developed in the *Constitutional Code*', he maintained, was 'not only a quite different concept' from that Bentham considered earlier in connection with the 'the possibility of limited sovereignty', but equally involved 'a quite different theory of law'. The *Constitutional Code* enjoyed the status of 'law', even though it was not the product of any sovereign command.[38]

Hart's argument concerning this rupture in Bentham's thought stimulated an important body of subsequent commentary. Although the scholarship in question is in no sense uniform in its objectives or findings, in various ways it warns against Hart's suggestion that Bentham's democratic radicalism entailed a 'quite different theory of law'. As already seen in Bentham's handling of judicial power, his shift to democratic politics did indeed introduce major new priorities and orientations in his law reform project. The political practices he found relevant to explain the reality of limited sovereignty were quite different from the experiences of political power he chose to mobilize for a normative theory of democratic government. Nonetheless, important elements of continuity remained, though their observation demands a more expansive consideration of the Bentham materials than Hart allowed. Gerald Postema, a sympathetic critic of Hart, has offered the richest reconsideration of these materials in his masterful reconstruction of Bentham's legal theory. For Postema, Bentham's jurisprudence contained much better resources for dealing with the challenges to the command theory than Hart recognized, including resources for understanding the distinctive manner in which questions of 'validity' formed part of what was recognized as law in a given community. These overlooked strengths of Bentham's legal theory required a different reading of the development and content of his discussion of sovereignty from that presented by Hart. But once assembled, Postema concluded, the 'democratic theory of sovereignty in the *Constitutional Code*' proved 'perfectly consistent' with the earlier discussion and theory of law.[39]

[37] *Constitutional Code: I* (*CW*), 25 (Ch. 3), and 27 (Ch. 4, Art. 6).

[38] Hart, *Essays on Bentham*, 228–9.

[39] G.J. Postema, *Bentham and the Common Law Tradition* (Oxford: Clarendon Press, 1986), 261; and see the fuller discussion at 237–62. A more extreme critique of Hart is offered by Oren

Hart's discussion also attracted scholars concerned with development of Bentham's political thought, who also perceived elements of continuity as well as significant change in the democratic materials. The idea of 'constitutive' power as a dimension of sovereignty, as J.H. Burns emphasized, was first explored by Bentham in the 1780s in *IPML*, in a lengthy passage that distinguished between '*investitive*' and other forms of political power. The account of popular sovereignty in *Constitutional Code*, and the more general distinction between 'constitutive' and 'operative' authority, thus involved a return to materials Bentham had developed much earlier. The key changes in Bentham's position owed less to the alterations in his theory of law and sovereignty than to the specific version of democratic statecraft he advanced.[40] Frederick Rosen returned to the same issues of continuity and change in his influential study of *Constitutional Code*. He too stressed how the most important changes in Bentham's position reflected the terms of his democratic advocacy. His treatment of political power was no longer oriented to questions of 'order, obligation, and law', as in the earlier discussions of sovereignty. Instead, questions of political power were now firmly focused on the best forms of political rule.[41]

The contributions of Burns and Rosen raise a final issue which deserves much greater prominence. This concerns whether the concept of sovereignty – notwithstanding the key conceptual work with which it is associated in the command theory of law – can actually carry the interpretative weight assigned to it in Hart's fertile analysis. As Burns noted of Bentham's early discussions of sovereignty, these 'themes' were always 'peripheral' to 'Bentham's main interests' in the compositions in which they appeared, and typically received rehearsal in the digressive form of 'an enormous footnote'.[42] Rosen rightly explained that *Constitutional*

Ben-Dor. Ben-Dor finds in Bentham a 'split concept' of sovereignty, in which the community's habits of obedience operate in critical relationship to the practice of legislative supremacy. For Ben-Dor, Bentham's position on sovereignty meant that he never embraced the form of command theory of law which Hart attributed to him, and that the democratic potential of his approach was already present as early as 'Fragment': see O. Ben-Dor, *Constitutional Limits and the Public Sphere: A Critical Study of Bentham's Constitutionalism* (Oxford: Hart, 2000), Chs. 2, 4–6.

40 See Burns, 'Bentham on Sovereignty', 403–5, 413–16. Hart responded briefly to Burns in *Essays on Bentham*, 229n.

41 See F. Rosen, *Jeremy Bentham and Representative Democracy: A Study of the* Constitutional Code (Oxford: Clarendon Press, 1983), 41–54.

42 Burns, 'Bentham on Sovereignty', 403, 404, 408. Burns's emphasis on the need for greater care in charting the development of Bentham's discussion of sovereignty over time and texts is reinforced by Schofield in 'Bentham and H.L.A. Hart's "Utilitarian tradition in Jurisprudence"', 164–5.

Code 'does not dwell on the problem of sovereignty'.[43] In fact, in a massive and putatively comprehensive three-volume plan for democratic rule, the term effectively vanished. 'Sovereignty' appeared in only one three-sentence chapter, the briefest of the thirty-one chapters comprising the work.[44] In other writings that accompanied the Code's composition, such as the 1823 *Leading Principles of a Constitutional Code*,[45] or the papers now assembled as *First Principles Preparatory to Constitutional Code*,[46] the term was simply absent. Of course, the omission of the term does not demonstrate the insignificance of the concept. But it does suggest that Bentham's concerns with law and public power in *Constitutional Code* were not framed in terms of the analysis of sovereignty. An alternative and sturdier bridge is required for connecting Bentham's jurisprudence and his mature political theory.

Codification and Democracy

As an alternative to Hart's approach, I propose to connect Bentham's jurisprudence and his democratic theory by emphasizing his codification ideal. This involves an account of Bentham's *Constitutional Code* as an exercise in codification, and an understanding of the manner in which Bentham sought to harness for democracy a logic of public power he elaborated in his legislative programme. Hart, whose knowledge of Bentham's writings was formidable, largely excluded the codification project from the discussion in *Essays on Bentham*. Given this, it is helpful to emphasize how much of the jurisprudence Hart so much admired was itself composed specifically for the sake of Bentham's legislative plan. Bentham did not develop a concept of law which he then applied to the task of legislative design. Rather, in seeking to produce a legislative code he encountered conceptual challenges which stimulated specific jurisprudential inquiries.

The material eventually published as *IPML* was initiated 'as an introduction to a plan of a penal code *in terminis*, designed to follow... in the same volume'.[47] The work that Hart praised as Bentham's greatest contribution, *Limits* (*Of Laws in General*, in Hart's edition), began as

43 Rosen, *Bentham and Representative Democracy*, 41.

44 *Constitutional Code: I* (*CW*), 25 (Ch. 4).

45 'Leading Principles of a Constitutional Code, for any state', *The Pamphleteer*, 22 (No. 44) (1823), [476]–86 (Bowring, ii. 267–74).

46 *First Principles Preparatory to Constitutional Code*, ed. P. Schofield (Oxford: Clarendon Press, 1989 (*CW*)).

47 *IPML* (*CW*), 1.

the continuation of the closing chapter of *IPML*, where Bentham tackled the distinction between the penal and civil branches of the law. This distinction, Bentham maintained, required an analysis of a more fundamental question. 'It will be necessary', he explained, 'to ascertain what *a law* is: meaning one entire but single law'.[48] The object of attention was not the frequently rehearsed modern question concerning 'the concept of law' or 'what law is'. Instead, Bentham's question was 'what *a law* is'. And the question of individuation – the challenge of determining what comprised 'one entire but single law' – again arose expressly in terms of his legislative project. As Bentham explained earlier in the same closing chapter of *IPML*, 'it is evident enough that the notion of a complete law must first be fixed before the legislator can in any case know what he is to do, or when his work is done'.[49] In completing the analysis and explaining its value, he again returned to his legislative programme. Among its several achievements, Bentham listed first and foremost its having established the foundation for 'the plan of a compleat and regular body of statute laws: and thereby . . . a compleat body of law for every purpose'.[50]

In his jurisprudence, Bentham expressly adopted a capacious definition of the term *law*: 'The latitude here given to the import of the word *law* is . . . rather greater than what seems to be given to it in common.'[51] But in his utilitarian programme for law reform, he presented his codification plan as the sole form of law that could fulfil the institution's moral goal to promote the greatest happiness.[52] In contrast to the reactive and ad hoc manner in which most laws were enacted, or which, in the case of customary law, had fashioned entire legal systems, Bentham's *Pannomion* was a prospective legislative design, whose detailed rules and procedures displayed the 'dictates of utility in every line'.[53] The principal branches of the *Pannomion* – the codes of penal, civil, constitutional, and procedure law – were each shaped by distinctive goals and organizing priorities. The Code's organizing divisions and categories were given a rigorously developed and maintained terminology designed to make clear the law's aims and functions. '*Clearness, correctness, completeness, conciseness,*

48 Ibid., 299.
49 Ibid., 283.
50 *Limits* (*CW*), 220.
51 Ibid., 25.
52 I draw here on my fuller discussion in 'Bentham on Codification', 464–70.
53 *IPML* (*CW*), 7.

compactness, methodicalness, consistency', Bentham emphasized in characterizing his codification ideal.[54]

Among the distinctive features of Bentham's mature political theory was that his plan for democracy took the form of a legal code. Bentham's democratic *theory* was elaborated through a variety of writings, directed at a range of distinct audiences. But his *plan* for a democratic state was formulated as a three-volume *Constitutional Code.* In the sole part of the work Bentham managed to bring to publication within his own lifetime, the 1830 Volume One, Bentham chose to begin not with democratic government, but instead with his legislative plan. Thus, his Preface introduced the work by locating *Constitutional Code* as a component part 'of my *all-comprehensive Code*' or 'say, in one word, of my *Pannomion*'.[55]

Like other advocates of democracy in his era, Bentham began with a comprehensive indictment of the then dominant state systems of monarchy and aristocracy.[56] The political structures, procedures, and ideologies of these states all served what he termed the 'sinister interest' of ruling elites, according to which public power and wealth were deployed to enhance the welfare of the 'ruling few' at the expense of the subject many. The task of democracy was to combat 'sinister interest' by introducing a radically altered pattern of political life devoted to the welfare of the entire community. This, for Bentham, involved an extensive democratic electorate who (as we have seen) held sovereign 'constitutive' authority. This authority chose legislative representatives who exercised supreme 'legislative' authority. The elected legislature made law and chose the state's most important government officials. It appointed a Justice Minister, who was responsible for the operation of community's elaborate network of local and appellate courts, and a Prime Minister, who oversaw an ambitious structure of thirteen administrative departments. All the political structures were designed to make clear the specific duties of each government

[54] Bentham, 'Codification Proposal, Addressed by Jeremy Bentham to All Nations Professing Liberal Opinions', in '*Legislator of the World': Writings on Codification, Law, and Education*, eds. P. Schofield and J. Harris (Oxford: Clarendon Press, 1998 (*CW*)), 241–384, at 268.

[55] *Constitutional Code: I* (*CW*), 3. (The 1830 *Constitutional Code* Volume One included a detailed Table of Contents for the Penal Code, and made reference to the anticipated publication of similar Tables for the Civil and Procedure Codes.)

[56] In surveying Bentham's democratic theory here, I draw on my fuller discussions in 'Bentham's Democracy', and 'Economy and Polity in Bentham's Science of Legislation', in *Economy, Polity, and Society: British Intellectual History 1750–1950*, eds. S. Collini, R. Whatmore, and B. Young (Cambridge University Press, 2000), 107–34, at 124–34.

official, to identify individual responsibility for each government decision, and to make the functioning of the state fully known to the democratic community, whose members monitored its activities, and enjoyed wide powers to criticize its failings, to accuse and condemn government officials who were held to have failed in their public responsibilities, and to remove from office those elected representatives who violated its trust.

Bentham's political design eschewed those constitutional devices that had already become familiar in the liberal political experiments of the American and French Revolutionary era, and to which Hart referred in his discussion of judicial review. Legally limited government, as Bentham's early discussions of sovereignty explained, was a well-established feature of political practice. But it was not part of his radical democratic programme. Bentham rejected not only structural arrangements to secure constitutional 'balance', or a 'separation' of political powers, but also enacting and entrenching 'declarations' of irrevocable individual rights. For example, the Constitutional Code identified many laws and policies the state should avoid because these measures violated the general happiness of the community. A leading example was the insistence that there should be no established church, no public system of religious instruction, and no laws supporting religious orthodoxy.[57] But this policy was not advanced through constitutional limitations on state authority or legislative capacity concerning religion. Rather, the legislature was 'omnicompetent', and there were 'no limits' to 'its power'. To prevent the abuse of political power and the adoption of policies contrary to the general happiness, Bentham designed a system 'checks' and 'securities', including those which rendered effective the community's control over those who exercised political power.[58]

Chief among such securities against misrule, Bentham emphasized the power of critical public opinion. 'Public Opinion', he maintained, 'may be considered as a system of law, emanating from the body of the people'.[59] He gave institutional expression to this claim through a body he termed the Public Opinion Tribunal, which functioned analogously to a judicial body in airing charges concerning individual misconduct and in issuing penalties where such charges proved convincing. The Public Opinion Tribunal imposed moral sanctions, principally in form of the suspicion

[57] See the extensive 'Note' on the 'subject of Religious Establishment' in 'Constitutional Code', Bowring ix. 452–3.

[58] See *Constitutional Code: I* (*CW*), 41–2 (Ch. 6, Art. 1).

[59] Ibid., 36 (Ch. 5, § 4, Art. 4).

and lowered reputation it attached to those public officials it convicted of misconduct. This tribunal – and the operation of critical public opinion generally – furnished the most important resource against political abuse and sinister interest. 'Of the aggregate mass of securities against the abuse of power . . . the greatest part . . . unavoidably depends upon the power of the Public Opinion Tribunal.'[60]

What does it mean to interpret this political programme as an exercise in codification? In its methods and presentation, the Constitutional Code displayed the general logic of the larger *Pannomion.* This part of the complete code distributed public offices and powers; and, as with the other principal parts, it was equipped with a defining set of subsidiary goals and priorities through which the foundational goal of general happiness was advanced. In the case of constitutional law, the unifying goals were 'official aptitude maximized' and 'expense minimized'. In his codification proposals, Bentham insisted that legal systems which relied on unwritten and customary rules actually lacked systems of authentic law. Likewise, in his democratic writings, he argued that states lacking written and authoritative constitutional texts likewise lacked authentic constitutional law. Inherited and customary legal rules and maxims, as he insisted at length in his attacks on England's common law, routinely preserved abuses, and masked professional self-interest from public scrutiny. So, in the case of political practice, established legal structures and conventional constitutional pieties served to protect the abuses and sinister interest the ruling few.[61] In the effort to achieve precision and clarity in his legislative programme, Bentham became notorious for his frequent word invention – his creation of novel terms and categories to denote more precisely and consistently the law's categories and designs. The practice was maintained in *Constitutional Code*, as Bentham developed a new terminology to describe the basic functions and responsibilities of government officials. Thus, for example, in delineating the administrative structure of the state under the direction of the Prime Minister, Bentham identified and described the principal functions assigned 'collectively' to all of the administrative departments – statistic function,

[60] Ibid., 125 (Ch. 6, § 31, Art. 33). On the importance of publicity in Bentham's jurisprudence, see Postema 'The Soul of Justice', Chapter 3 in this volume, and 'Bentham on the Public Character of Law', *Utilitas* 1 (1989): 41–61; and in relation to Bentham's political theory, see Schofield, *Utility and Democracy*, 250–71, 293–6.

[61] For brief presentations of these major themes, see: 'Constitutional Code', Bowring ix. 9–11; *Official Aptitude Maximized, Expense Minimized*, ed. P. Schofield (Oxford: Clarendon Press, 1993 (*CW*)), 30–7; and *First Principles Preparatory to Constitutional Code* (*CW*), 252–69.

encourage proposals concerning how in future government activity might be improved.[73] Accompanying this official archive was a separate structure of official 'Registration and Publication' by which this information circulated among government officials; was transferred upwards through a hierarchically structured network of government superiors, culminating in the Prime Minister; and was further conveyed to the community's elected legislative representatives and to the community at large.

On one dimension, official public records were instruments of power. The gathering and circulation of information served to enhance the efficacy and thereby the capacity of the state. Local government officials collected demographic and economic information concerning the districts in which they served; courts collected information concerning the implementation of the law, and identified areas which needed improvement; ministers assembled and analyzed information on the performance of their departments; the Prime Minister assembled and analyzed information on performance of ministers and their ministries; the Legislature assembled and analyzed its own information concerning government performance and the welfare of the community. The quality and availability of this information were a vital resource for 'official aptitude', and was critical to the state's successful promotion of general happiness. 'As in all private so in all public business', Bentham observed, 'apt operation' required 'appropriate and correspondently extensive information'.[74] Such 'extensive information' was particularly vital given the increased range of public responsibilities assigned to the state, as in the case of health, education, and indigence relief.

But at the same time that 'extensive information' increased the efficacy of the state, it also created instruments to thwart the abuse of public power. The public archive enabled the Prime Minister to analyze and evaluate the performance of the administrative officials under his or her authority; the elected representatives were better able to analyze and evaluate the performance of those charged to implement their legislative will; and, most important, the democratic populace acquired the information to analyze and evaluate the performance of all who ruled, elected representatives included. Thus, the dissemination of official records comprised a key element in what Bentham termed the 'completeness of the subjection to the power of the Public Opinion Tribunal'. The activities of the rulers

[73] See the 'Instructional' discussion in *Constitutional Code: I* (*CW*), 222–5 (Ch. 9, § 7 (1st), Arts. 18–21).

[74] Ibid, 283 (Ch. 9, § 10, Art. 1).

were archived so fully, consistently and legibly that the state itself became firmly placed 'under the surveillance of the public'.[75]

Constitutional Code can be understood as the ultimate embodiment of Bentham's codification ideal as system of known and public law. In this setting, the law's required 'perpetual commentary of reasons' was supplied to the community through the body of the code itself. Each of *Constitutional Code*'s elaborate provisions was identified and labelled according to its specific purpose as 'Enactive', 'Instructional', 'Ratiocinative', 'Expositive', or 'Exemplificational'.[76] Under these provisions, the democratic citizenry enjoyed sovereignty as a supreme 'Constitutive' authority. But the power so exercised operated within a field of publicity and criticism that simultaneously enhanced state power and stifled abuse. In designing democracy, Bentham drew on an institutional logic he had elaborated in his earliest writings on codification, and this approach served to bring into unity his legislative project and his democratic statecraft. Codification furnished a vital and foundational link between jurisprudence and political theory.

[75] Ibid., 427–8 (Ch. 9, § 25, Art. 30).

[76] See Bentham's discussion of this feature of the Constitutional Code in *Official Aptitude Maximized* (*CW*), 30–7.

7

Bentham's Natural Arrangement and the Collapse of the Expositor–Censor Distinction in the General Theory of Law

XIAOBO ZHAI[1]

Introduction

In his unduly neglected *Essays on Bentham*, Hart writes:

> among Bentham's many claims to be an innovator none is better founded nor, I think, more important than his insistence on a precise and so far as possible a morally neutral vocabulary for use in the discussion of law and politics. This insistence, though it may seem a merely linguistic matter, was the very centre, and I would say the sane and healthy centre, of the legal positivism of which Bentham may be regarded as the founder. It accounts for many important themes in his general theory including the form of his own definition of law. The terms that Bentham uses to define law are all flatly descriptive and normatively neutral.[2]

By 'his general theory', Hart means Bentham's 'universal expository jurisprudence' (hereafter UEJ).[3] In his *Postscript* to *The Concept of Law*, Hart claims that his legal theory is 'descriptive in that it is morally neutral'.[4] It is clear that Hart attributes his self-professed 'morally neutral' description (hereafter MND) to Bentham, and thinks that Bentham's method of UEJ was the same as his MND, although his legal theory has significantly different content. In relation to this interpretation, Hart even argues that

[1] I would like to thank Michael Quinn, Philip Schofield, Stephen Guest, Gerald Postema, David Lieberman, and Seth Mehl for their comments on the draft. For Bentham's manuscripts, I rely on the transcripts of the Bentham Project. I am indebted to Michael Quinn for his help with my written English. All infelicities and errors are mine.

[2] H.L.A. Hart, *Essays on Bentham* (Oxford: Clarendon Press, 1982), 28; see also Hart, 'Bentham's Principle of Utility and Theory of Penal Law', in Bentham, *An Introduction to the Principles of Morals and Legislation* (first published 1789), eds. J.H. Burns and H.L.A. Hart, with a new introduction by F. Rosen (Oxford: Clarendon Press, 1996 (*CW*)) (henceforth *IPML* (*CW*)), lxxix–cxii, at lxxxv.

[3] See Hart, *Essays on Bentham*, 163–4.

[4] H.L.A. Hart, *The Concept of Law*, 2nd edn. (Oxford University Press, 1994), 239–40.

Bentham's legal positivism or 'analytical vision' is logically independent of his utilitarianism, and that the latter often 'gets in the way of' the former.[5]

Hart's standard interpretation of Bentham's approach has received strong criticism from Gerald Postema, who argues that, despite Bentham's insistence on 'the importance of the distinction between the Expositor and the Censor', and of laws' being purged of all moral or evaluative conditions, Bentham does not seek to construct a value-free theory of the nature of law by appeal 'solely to morally neutral social facts, or *a priori* conceptual or linguistic analysis'[6]; instead, Bentham resorts to utilitarian morality in 'determining necessary formal features of law'.[7] Bentham's UEJ is 'guided by utilitarian considerations just as censorial jurisprudence is'.[8] In contrast with Hart's reading, Postema contends that Bentham's direct-utilitarian practical reasoning leads to, rather than impedes, his normative positivism. Even when denying common law the status of law by reason of it being a fiction, the basis of Bentham's argument, in Postema's view, is still not 'neutral' and 'logical', but 'practical and ultimately utilitarian'.[9] Postema even claims that Bentham's theory of real and fictitious entities depends on his utilitarianism.[10]

In his recent book *Utility and Democracy*, and related articles,[11] Philip Schofield argues provocatively that Bentham's enterprise is completely different from Hart's, and that 'Bentham was not a legal positivist in the senses in which Hart understood that notion'.[12] Borrowing Stephen Perry's distinction,[13] Schofield writes that 'neither methodological legal positivism nor substantive legal positivism . . . can be attributed to Bentham'.[14] Schofield agrees with Postema in rejecting Hart's

[5] Hart, *Essays on Bentham*, 62; see also 'Bentham's Principle of Utility and Theory of Penal Law', xcix.

[6] G. Postema, *Bentham and the Common Law Tradition* (Oxford: Clarendon Press, 1986), 328.

[7] G. Postema, 'The Expositor, the Censor, and the Common Law', *Canadian Journal of Philosophy*, 9 (1979), 643–70, at 645.

[8] Ibid., 664.

[9] Ibid., 650, 656, 659.

[10] See ibid., 657n.

[11] P. Schofield, *Utility and Democracy: The Political Thought of Jeremy Bentham* (Oxford University Press, 2006); 'Jeremy Bentham, the Principle of Utility, and Legal Positivism', in *Current Legal Problems*, 56 (2003), 1–39; 'Jeremy Bentham and H.L.A. Hart's "Utilitarian Tradition in Jurisprudence"', *Jurisprudence*, 1 (2010), 147–67.

[12] Schofield, 'Jeremy Bentham and H.L.A. Hart's "Utilitarian Tradition in Jurisprudence"', 150.

[13] Perry divides Hart's legal positivism into two parts: substantive and methodological. See S.R. Perry, 'Hart's Methodological Positivism', in *Hart's Postscript: Essays on the Postscript to The Concept of Law*, ed. J. Coleman (Oxford University Press, 2001), 311–54, at 311–13.

[14] Schofield, 'Jeremy Bentham and H.L.A. Hart's "Utilitarian Tradition in Jurisprudence"', 151.

attribution of MND to Bentham, and in highlighting the utilitarian character of Bentham's UEJ. The expositor–censor distinction, Schofield stresses, is employed by Bentham to condemn Blackstone 'not for linking law to a particular substantive content, but for linking it to the wrong substantive content'.[15] Schofield states that the basic ideas of Bentham's theory of real and fictitious entities, or his empiricist nominalism,[16] antecede, not only historically but also philosophically, his principle of utility,[17] and form the 'logical starting point for his philosophy'. Bentham's theory of real and fictitious entities serves as the 'foundation' of Bentham's legal theory.[18] Schofield declares that a framework based on Bentham's theory of real and fictitious entities, and its associated philosophy of language, would produce a better understanding of Bentham's UEJ, and of its potential contribution to contemporary debates in legal philosophy.[19] Unlike Hart – who sets out from his own version of legal positivism – or Postema – who begins with Bentham's principle of utility – Schofield's starting point is Bentham's theory of real and fictitious entities.

This chapter develops and modifies the challenges to Hart's MND interpretation inaugurated by Postema and carried forward by Schofield. My main claim is that the key to understanding Bentham's UEJ is his theory of natural arrangement, which receives a detailed account in Part One. Part Two explores the sophisticated interrelations between natural arrangement, the principle of utility and the investigation of truths. It is argued that Hart's MND interpretation as conventionally understood is mistaken, and that Bentham's expositor–censor distinction virtually collapses in his general theory of law. Part Three presents an interpretation of Bentham's insistence on neutral vocabulary, and argues that Hart misconstrues that insistence. In summary, the theses presented in this chapter are, first: Bentham's UEJ is not any kind of Hartian MND; 'neutral vocabulary' is indeed entailed by Bentham's UEJ, but it is neither morally neutral, nor central to Bentham's UEJ. Second, Bentham's empiricist nominalism and his utilitarianism are united in his UEJ by his idea of natural arrangement, through which Postema's and Schofield's different interpretations can be reconciled, and their limitations transcended.

[15] Ibid., 157.

[16] Postema uses 'empiricism and materialist nominalism' to refer to Bentham's theory of real and fictitious entities: see 'The Expositor, the Censor, and the Common Law', 657.

[17] See Schofield, *Utility and Democracy*, 2, 7.

[18] Ibid., 9.

[19] Schofield, 'Jeremy Bentham and HLA Hart's "Utilitarian Tradition in Jurisprudence"', 167.

Part One: Natural Arrangement

Universal Expository Jurisprudence and Natural Arrangement

When criticizing Blackstone's eulogy of common law, which is disguised as an explanation, Bentham offers a compact account of the distinctions between expository and censorial jurisprudence. The expositor 'explain[s] to us what, as he supposes, the Law is', principally occupies himself in 'stating, or in inquiring after facts', and shows 'what the legislator and his underworkman the judge have done already'. In contrast, the censor 'observe[s] to us what he thinks it [that is the law] ought to be', occupies himself in 'discussing reasons', and 'suggest[s] what the legislator ought to do in future'.[20] The censor deals to a large extent with affections, and expresses judgments or sentiments of approbation or disapprobation; he addresses, or seeks to influence, the volitional faculty. The expositor, however, applies himself to the intellectual faculty, that is, the understanding, and deploys the faculties of 'apprehension, memory and judgment'.[21]

In its extent, expository jurisprudence is either local or universal: the former concerns the laws of a particular nation or nations, the latter concerns the laws of all nations.[22] When Bentham says that the expositor is always the citizen of a particular country,[23] he means the local expositor, since law as it is varies widely in different countries. Expository jurisprudence, to be universal, has to confine itself to terminology, dealing with the import of words that are equivalent or correspondent to one another, and that refer to nearly the same things, such as law, duty, obligation, right, and power. In contrast with the local expositor, the censor and the universal expositor share at least one feature: they are the citizens of the world.[24]

[20] Bentham, 'A Fragment on Government' (henceforth 'Fragment'), in *A Comment on the Commentaries and a Fragment on Government*, eds. J.H. Burns and H.L.A. Hart (London: Athlone, 1977 (*CW*)) (henceforth *Comment/Fragment* (*CW*)), 391–551, at 397–8.

[21] 'Fragment', in *Comment/Fragment* (*CW*), 397. See also Bentham, *Chrestomathia*, eds. M.J. Smith and W.H. Burston (Oxford: Clarendon Press, 1983 (*CW*)), 188, 202.

[22] See Bentham, *Of the Limits of the Penal Branch of Jurisprudence* (henceforth *Limits* (*CW*)), ed. P. Schofield (Oxford: Clarendon Press, 2010 (*CW*)), 17. See also Bentham, 'Pannomial Fragments', in *Jeremy Bentham: Selected Writings*, ed. S.G. Engelmann (New Haven and London: Yale University Press, 2011), 253.

[23] 'Fragment', in *Comment/Fragment* (*CW*), 398.

[24] Bentham (ibid.) says that 'the Censor is, or ought to be the citizen of the world', because what ought to be law 'is in all countries to a great degree the same'; see also *IPML* (*CW*), 295.

The function of expositor, according to Bentham, is divided into that of history and that of simple demonstration.[25] To 'represent the law in the state it is for the time being' is the business of simple demonstration, which consists of 'arrangement, narration and conjecture'.[26] Laws that are 'explicit, clear and settled' are matter of narration; conjecture or interpretation is needed when laws are 'obscure, silent, or unsteady'. 'It is matter of arrangement to distribute the several real or supposed institutions into different masses, for the purpose of a general survey; to determine the *order* in which those masses shall be brought to view; and to find for each of them a *name*.'[27] Narration and interpretation treat chiefly of particular institutions, and consequently do not interest Bentham. The business that Bentham was determined to grapple with was that of arrangement, which he regards as 'the most difficult and the most important of the functions of the demonstrator'.[28]

Bentham identifies two ways of arranging legal materials: technical and natural. To mark out and denominate legal materials according to a nomenclature which makes sense only to persons trained in particular professions, such as lawyers and priests, is to arrange them technically, whereas a natural arrangement characterizes the materials according to the properties which man in general is, 'by the common constitution of man's nature, disposed to attend to', which engage or fix man's attention 'naturally', 'readily' and 'firmly', and which are 'most easy to be understood and remembered':[29]

> Now by what other means should an object engage, or fix a man's attention, unless by interesting him? And what circumstance belonging to any action can be more interesting, or rather what other circumstance belonging to it can be at all interesting to him, than that of the influence it promises to have on his own happiness, and the happiness of those who are about him?[30]

Natural arrangement presents objects 'according to their most striking and interesting qualities'.[31] The interesting properties are the tendency

[25] 'Fragment', in *Comment/Fragment* (*CW*), 414.
[26] Ibid.
[27] Ibid.
[28] Ibid.
[29] Ibid., 415; and see also *IPML* (*CW*), 272–3. For a general account of Bentham's natural arrangement, see D. Lieberman, *The Province of Legislation Determined* (Cambridge University Press, 1989), 257–66.
[30] *IPML* (*CW*), 272–3.
[31] Bentham, 'A General View of a Complete Code of Laws', Bowring, iii. 154–210, at 171.

toward, or divergence from, pleasure or pain, which 'may be called by one general word, interesting perceptions',[32] and for the meanings of which a man need not consult a lawyer.[33] The tendency to produce a positive balance of pleasure over pain is utility, whereas the opposite tendency is mischievousness. To point out to a man, directly or indirectly, the utility or the mischievousness of real legal materials is 'the only way to make him see clearly the property of them which every man is in search of; the only way, in short, to give him satisfaction'.[34]

I would argue that natural arrangement is Bentham's most original contribution to legal elucidation, and the very kernel of his UEJ: 'the only universal way'[35] in which legal materials can be characterized. It is only in relation to this idea that many crucial themes in his legal philosophy can receive adequate explanation. David Lieberman takes natural arrangement as 'a fundamental tenet of Benthamic jurisprudence' which marks 'a final stage in the creation of an authentic science of jurisprudence'.[36]

Natural Arrangement and the Defects of Ordinary Language

The first task of natural arrangement is 'to distribute the several real or supposed institutions into different masses, for the purpose of a general survey; to determine the order in which those masses shall be brought to view'.[37] This distribution and ordering are highly complex operations of the human mind, and they rely on language as the instrument not only of communication, but also of thought. Nouns – that is, words that name – are the main medium by which the ideas of things can be presented to the mind and arranged when the things themselves are absent.[38] Things without names cannot be fashioned and fixed in the mind, cannot be expressed and communicated, and hence cannot be thought of consistently and productively. Without language, especially its system of designations, none of the faculties of the human mind,

[32] *IPML* (*CW*), 42; see also *Chrestomathia* (*CW*), 180.
[33] 'Fragment', in *Comment/Fragment* (*CW*), 418.
[34] Ibid., 416.
[35] Ibid; see also *IPML* (*CW*), 274; 'General View of a Complete Code of Laws' Bowring, iii. 161–2.
[36] Lieberman, *Province of Legislation Determined*, 259.
[37] 'Fragment', in *Comment/Fragment* (*CW*), 414.
[38] See UC ci. 340–1 (Bowring, viii. 262).

except perception, can work stably and beneficially.[39] However, ordinary language is full of imperfections, which are best illustrated in the technical arrangement perfected by William Blackstone.

In nearly every page of his 'Comment on the Commentaries' and 'Fragment on Government', Bentham complains that he cannot find 'sense' in Blackstone's 'sounds'. He took great efforts to 'hunt after meaning' in Blackstone's *Commentaries*,[40] but finally had to accept that the whole book was just a 'labyrinth of confusion', or a 'whirlpool of undefined and fluctuating words', which even the author himself did not understand.[41] In short, he found Blackstone's *Commentaries* a pile of beautiful nonsense: elegant, smooth, flowery, ear-tickling or imagination-dazzling, but mind-vexing, ambiguous, obscure, confusing, incomprehensible or meaningless; the few intelligible lines were obviously mistaken or self-contradictory.[42] What Blackstone pursued was not instructive accuracy, but alluring and blinding ornaments, not 'the firm beauties of precision' in 'a purer air', but 'the flaccid fopperies of Poetry and Rhetoric'.[43] Blackstone's problem epitomizes the defects of ordinary or common language, especially in legal field.

First, ordinary language in the legal domain is ambiguous, jargonized, and mysterious. It contains many words without any meaning, or with plural and even opposite meanings which are used indiscriminately.[44] The meaning of words is 'commonly neither determinate nor uniform'.[45] An inference relying on one sense of a word is often drawn from a premise using the word in a very different sense. Different objects are frequently treated of as the same, and vice versa.[46] One of the greatest absurdities is that the proximity in importance and quality between two things very often becomes the very cause of the aversion to extending to one the name given to the other.[47] Failing to mark the similarities and differences which

39 See *Rationale of Judicial Evidence, Specially Applied to English Practice* (first published in 5 vols., 1827), Bowring, vi. 189–585, and vii. 1–644 (henceforth 'Rationale of Judicial Evidence'), at Bowring, vi. 205 ('Prospective View'); 'Essay on Language', Bowring, viii. 294–338, at 298.

40 W. Blackstone, *Commentaries on the Laws of England*, 4 vols. (Oxford: Clarendon Press, 1765–9).

41 Bentham, 'A Comment on the Commentaries' (henceforth 'Comment'), in *Comment/Fragment* (*CW*), 1–273, at 17–18, 64, 96.

42 See ibid., 13–14, 17, 22, 40, 50, 52, 61–2, 64, 96.

43 Ibid., 10.

44 UC ci. 265 (Bowring, viii. 249).

45 *IPML* (*CW*), 230.

46 See ibid., 187n.

47 See *Limits* (*CW*), 31.

are interesting and important, ordinary language often blurs and conceals the lines and issues really at stake.

Second, ordinary language is heavy with dyslogistic and eulogistic expressions, and lacking in neutral names.[48] This 'scantiness' of neutral names is regarded by Bentham as a major vice, as opposed to the leading virtue of copiousness.[49] Eulogistic appellatives mark objects with approbation, and dyslogistic appellatives mark them with disapprobation. Neutral appellatives describe objects simply, that is with neither approbation nor disapprobation. An action or a motive may be undesirable only in some situations, but not in others, and designating it with a dyslogistic appellative may operate as an undiscriminating condemnation of the whole group of corresponding actions. Conversely, when an eulogistic name is given to an action or a motive which may be desirable in only some situations, all the mischievous effects that are liable to be produced by the corresponding group of actions or motives in these and other situations may be covered up and kept out of sight.[50] Bentham labels dyslogistic and eulogistic names '*impostor* terms', because they are question-begging. The propositions containing these terms as subjects, although they demand evidence, are only asserted and affirmed. The process of proving merely consists of giving bad or good names, which themselves are 'instruments of deception'. By employing these impostor names, intentionally or unintentionally, the author on the one hand secretly incorporates his own prejudices into his description, and, on the other, blinds himself to the real nature of the objects under study. These impostor names short-circuit investigation and close down argument with 'the greatest effect, and least risk of detection'.[51] Man falls into fallacies of this kind 'but too naturally of himself'.[52]

Third, the fundamental flaw of ordinary language is that the way that names are used suggests that their referents really exist, when in fact

[48] See 'A Table of the Springs of Action', 'Explanations', in *Deontology together with a Table of the Springs of Action and Article on Utilitarianism*, ed. A. Goldworth (Oxford: Clarendon Press, 1983 (*CW*)), 87–98, at 96.

[49] See UC cii. 319 (Bowring, viii. 304).

[50] See 'Table of the Springs of Action', 'Explanations', *Deontology* (*CW*), 95.

[51] 'The Book of Fallacies', Bowring, ii. 375–487, at 436. To avoid misunderstanding Bentham on this point, it should be noted that Bentham does not oppose the use of evaluative terms, if the properties presented by these terms are confirmed beforehand by careful investigations, which are guided by the principle of utility, and supported by evidence itself presented in neutral language. By imposter terms, Bentham means naming eulogistically or dyslogistically without this kind of investigation, and thereby naming out of prejudice.

[52] Ibid.

most of them do not.[53] Nouns represent names of either real or fictitious entities, which is a 'comprehensive and instructive' distinction, according to which all objects that were or can be presented to human faculties can be designated.[54] The distinction between real and fictitious entities (for shortness, Bentham often omits the words 'names of')[55] must be first comprehended in order for the nature of language to be understood.

A real entity is an entity to which existence is really and seriously meant to be ascribed.[56] It really exists, and can be perceived individually by the senses.[57] Objects that are bodies, also called physical real entities, might be considered really existing and possessing reality. However, objects that are individual perceptions – that is, psychical real entities – possess a better title to reality which is supported by more immediate evidence: 'Of the reality of perceptions, they are themselves their own evidence: it is only by the evidence afforded by perceptions that the reality of a body of any kind can be established.'[58] Strictly speaking, individual impressions (which are made on senses when perceptions take place) and ideas (which are formed by recollection and imagination) are the 'sole perceptible' entities, our perceptions of which are 'more direct and immediate', and our persuasion 'of their existence... more intense and irresistible'.[59] However, Bentham emphasizes that a perception is necessarily accompanied by a corresponding judgment, which can always be wrong.[60] Corporeal substances – the supposed source of perceptions – are only 'in a secondary and comparatively remote way, the object or subject of

[53] See UC ci. 341 (Bowring, viii. 262).

[54] Ibid; and see UC cii. 21, 23 (*De l'ontologie, et autres textes sur les fictions*, ed. P. Schofield, trans. J.-P. Cléro and C. Laval (Paris: Seuil, 1997), 80–2, 84; Bowring, viii. 198); UC cii. 462 (Bowring viii. 331). Despite reiterating this view, Bentham seems inconsistent, or has not fully developed his ontology. Names of fabulous entities doubtless are also substantive nouns: see UC ci. 322, 342 (Bowring, viii. 262–3). For detailed accounts of Bentham's theory of real and fictitious entities, see Schofield, *Utility and Democracy*, Ch. 1; R. Harrison, *Bentham* (London: Routledge & Kegan Paul, 1983), Chs. 2 and 3; M. Quinn, 'L'archetypation et la recherche d'images significantes: significant et signifié dans la logique de Bentham', *Essaim* 28 (2012), 171–81; Quinn, 'Which Comes First, Bentham's Chicken of Utility or His Egg of Truth?' *Journal of Bentham Studies* 14 (2012); Quinn, 'Fuller on Legal Fictions: A Benthamic Perspective', *International Journal of Law in Context* 9 (2013), 466–84.

[55] See UC cii. 25 (*De l'ontologie*, 86–8; Bowring, viii. 199).

[56] See UC cii. 16 (*De l'ontologie*,164; Bowring, viii. 196).

[57] See Schofield, *Utility and Democracy*, 8.

[58] UC cii. 14 (*De l'ontologie*, 174; Bowring, viii. 196); see also UC cii. 13 (*De l'ontologie*, 172–4; Bowring, viii. 196), UC ci. 347 (Bowring, viii. 267).

[59] UC cii. 15 (*De l'ontologie*, 180; Bowring, viii. 196).

[60] UC ci. 118 (Bowring, viii. 224); see also UC cii. 298 (Bowring, viii. 299).

perception'[61]; to be precise, their existence is a subject of inference, judgment and ratiocination, which is more liable to be erroneous, and 'in experience is very frequently found to be so'.[62] Nevertheless, if substances only are the subject in question, 'the characteristic and differential attributive perceptible' is better applied to corporeal substances, the term inferential to incorporeal ones, considering that the inference of the existence of the former from the existence of perceptions – the impressions that they make on the senses – is 'much stronger and more irresistible' than the inference of that of the latter.[63]

A fictitious entity is an entity 'to which, though by the grammatical form of the discourse employed in speaking of it existence is ascribed, yet in truth and reality existence is not meant to be ascribed'.[64] For the purpose of discourse, fictitious entities are spoken of as existing in the same manner as real entities, but speakers do not intend to produce the persuasion that each of them has any separate and real existence.[65] They of themselves are nothing, and their names do not correspond to objects in the physical world. They owe their 'impossible yet indispensable' existence only to language[66]: without them, 'nothing can be said', 'scarce any thing can be done', and language superior to that of the brute animals could not exist. They are imagined, contrived entities, created and invented by the mind, 'dressed up in the garb, and placed upon the level of real [entities]'.[67] Even worse, the contriving or creating is always prior to the true knowledge of things,[68] and often has nothing to do with things. This process of contriving or creating leads to three features of names of fictitious entities. First, names of fictitious entities in and of themselves are nothing, but they can have meanings or senses. A fictitious proposition can be true and instructive, although not in and of itself, but only in terms of representing 'some proposition having for its subject some real entity'.[69] Second, they can have ambiguous or obscure senses. Third, they can be nonsensical, in which case the propositions containing them can only be equally meaningless.

61 UC ci. 118 (Bowring, viii. 224).
62 Ibid.
63 UC cii. 15 (*De l'ontologie*, 180; Bowring, viii. 196).
64 UC cii. 16 (*De l'ontologie*, 164; Bowring, viii. 197).
65 See UC ci. 322 (Bowring, viii. 262), cii. 24 (*De l'ontologie*, 86; Bowring, viii. 198).
66 See UC cii. 23 (*De l'ontologie*, 84; Bowring, viii. 198).
67 UC cii. 21, 23 (*De l'ontologie*, 82, 84; Bowring, viii. 198).
68 *IPML* (*CW*), 187n.
69 UC ci. 217 (Bowring, viii. 246).

At the earliest stage of human communications, one of the most urgent necessities is to name real entities with words. For a time, 'to judge from the structure of language',[70] words were all names of real entities; and even today, many words, the most basic ones in particular, are still so. Children start to learn language generally from names of real entities. This historical and personal or psychological process, over time, builds up a strong and habitual association between the idea of names and that of the reality of the objects to which those names are applied. From this intimate connection, springs a very natural and extensive propensity of 'ascribing reality to the objects designated by words which, upon due examination, would be found to be nothing but so many names of so many fictitious entities'.[71] This propensity, if submitted to without sufficient caution, is a recurrent cause of confusion, perplexity and error.[72]

Apart from the aforementioned imperfections, which have very much to do with the structure of language, what makes the situation worse is the intervention of corruption and intellectual weakness: that is to say, the sinister interest of the ruling few, which produces interest-begotten prejudice, and its exploitation of intellectual weakness among the subject many, which results in adoptive prejudice.[73] These factors in turn form the most fertile sources for the perverse association of ideas, fallacious arguments, and delusive nonsense. Owing to these imperfections, the 'ruling few' are able easily to obscure and conceal the true state of the law. These few fill the brains of the public with numerous enervating delusions, which vitiate public understanding, blind subjects to their true interest, and inculcate among them abject and indiscriminating homage to sham laws, thereby leaving them in total darkness as to the really existing laws. Bentham protests against the 'tyranny' or 'shackles' of ordinary language, which is 'the work of popular caprice'.[74] He warns us not to confine ourselves to the language most in use; otherwise, our propositions will be repugnant to truths, to 'real fact[s]', to 'the experience of every instant', and thereby adverse to utility.[75]

Bentham's account of the wretchedness of ordinary language could not be further removed from Hart's ordinary language analysis, which states that '[m]any important distinctions, which are not immediately

70 'Rationale of Judicial Evidence', Bowring, vi. 237 (Bk. I, Ch. 7).

71 UC cii. 24 (*De l'ontologie*, 86; Bowring, viii. 199); see also UC ci. 341 (Bowring, viii. 262).

72 See UC ci. 341 (Bowring, viii. 262).

73 See UC cii. 394 (Bowring, viii. 318).

74 *IPML* (*CW*), 190n.

75 'Comment', in *Comment/Fragment* (*CW*), 13, 19.

obvious, between types of social situation or relationships may best be brought to light by an examination of the standard uses of the relevant expressions and of the way in which these depend on a social context, itself often left unstated'.[76] Many differences between Bentham's and Hart's legal theories can be traced to their different attitudes towards ordinary language. Bentham does not think that there is any reliable or accurate standard in the current usage of nouns. His project is first to break the witchery of the current or common language, and then remake it in the light of the real state of things.

Here lies a fundamental paradox: imperfections in language and errors in thought are apparently like the chicken and the egg. Terminology can only be improved by clear and correct thought. It is impossible, however, to think clearly and correctly, while words are seriously flawed. There is no easy way out of this dilemma.[77] Bentham himself admits that complete success is unattainable:

> Striving to cut a new road through the wilds of jurisprudence, I find myself continually distressed, for want of tools that are fit to work with. To frame a complete set of new ones is impossible. All that can be done is, to make here and there a new one in cases of absolute necessity, and for the rest, to patch up from time to time the imperfections of the old.[78]

The important lesson to be learnt from the abject state of ordinary language is that names and their ideas in current use are only the starting points: they cannot and should not be guides, still less standards.

Natural Arrangement: Individualization, Definition, Paraphrasis and Naming

Language is a basic medium by means of which man deals with the world. Man habitually treats of ideas, things, and their properties with the help of relevant names. When exploring the world, before embarking on any conscious research, a man should choose names that he conceives to be interesting, that is, having to do with his pleasure or pain. Only after making this choice can he start the effort of understanding. However, we must 'pierce through' the words before we can understand clearly 'the real state of things'.[79] Once following names to the field of things,

[76] Hart, *Concept of Law*, vi.
[77] See *IPML* (*CW*), 187n.
[78] Ibid., 215.
[79] *Limits* (*CW*), 287.

we should leave behind the initially helpful but perhaps misleading and imposturous name, the fate of which has to await the ultimate verdict of the investigation of things. Only after the nature of things is known can a proper nomenclature be formed for them.[80] The original name itself and its meaning may be discarded, recoined, modified, or refixed. Bentham's methodology of piercing through words to things, generally speaking, can be summarized by the concept of individualization.

Individualization

The path of knowledge 'as chalked out by the hand of nature' starts from individual things. The senses are the fountain of all perceptions. It is only through sense perception that any persuasions concerning objects can be obtained, or roughly speaking, that things can be known. 'To *sense* no objects but individual ones ever present themselves.'[81] The senses perceive objects individually, and the only existing objects are individual real entities. The proper course of knowing and naming the world sets out from 'individuals and those determinate', and arrives at extensive aggregates through generalization and abstraction.[82] In order to know what a name means, to discern and rectify the mistakes lurking behind name-creation, the initial process of name-creation has to be unpacked, recovered, corrected and reconstructed. This involves a further converse process, that of division or generic individualization, which is the operation of instruction that causes men

> to be agreed in determining within what limits or bounds an individual when designated by and under [a generic] name shall be considered as limited, so as to be distinguished from all objects which are regarded as liable to be confounded with it: or in relation to any individual likely to be considered as designated by that name, of what elements that aggregate shall be considered as composed.[83]

The core idea of individualization is that the correct way to understand, expound, and determine the idea represented by a name is to retrieve the relation between this name and relevant real entities, because the only objects, that is, the only fountains of sense or meaning that exist, are real entities which are 'the real source, efficient cause, or connecting

[80] See 'General View of a Complete Code of Laws', Bowring, iii. 171.
[81] UC ci. 332 (Bowring, viii. 265); see also UC cii. 300 (Bowring, viii. 256).
[82] See UC ci. 336 (Bowring, viii. 266); UC ci. 124 (Bowring, viii. 225).
[83] UC ci. 207 (Bowring, viii. 243).

principle'.[84] 'The field of law', according to Bentham, is 'the field in which the demand for this mode of individualization – for this mode of exposition – is most copious and most urgent, and the use of it most conspicuous and the utility of it most obvious and incontestable'.[85]

Definition, Bifurcation, and Abstraction

There are two distinct but interconnected ways to individualize a common name: definition and paraphrasis. The nature of the subject dictates the mode of the exposition.[86] When facing an ambiguous or obscure common noun, the first thing that springs to mind is to define it:[87]

> To *define* a word is to indicate some aggregate, in which the object of which it is the sign is comprehended, together with an indication of some quality which, being possessed by that same object, is not possessed by any other object included in that same aggregate. Elliptically but more familiarly – to define is to expound, by indication of the genus and the difference.[88]

In order for a definition to be possible, the object in question must belong to an aggregate the meaning of which has already been established. Put differently, the import of the word to be defined should be included in that of another word which can be employed in the definition.[89] A word representing an entity with no superior genus, although most imperiously demanding exposition, is clearly incapable of being defined by differentiating it from other species of the same genus. An alternative mode of exposition has to be found for it.[90] When giving a definition, if the word to be defined tends to be used by different speakers in multifarious senses, distinction or disambiguation will be 'an operation necessarily preliminary to that of definition'.[91] 'Division and definition go hand in hand'; 'Without division there could be no definition'.[92] As explained earlier, to define is to find a higher genus containing the object represented by the word to be defined, and then to differentiate this object from others belonging to the same genus by means of indicating some distinguishing

84 UC ci. 218 (Bowring, viii. 246).
85 UC ci. 207 (Bowring, viii. 243).
86 See UC ci. 203 (Bowring, viii. 243).
87 Ibid.
88 UC ci. 215 (Bowring, viii. 245).
89 See ibid.
90 See UC ci. 216 (Bowring, viii. 246).
91 UC ci. 265 (Bowring, viii. 249).
92 UC ci. 286; UC ci. 351–2 (Bowring, viii. 268).

qualities[93] appertaining to the former but not the latter. Once we follow the name to its higher aggregate of things, to define is simply to know and understand the object's distinguishing qualities, and to be acquainted with its differences from other species of the same genus, which obviously requires the operations of distinction and division: once division has been made, the need for further exposition by way of definition may be effectually superseded.[94]

The really tough job in defining is to divide or to distinguish. The only complete and correct way to do this job is by bifurcation: 'distributing them into a system of parcels, each of them a part, either of some other parcel, or, at any rate, of the common whole'.[95] Bifurcation or exhaustive division applies logic to legal materials. In order for a bifurcation to be conducted, we need to first determine the *fundamentum divisionis*, that is, the characteristic qualities in light of which objects are divided.[96] Any object may present to man's senses innumerable perceptions in conjunction.[97] It is impossible, and also pointless, to take all the perceptions into consideration, so what perceptions should be considered? Since the desire of pleasure and that of exemption from pain, or man's interest in various shapes, is the source of every thought as well as the cause of every action, the choosing of the characteristic and distinguishing properties must 'bear an indispensable . . . relation to the particular end or purpose' of human activities: happiness.[98] At the same time, Bentham also warns that this relation does not have to be 'a very prominent' one, that the choosing has to depend on the objects themselves, and that the qualities have to be the interesting qualities of the objects themselves.[99] The mind will, and also ought to, conduct the operation of abstraction, by which 'the mind by its apprehensive faculty lays hold of some one alone or some other part of the whole number, leaving the rest unnoticed and unheeded'.[100] The perceptions – impressions and ideas – that are picked out by the mind are the pathematic ones, that is, those which are interesting in that they relate to pleasures and pains. Among all real entities,

93 For discussion of the idea of quality, see UC cii. 42 (*De l'ontologie*, 98; Bowring, viii. 202–3).
94 See UC ci. 272 (Bowring, viii. 251).
95 *IPML* (*CW*), 187n.
96 See UC ci. 351 (Bowring, viii. 268).
97 See UC ci. 124 (Bowring, viii. 225).
98 UC ci. 312 (Bowring, viii. 260).
99 Ibid.
100 UC ci. 124 (Bowring, viii. 225).

> the two of which are as it were the *roots*, the main pillars or *foundations* of all the rest, the *matter* of which all the rest are composed – or the *receptacles* of that matter . . . will be, it is believed, if they have not been already, seen to be, PLEASURES and PAINS. Of these, the existence is matter of universal and constant experience. Without any of the rest, *these* are susceptible of, – and as often as they come *unlooked* for, do actually come into, *existence*: without these, no one of all those others ever had, or ever could have had, existence.[101]

With a real and interesting *fundamentum divisionis*, bifurcation can produce a complete knowledge of the interesting properties of things. Bentham is obsessed with bifurcation in nearly all of his writings. It is so important for Bentham that he declares that he owes all his new and original insights to it.[102] By means of bifurcation, objects which agree in important features can be classed together, and be distinguished from objects which are really different. In a word, objects of different or similar interesting qualities are ready to be arranged or methodized naturally in the order of subalternation.[103] Considering the fallibility of the human mind, this bifurcation needs impartial and penetrating eyes to detect points of real agreement and of difference. Some imports, although apparently widely and importantly different, might actually be interconnected, associated or similar at implicit but equally important levels, and vice versa.[104] In the current period of science, writes Bentham, to pursue bifurcation strictly to its utmost length would be too fatiguing for the author and disagreeable for the reader[105]; however, people should be encouraged to carry this 'eminently instructive' method to 'whatever length it is capable of being followed'.[106]

Paraphrasis

If it lacks a superior genus, the name of a fictitious entity is not capable of being individualized through definition, and the only instructive mode of expounding it is paraphrasis. The principle behind paraphrasis is the same as that behind definition: to individualize words to real entities which can be expounded by definition. 'To understand abstract terms, is to know how to translate figurative language into language without figure', and

[101] 'Table of the Springs of Action', 'Observations' in *Deontology* (*CW*), 98–115, at 98.
[102] See *IPML* (*CW*), 196n.
[103] See UC cii. 313, 314 (Bowring, viii. 260), 331 (Bowring, viii. 265).
[104] See UC ci. 273–4 (Bowring, viii. 251).
[105] See *IPML* (*CW*), 196n.
[106] Ibid.; see also *Chrestomathia* (*CW*), 157.

to 'decipher' it into 'the language of pure and simple truth – into that of fact'.[107] Paraphrasis is the operation of translating or recasting into propositions having for their subjects real entities, propositions which have for their subjects fictitious entities.[108]

A preliminary and subservient operation to paraphrasis is phraseoplerosis, by which the name of a fictitious entity is filled up into a fictitious proposition capable of being paraphrased.[109] As illustrated earlier, sense can only come from the senses: the world of real entities exhausts the universe of meaning or sense, and there is no sense or meaning outside or separate from it. A fictitious entity in and of itself is nothing, and nothing has no properties, so a fictitious proposition in and of itself cannot be true and instructive. However, this does not mean that a fictitious proposition is necessarily untrue and useless: its meaning and truth depend on its relation with names of real entities. Only by representing or being connected to a proposition (Bentham also calls this proposition 'a paraphrastically-expository proposition')[110] having for its subjects real entities, can fictitious propositions be instructive and true. If a fictitious proposition presents to the mind an image of 'some real action or state of things', which Bentham calls the archetypal or emblematic image,[111] then the meaning of the phraseoplerosized fictitious entity is made clear and determinate. Expounding the fictitious entity in terms 'calculated' to raise images of substances perceived, that is, of the sources of every idea, is 'the only method' by which any abstract terms can be expounded 'to any instructive purpose'.[112] In this paraphrasis – phraseoplerosis plus archetypation – aiming at the idea represented by the subject-noun in a fictitious proposition, etymological analysis aiming at the root of the word might be helpful, and provide clues to the route to paraphrase or archetypify the ideas, especially for the primitive abstract nouns whose material images have a strong analogy with the immaterial ideas. However, it can also be misleading, considering that the connection between ideas and their signs may be completely arbitrary.[113] If this paraphrastic operation proves impossible, then the noun in question is 'a mere

107 'General View of a Complete Code of Laws', Bowring, iii. 181.
108 See UC ci. 217 (Bowring, viii. 246).
109 UC ci. 219 (Bowring, viii. 246–7).
110 Ibid. (Bowring, viii. 247).
111 UC ci. 218 (Bowring, viii. 246); see also UC cii. 546 (Bowring, viii. 345n).
112 'Fragment', in *Comment/Fragment* (*CW*), 495.
113 For a slightly different interpretation, see Quinn, 'L'archetypation et la recherche d'images significantes'.

nothing',[114] a meaningless sound, and any proposition which includes it is nonsense. A fictitious proposition abstracted from all relations to some real-entity-proposition can only be a falsehood or nonsense.

The meanings of many terms in morals, law and politics are the foundations of 'questions of prime and practical importance'.[115] According to Bentham, these terms, including obligations, powers, rights, and the whole tribe of terms of same or similar stamp, are all names of fictitious entities.[116] In fact, people very generally try to define them, but these efforts are futile and foolish, because these terms are often not species of any superior genus, and are thus incapable of being defined: they are not species of anything. They all share one 'real source', that is, one and the same sort of real entities: sensations of pain or pleasure. Their import can only be illustrated by paraphrasis, that is, by showing the relation which they bear to real entities. Fortunately, Bentham thinks, they are also 'the most instructive examples for exposition and explanation of paraphrasis and of the other modes of exposition connected with it and subsidiary to it'.[117]

It is worth noting that definition and paraphrasis, as two ways of individualization, are not independent of and separate from each other. Through paraphasis, fictitious entities are connected to real entities, which, except pleasure and pain, may need, and may be capable of, definitions. In order to define real entities, people need to know their properties, which are in turn fictitious entities and may need paraphrasis. In practice, definition and paraphrasis are always interwoven with each other: they serve each other and call for each other's service.

Naming

By means of individualization, we harvest many clear, exact, and interesting ideas, which would just be floating, indeterminate and ephemeral dreams or clouds, unless they were fixed, expressed, arranged, and regulated by words. This ability of naming by words makes man, 'in the scale of perfection and intelligence', superior to, and distinct from, animals.[118] A general name is 'the *common* – the necessary – tie, by which a number of general or abstract ideas are fixed and fastened together in the mind'.[119]

114 UC ci. 217 (Bowring, viii. 246).
115 'Radical Reform Bill', 'Appendix', Bowring, iii. 592–7, at 593n.
116 'Fragment', in *Comment/Fragment* (*CW*), 495.
117 UC ci. 221 (Bowring, viii. 247).
118 UC ci. 423 (Bowring, viii. 229); and see also *Limits* (*CW*), 224.
119 UC ci. 128 (Bowring, viii. 226).

A system of collective denominations is an 'indispensable requisite' to the collective and subalternate methodization of a multitude of general ideas.[120]

It is extremely difficult to find out or make up more apposite denominations to express new ideas, or to make old ideas more clear and determinate.[121] Ideally, ideas capable of interpretation in terms of real entities should be the only guide, and every real and interesting difference should have a different denomination. Out of this ideal, Bentham takes precision as 'the very life and soul' of legal science,[122] which requires copiousness to be the principal and highest virtue of language. Copiousness means that language should be capable of affording an adequate expression for all useful ideas:

> It is only in proportion as it is *copious* that in a direct way language contributes any thing to its *end*: to any of the modifications of which the *universal end, well-being,* is susceptible. Reduce its copiousness, and in proportion as you reduce it, the height of the place occupied by man on the scale of being is reduced from that of a member of the best governed and mannered community down to that of a barbarian, of a savage, of a beast.[123]

Bentham unreservedly sings the praises of copiousness. The general rule of language improvement is 'The more copious a language, the better'.[124] Any addition of new words and combinations to the pre-existing stock of instruments of discourse is prima facie, and saving particular exceptions, an improvement.[125] This general rule has one exception – namely simplicity. Simplicity is not an enemy of copiousness: 'a language is copious, in so far as it is replete with useful matter; it is simple, in so far as it is unencumbered with matter which, being useless, is at best superfluous',[126] and at worst extremely harmful. Simplicity is the opposite of technicality – lawyers' or professional technicality. So copiousness must be distinguished from technicality. The virtue adjacent and attached to copiousness, but seated on the same lofty eminence, is *clearness*, that is, the absence of ambiguity and obscurity.[127] It is necessary to clearness that the name

120 Ibid.; see also UC ci. 312 (Bowring, viii. 260).
121 *IPML* (*CW*), 187n.
122 'Comment', in *Comment/Fragment* (*CW*), 11–12.
123 UC cii. 352 (Bowring, viii. 310).
124 UC cii. 392 (Bowring, viii. 318).
125 Ibid.
126 UC cii. 350 (Bowring, viii. 310).
127 See UC cii. 392–3 (Bowring, viii. 318).

must reflect or unambiguously indicate the idea that we intend to bring to view,[128] and should therefore refer to nothing other than the idea. For this reason, the name should aspire to be as specific and as neutral as possible. Bentham stresses that 'the only novelty' of his methodology of naming 'consists in the steady adherence to the one neutral expression, rejecting altogether the terms, of which the import is infected by adventitious and unsuitable ideas'.[129]

Bentham's standards of copiousness, simplicity, clearness, and neutrality imply that a new, and hence unusual, language should be invented. Although Bentham believes that improvement in language is capable of being introduced by simple practice – by mere individual practice of instruction, and by the apparent solidity and conclusiveness of the reasons the instructor offers[130] – he is also very clearly aware of the difficulty: 'every where the state of the language is what it is, and it lies not in the power of any individual, by any act of his own, to render it in any degree worth mentioning either materially better or worse':[131] 'change the import of the old names, and you are in perpetual danger of being misunderstood; introduce an entire new set of names, and you are sure not to be understood at all'.[132] It is neither practicable nor expedient to destroy ordinary language altogether.[133] Bentham's strategy is, first, to address things 'as much as possible under their accustomed names'.[134] Second, if the first operation proves impossible, new names have to be invented or fabricated. In most cases, given the desire to avoid the inconvenience of fabricating words that are absolutely new, the way of inventing them consists of bringing two or three existing words together,[135] and trying to make sure that his coinage of words has 'already a footing in the language', and to avoid being too long-winded.[136] However, in both cases, the author has to 'enter into a long discussion, to state the whole matter at large, to confess, that for the sake of promoting the purposes, he has violated the

128 See *IPML* (*CW*), 214.
129 Ibid., 102.
130 See UC cii. 364–5 (Bowring, viii. 313).
131 UC cii. 315 (Bowring, viii. 303).
132 *IPML* (*CW*), 187n.
133 See *Limits* (*CW*), 287.
134 *IPML* (*CW*), 190n.
135 See ibid., 102.
136 *Chrestomathia* (*CW*), 185.

established laws of language, and to throw himself upon the mercy of his readers'.[137]

When discussing Bentham's paraphrastic analysis, Ross Harrison suggests that we should give up the idea that the sentence to be analysed has any precise pre-analysis meaning or truth which needs to be captured in the analysis: instead, we must take the analyzing sentence as giving the analysed sentence whatever truth it has, and thereby giving it a sense. In Hart's view, 'this apparently stipulative conception of analysis' is 'mistaken and unnecessary'. Hart makes a distinction between the ability to use correctly and the ability to specify. According to Hart, a competent speaker can use correctly the general terms and sentences of his language, and in this sense knows their meanings, even if he is not able to specify those features of such objects or situations with reference to which he is using general terms and sentences, and therefore needs a philosopher-paraphraser to 'produce an explicit statement of the features of the relevant objects or situations which guide and are the criteria for its correct use'.[138]

Neither Harrison's nor Hart's interpretation is justified. Bentham's paraphrastic analysis, as part of his natural arrangement, combines two functions: testing and reforming. General terms, prior to paraphrastic analysis, might or might not have clear or ambiguous or obscure meanings, that is, might or might not refer directly or indirectly, determinately or indeterminately, to real entities. Paraphrastic analysis will examine whether a general term has this kind of true and instructive meaning; disambiguate different mixed ideas; fix and solidify some inexact ideas; and rearrange these ideas naturally, by way of tracing them up or individualizing them to real entities. In this operation, a natural arranger may 'produce an explicit statement of the features of the . . . situations which guide and are the criteria for its correct use', but equally, and more likely, the analysis may give the words analysed a meaning which they do not have prior to analysis. Important new ideas may emerge from this operation through bifurcation or paraphrasis, the original terms may be discarded or given new meanings, or proper new names will be found out or fabricated for new ideas. Language thereby is reformed and improved. Thus, expository jurisprudence, as Bentham argues, is 'the art of finding clear ideas to annex

137 *IPML* (*CW*), 102; see also ibid., 216, 275.

138 Hart, 'Book Review of *Bentham* by Ross Harrison', *Mind*, 94 (1985), 153–8, at 155–6.

to the expressions of men whose ideas were not clear'.[139] In fact, Hart did recognize this reformative and constructive dimension of Bentham's natural arrangement a dozen years before his criticism of Harrison. When commenting on Maine's reading of Bentham's idea of rights, Hart says:

> [Bentham] did not think that... he was strictly bound by common usage... which at points he found to be confused, arbitrary, and vague and in various other ways unsatisfactory. Quite frequently and explicitly, he departed from usage in order to construct a meaning for a term which, while generally coinciding with usage and furnishing an explanation of its main trends, would not only be clear, but would pick out and collect clusters of features frequently recurrent in the life of a legal system, to which it was important to attend for some statable theoretical or practical purpose. Hence Bentham spoke of himself as expounding the meaning of terms by 'fixing' rather than 'teaching' their import.... In modern terminology, Bentham's conception of analysis is that of 'rational reconstruction' or refinement of concepts in use: his general standpoint is critical and corrective.[140]

It is indeed very puzzling that Hart gave up this more elaborate, more faithful and more correct reading of Bentham.

Two Examples

Bentham's expositions of such basic terms as law and obligation are two classic examples of his method of natural arrangement. The word 'law', according to Bentham, is used in widely different ways, referring to entirely diverse things, including common law, natural law and statutory law, and so forth. For Bentham, therefore, 'the idea of law has never been precisely settled', and 'no one certain thing is as yet meant by a law'.[141] His business 'is therefore not to remind the reader what *is* meant by a law'.[142] *Law* or *the law*, 'taken indefinitely, is an abstract and collective term; which, when it means anything, can mean neither more nor less than the sum total of a number of individual laws taken together'.[143] Put another way, *law* or *the law* signifies a fictitious entity or logical whole. To make sense of the word *law*, we have to individualize or paraphrase it, to be acquainted with and to describe the real entities to which *law* refers; each of these real entities should constitute 'neither more nor less than one

139 *Limits* (*CW*), 220.
140 Hart, *Essays on Bentham*, 164.
141 'Preparatory Principles Inserenda', UC lxix. 86.
142 Ibid. (emphasis original).
143 *IPML* (*CW*), 294.

entire law'.[144] When expounding the name of *a law*, Bentham employs the method of definition. By means of a series of definitional bifurcations, Bentham finds that some sign of the legislator's will imperating the subjects' behaviour is the real entity or archetype of the name law.[145] He then begins his investigation of things, ransacking human experience for the things sharing essential qualities with the archetype and classifying them. Bentham discovers that the things sharing essential qualities with the archetypal real entity named a law include the expressions of will backed or sanctioned by the sovereign authority, whether they are immediately conceived or indirectly adopted, whether public (legislative, judicial, military or executive), private or domestic, whether permanent or temporary, commanding or countermanding, statutory or customary, issued from an individual or a body, *propter quid* or *ex mero motu*. These various sorts of expressions of will, although men, for different reasons, tend to deny many of them the appellation of *a law*, share the same nature in every point with law's archetypal real entity, except their immediate source, that is, their manner of appertaining to the sovereign.[146] These objects are so intimately allied and so frequently susceptible of the same propositions that it is necessary to characterize them with, or find for them, a common exposition and appellation. The genus is 'an assemblage of signs declarative of a volition'; the differentia is

> conceived or adopted by the sovereign in a state, concerning the conduct to be observed in a certain case by a certain person or class of persons, who in the case in question are, or are supposed to be subject to his power: such volition trusting for its accomplishment to the expectation of certain events which it is intended such declaration should upon occasion be a means of bringing to pass, and the prospect of which it is intended should act as a motive upon those whose conduct is in question.[147]

The 'least exceptionable'[148] appellation is the term 'law', which is also frequently used in this sense.[149] There are many competing appellations, and Bentham then explains carefully and meticulously, with reference to the ordinary usage of words, why the name 'law' is to be preferred to other names.

[144] *Limits* (*CW*), 237.
[145] Ibid., 250.
[146] See *Limits* (*CW*), 32.
[147] Ibid., 24.
[148] Ibid., 32.
[149] See ibid., 34–5.

Bentham is fully aware that 'the latitude he gives to the import of the word "law" is rather greater than what seems to be given to it in common'.[150] He warns readers, by stressing the difference between his idea of law and that of legislation, that he has 'outstretched' the idea which common usage has annexed to the word law when he 'appropriate[s] the term law' to 'the large and comprehensive idea'.[151] In this way, by means of definition, Bentham annexes to the word *law* a meaning or an idea which he thinks ought to be meant by it. This idea can serve as a pattern to which legal materials can be reduced, and is the monad of which the vast universe of jurisprudence is composed.[152]

As mentioned earlier, ethical fictitious entities, of which obligation constitutes the basis, afford 'the most instructive' examples for the explanation of paraphrasis. The real source of all the ethical fictitious entities is the perception productive of pain or pleasure or both. Regarding obligation, the first step is still to individualize the collective noun 'obligation' into 'an obligation', which is still the name of a fictitious entity having no superior genus, and therefore not susceptible of definition, but only of paraphrasis. In order to be paraphrased, it has to be made up, by means of phraseoplerosis, into a fictitious proposition: 'an obligation is incumbent on a man'. Through etymological analysis, Bentham thinks that the 'emblematic or archetypal image' of an obligation is

> that of a man lying down, with a heavy body pressing upon him, to wit in such sort as either to prevent him from acting at all, or so ordering matters that if so it be that he does act, it can not be in any other direction or manner than the direction or manner in question – the direction or manner requisite.[153]

With this clue of the archetypal image, Bentham completes his paraphrasis with the following exposition: an obligation of conducting oneself in a certain manner is spoken of as incumbent on a man, 'in so far as, in the event of his failing to conduct himself in that same manner, pain or loss of pleasure is considered as about to be experienced by him'.[154] The source of the explanation is 'the idea of eventual sensation' of pleasure or pain, and

150 See ibid., 25.
151 See ibid., 26–36.
152 See ibid. 34–5, 269.
153 UC ci. 223 (Bowring, viii. 247).
154 UC ci. 222 (Bowring, viii. 247).

'the designation of the event on the happening of which such sensation is considered as being about to take place'.[155]

Part Two: Utility, Truth, and the Collapse of the Expositor–Censor Distinction

Natural Arrangement and the Principle of Utility

Having spelt out Bentham's UEJ, with natural arrangement as its basis, let us turn to the question of whether Bentham's UEJ can be characterized as one kind of Hartian morally neutral description. Any sensible answer to this question will depend on what 'morally neutral' means. One very influential reading is that it means 'normatively inert. It does not provide any guidance at all on what anyone should do about anything on any occasion'.[156] Understood this way, Hartian MND would certainly have made no sense to Bentham. Hart's comment that Bentham's utilitarianism gets in the way of his analytical vision would certainly have surprised Bentham. As Bentham himself says very clearly, the principle of utility 'preside[s]over and govern[s]' natural arrangement,[157] and his UEJ is the fruit of 'a method planned under the auspices of the principle of utility'.[158] Bentham's natural arrangement is morally utilitarian, and even the expositor–censor distinction seems to collapse, or at least to lose much of its significance.

A Branch of Eudaemonics

Mankind is 'under the governance of two sovereign masters, pain and pleasure', which are the source of every thought and the cause of every action. Recognizing this subjection, Bentham's principle of utility approves or disapproves of 'every action whatsoever', depending on a judgment of future fact, namely whether it will tend to promote or to diminish the happiness of the affected parties.[159] The principle of utility is 'the sole and all-sufficient reason for every point of practice whatsoever'[160]; 'used to

155 Ibid.

156 John Gardner, *Law as a Leap of Faith: Essays on Law in General* (Oxford University Press, 2012), 23.

157 'Fragment', in *Comment/Fragment* (*CW*), 416.

158 *Limits* (*CW*), 219n; see also *IPML* (*CW*), 272.

159 See *IPML* (*CW*), 11–12.

160 'Fragment', in *Comment/Fragment* (*CW*), 448.

prove everything else, it cannot itself be proved'. To prove it is impossible and needless: it is the all-comprehensive principle, and there is no fulcrum outside it.[161] It is, as Bentham claims, the foundation of all of his works. The science which recognizes our subjection to pain and pleasure, and therefore follows the principle of utility, is named by Bentham as Eudaemonics, which is 'the pursuit of happiness' or 'the art of well-being'.[162] Beyond Eudaemonics, there is nothing worth knowing. Knowledge has no value at all unless it leads to a balance on the side of pleasure.[163] The central teaching of Eudaemonics is that well-being in different shapes, 'directly or indirectly', is, 'constantly and unpreventably', 'the subject of every thought, and object of every action' of every 'sensitive and thinking Being'.[164] Operations of the mind and body are the results of the exercise of the volitional faculty in the field of desire, and the objects of the desire can only be pleasure or pain.[165] 'Nor can any intelligible reason be given for desiring that it should be otherwise.'[166] A thing can claim man's regard, only because it is in different ways 'a source of happiness' or 'a security against unhappiness'.[167] Eudaemonics is 'the Common Hall or central place of meeting, of all the arts and sciences. . . . Every art, with its correspondent science, is a branch of Eudaemonics'.[168] Bentham's UEJ is just one chamber in his magnificent edifice of Eudaemonics.

The Purposes of Natural Arrangement

Bentham's UEJ is a division of Eudaemonics. Its ultimate purpose is the pursuit of happiness. Confined to legal theory, it should be borne in mind that UEJ is only a means which Bentham deems necessary to the end of accomplishing his project to 'rear the fabric of felicity by the hands of reason and of law'.[169] Bentham believes that legislation is the most important of all earthly pursuits, and that he has a genius for it. Legislation is the branch of jurisprudence which 'teaches how a multitude of men, composing a community, may be disposed to pursue that course which upon the whole is the most conducive to the happiness of the

161 See *IPML* (*CW*), 13–15.
162 *Chrestomathia* (*CW*), 181.
163 See UC ci. 153 (Bowring, viii. 233).
164 *Chrestomathia* (*CW*), 179.
165 See UC ci. 409–10 (Bowring, viii. 279).
166 *Chrestomathia* (*CW*), 179.
167 Ibid. 180.
168 Ibid.
169 *IPML* (*CW*), 11.

whole community, by means of motives to be applied by the legislator'.[170] It includes ascertaining the principles of right and wrong, applying them to laws and modes of conduct, determining upon them the best laws, and then reforming existing laws accordingly.[171] Bentham levelled many criticisms against Blackstone, amongst many capital blemishes of whose work the 'grand and fundamental one' is 'the antipathy to reformation'.[172] Bentham took legislative reform as the 'great and only legitimate end of all political speculations',[173] and the completion of it as the business of his whole life.[174] His UEJ surveys objects from the perspective of the legislator. He would endorse Helvétius's judgment that 'morality is evidently no more than a frivolous science, unless blended with policy and legislation'.[175] In order to complete his life's work of legislation, Bentham needs a 'good nomenclature'[176] and language, the improvement of which is pre-requisite to attaining fully 'the great end of good government'[177]: Blackstone's ambiguous, obscure and degenerate nomenclature of itself promises 'a general vein of obscure and crooked reasoning, from whence no clear and sterling knowledge could be derived'.[178] This abject state of understanding necessarily corrupts the affections of the heart. Bentham's discussion of the characters of the expositor and the censor follows immediately his statement that he wages war against Blackstone's book 'for the interests of true science, and of liberal improvement'.[179] As Ross Harrison rightly points out: 'The explicit interest in close and precise analysis and in the exact signification of language marks off Bentham both as a philosopher of a notably modern temper and also as a *philosophe*, who believed that clarification, illumination, revelation of the truth, would help to bring about a better world.'[180]

Apart from furnishing a good nomenclature, UEJ has another cardinal purpose. A preliminary task for Bentham's project of legal reform is to

170 *Limits* (*CW*), 15.

171 See *The Correspondence of Jeremy Bentham*, vol. 1, ed. T.L.S. Sprigge (London: Athlone, 1968 (*CW*)), 367.

172 'Fragment', in *Comment/Fragment* (*CW*), 394.

173 UC cxl. 2.

174 See *The Correspondence of Jeremy Bentham*, vol. 2, ed. T.L.S. Sprigge (London: Athlone 1968 (*CW*)), 100.

175 Helvétius, *De l'esprit: or, Essays on the Mind, and Its Several Faculties* (London, 1759), 81.

176 'General View of a Complete Code of Laws', Bowring, iii. 169.

177 'Nomography; or The Art of Inditing Laws', Bowring, iii. 231–83, at 271.

178 'Fragment', in *Comment/Fragment* (*CW*), 394.

179 Ibid., 397.

180 Harrison, *Bentham*, 13.

clear the field of jurisprudence of irrational and oppressive rubbish, especially the fraudulent nonsenses composed of common law and natural law. In order to instruct, Bentham has to 'undeceive' first.[181] One of his primary aims is the emancipation of the judicial faculties of the public from the shackles of corrupt and imposturous charlataneries. Before embarking on his project, he needs to 'pluck the mask of mystery from the face of jurisprudence',[182] and open people's eyes to the truth of laws, thereby cleansing their minds of all deceptive superstitions and breaking the sedative spell of the prevailing misconceptions. UEJ meets this expectation by exploring and telling important truths of legal practice, which can 'throw the light of day upon the dark den of Cacus'.[183] This is exactly the way that Bentham has prepared before the expositor.[184]

Abstracting Interesting Properties

Bentham's natural arrangement is one kind of abstraction and arrangement of interesting properties of real legal materials. What is important is not that Bentham is abstracting and describing facts or factual properties, but rather the particular facts and properties he is abstracting, and how he describes them. Legal materials have numerous aspects, and can be given many different but equally true descriptions. For a blank mind, legal phenomena by themselves are total chaos. Observing and describing cannot start without a prior perspective, which cannot be separate from the observer's purpose. Purpose contains the germ of everything. Only with some purpose and perspective can one decide what aspects of what materials are relevant, important or characteristic when abstracting and describing. Revealing the truths of some aspects entails neglecting the remainder. This should not be regretted because, of the particular subject under description, only some aspects or dimensions are interesting and deserve our attention; as quoted earlier: 'the mind by its apprehensive faculty lays hold of some one alone or some other part of the whole number, leaving the rest unnoticed and unheeded'.[185] Bentham's UEJ is description of some kind. However, its purposes of producing a good nomenclature for utilitarian legislation and undeceiving the public's legal understanding

181 'Fragment', in *Comment/Fragment* (*CW*), 500.

182 Ibid., 410.

183 'On Public Account Keeping', in *Official Aptitude Maximized; Expense Minimized*, ed. P. Schofield (Oxford: Clarendon Press, 1993 (*CW*)), 293–301, at 298.

184 See 'Fragment', in *Comment/Fragment* (*CW*), 501.

185 UC ci. 124 (Bowring, viii. 225).

require it to describe the interesting properties of real legal materials. For Bentham, the only universal, satisfactory, and clear method of description is to point out with natural language – directly or indirectly – the most striking, interesting, and characteristic properties – that is, the utility or disutility – of real legal materials, which will serve to engage and fix the subjects' attention naturally and firmly. Only the properties which have a direct or indirect influence on human beings' pleasure or pain are entitled to our attention. A thing or property that has nothing to do with pleasure or pain is simply irrelevant to a human being, for whom nothing matters but pleasure and pain.

The Collapse of the Expositor–Censor Distinction

To point out the utility or disutility of real legal materials is at the same time to engage with reasons. It is just here that the expositor–censor distinction obviously and decidedly falls apart, and that Bentham starts to give up or forget his earlier seemingly crystal-clear distinction. As has been argued, Bentham bases his expositor–censor distinction upon the distinction between facts and reasons: the expositor states and enquires after facts, and the censor discusses reasons. However, now Bentham argues that the only natural way to arrange legal materials is to abstract and describe their interesting properties, their utility and disutility, which are 'reasons' for their being arranged this or that way,[186] and 'why they ought to be so'. 'By this means, while it [natural arrangement] addresses itself to the understanding, it recommends itself in some measure to the affections.'[187] This seems unavoidable, because among all experienced or imaginable qualities, 'goodness and badness' are 'the very first' that come to people's notice, and that obtain names from the faculty of discourse.[188] This is not to deny that the expositor states and enquires after facts, but it does remind us that the relation between facts and reasons is more complex and sophisticated: reasons should also be facts. At the level of universal expository jurisprudence as opposed to local expository jurisprudence, reasons are present in the form of true beliefs about universal facts, and beliefs about universal facts are laden both with reasons and with values. Following this thread, a universal expositor metamorphoses into a censor, as is illustrated very clearly in Bentham's discussion of the arrangement of offences:

186 See 'Fragment', in *Comment/Fragment* (*CW*), 416.
187 *IPML* (*CW*), 273.
188 UC cii. 42 (*De l'ontologie*, 98; Bowring, viii. 203).

> These offences would be collected into classes denominated by the various modes of their divergency from the common end; . . . by their various forms and degrees of mischievousness: in a word, by those properties which are reasons for their being made offences: and whether any such mode of conduct possesses any such property is a question of experience. Now, a bad Law is that which prohibits a mode of conduct that is not mischievous. . . . Thus cultivated, in short, the soil of Jurisprudence would be found to repel in a manner every evil institution.[189]

By means of natural arrangement,

> The mischievousness of a bad law would be detected, at least the utility of it would be rendered suspicious, by the difficulty of finding a place for it in such an arrangement: while, on the other hand, a technical arrangement is a sink that with equal facility will swallow any garbage that is thrown into it.[190]

Bentham seems to have realized this difficulty or tension in his theory. After his account suggesting the metamorphosis of his universal expositor into a universal censor, he quickly adds that the distinction still exists, but that UEJ would also be a compendium of censorial jurisprudence, and thus serve to instruct the subjects, and to help, correct or check the legislator[191]: it is to legislation what anatomy is to medicine.[192] The question for Bentham is: how can he deny that this kind of expositor is at the same time also a censor? Put differently, how can his expositor–censor distinction still be an important and valid distinction? Even if it is still possible to insist on the logical possibility of this distinction, the work left for his censor seems very trivial and insignificant once natural arrangement has been properly conducted.

Failure to appreciate this inevitable collapse of the expositor–censor distinction leads to many misunderstandings or misplaced criticisms of Bentham. Hart drives a huge wedge between, and indeed completely severs, the work of the expositor and of the censor. He thinks that, as an expositor concerned with analysing law's structure, Bentham 'would, or at any rate could' endorse Hart's own analysis based on established usage, but as a utilitarian censor, Bentham

> could argue that the purpose of the analysis . . . was to provide a set of clear terms to be used in describing a legal system in a way which would focus

[189] 'Fragment', in *Comment/Fragment* (*CW*), 416–17.
[190] Ibid., 416.
[191] See ibid., 417; and also *IPML* (*CW*), 273–4.
[192] *IPML* (*CW*), 9.

> attention on aspects of prime importance to the critic, and among these aspects of the law to which it was important to the critic to attend are those points at which the legal system itself creates human suffering or makes it likely.[193]

As argued earlier, this interpretation, by identifying Bentham's expositor with Hart's morally neutral describer, who 'has no justificatory aims . . . does not seek to justify or commend on moral or other grounds the forms and structures' that he is describing,[194] is straightforwardly mistaken as an interpretation of Bentham's UEJ: the work that Hart attributes to the utilitarian censor actually belongs to the expositor as a natural arranger.

Postema recognizes the inseparability of the roles of expositor and censor: 'while Bentham insists on a sharp distinction between . . . the functions of expositor and censor at the level of particular laws, his distinction is much less sharp at other levels, especially at the level of general reflection on the nature and proper forms of laws'.[195] However, the reason, Postema explains, is that the need for this sharp distinction arises from 'consideration of the proper functions of law and a conception of society which it was to serve'.[196] He asserts that Bentham 'overstates his own views' when he gives the first brief but comprehensive account of this distinction in 'Fragment', because 'later . . . while discussing the task of exposition, he makes it clear that recommendation, reasons for laws, and the principle of utility, are involved both directly and indirectly'.[197] In consequence, 'the functions of Expositor and Censor are not as clear cut as he suggests in the earlier passage'.[198] But Postema still accepts that this distinction is fundamental to Bentham's approach to jurisprudence, and his view is only that the standard interpretation of this distinction is 'much too wide'.[199] He then criticizes Bentham for confusion over the distinction:

> I do not think Bentham always kept clearly before his mind the difference between developing an account of the nature of law (inevitably drawing upon normative or evaluative considerations) – an account of law *as it is* – on the one hand, and arguing for a set of concepts it would be useful to

193 Hart, *Essays on Bentham*, 137.
194 Hart, *Concept of Law*, 240.
195 Postema, *Bentham and the Common Law*, 308
196 Ibid.
197 Postema, 'The Expositor, the Censor, and the Common Law', 662.
198 Ibid., 663; see also *Bentham and the Common Law*, 308.
199 Postema, 'The Expositor, the Censor, and the Common Law', 661.

> adopt in order to make law more useful to us, on the other. . . . His account of the nature of law would probably have been different, and to my mind more plausible, if he had paid more attention to the distinction.[200]

In response to Postema's criticism, it should be stressed that for Bentham, developing a general account of law as it is, and arguing for a set of useful concepts are processes or tasks of natural arrangement. A really meaningful account of the nature of law as it is abstracts and describes the interesting properties of really existing laws. Postema is right that this kind of account inevitably draws on evaluative considerations. However, the concepts arising from this account, for Bentham, are necessarily or naturally useful. The distinction between two projects that Postema has in mind does not exist for Bentham. So Bentham's account of the nature of law could not have been different, given his empiricist materialism and utilitarianism.

Natural Arrangement and Truths[201]

Some of Hart's followers now like to say that what Hart means by MND is that his jurisprudence seeks to produce truths: Joseph Raz says that it is after necessary and appropriate truths[202]; John Gardner says that it is after something 'both interesting and true to say about law in general, law as such, law wherever it may be found'.[203] Although they do not have a theory of truth, truths for them seem to mean propositions conforming to reality. Would Bentham view his theory this way?

As a general rule, Bentham would agree that legal theory is looking for interesting truths. In Bentham's view, for a proposition to be true is for it to agree with reality, which in the legal field means to agree with the 'facts' of 'the existence of human feelings, pains, or pleasures, as the effects of this or that disposition of law, or of this or that state of human affairs calling for a correspondent disposition and exercise of the power of the law', which are 'the only true and useful foundations' of legal science.[204] The truth of a proposition is destroyed to the extent that it disagrees with

[200] Postema, *Bentham and the Common Law*, 331.

[201] My account here draws on Quinn 'Which Comes First, Bentham's Chicken of Utility or his Egg of Truth?'

[202] J. Raz, 'Can There Be a Theory of Law', in *Blackwell Guide to the Philosophy of Law and Legal Theory*, eds. M.P. Golding and W.A. Edmundson (Oxford: Wiley-Blackwell, 2005), 324–42, at 324.

[203] Gardner, *Law as a Leap of Faith*, 301.

[204] 'Rationale of Judicial Evidence', Bowring, vii. 81 (Bk. V, Ch. 16).

reality.[205] Bentham believes in the objectivity of the reality: 'at this present time, whatsoever does exist has existence; whatsoever does not exist has not existence: and so at any and every future point of time'.[206] However, the only meaningful reality, or the only reality that matters, is the reality that can be accessed by man's senses: 'experience is the foundation of all our knowledge'.[207] According to human experience, truths in most cases promote utility: it is 'the general conformity of testimony to the real state of things – of the real state of things to testimony: of the facts reported upon to the reports made concerning them' that renders it a man's interest to believe the testimony.[208] It should be noted that 'conformity' is 'but a word expressive of the state our minds are put into by the contemplation of those facts'[209]; it expresses a persuasion supported by evidence. Truths operate by evidence: 'when all the evidences are equally present to his observation, and equally attended to, to believe or disbelieve is no longer in his power. It is the necessary result of the preponderance of the evidence on one side over that on the other'.[210] Bentham believes that his principle of utility is a truth, and that his Natural Arrangement is after useful truths.[211]

First, the supreme guiding principle of utility cannot and need not be proved. However, Bentham doubtless thinks that it is true and instructive. Its truth can be shown or expounded by means of paraphrasis in terms of such real entities as pleasure and pain.[212] As Bentham famously writes, the principle of utility is the principle 'which approves or disapproves of every action whatsoever, according to the tendency which it appears to have to augment or diminish the happiness of the party whose interest is in question'.[213] This can be seen more clearly if it is contrasted with the principle of sympathy and antipathy. Both the principle of utility and the principle of sympathy and antipathy are kinds of sentiment – that is, acts of mind. However, they are different: the principle of utility is 'founded', whereas the principle of sympathy and antipathy is 'unfounded',[214] in that, the former 'recognizes' mankind's universal and factual subjection

205 See *Chrestomathia* (*CW*), 347–8.
206 UC cii. 75 (*De l'ontologie*, 152; Bowring, viii. 211).
207 'Rationale of Judicial Evidence', Bowring, vi. 241 (Bk. I, Ch. 7).
208 Ibid., 236.
209 Ibid., Bowring, vii. 83 (Bk. V, Ch. 16).
210 'Memoir and Correspondence', Bowring, x. 146.
211 See 'Comment', in *Comment/Fragment* (*CW*), 51.
212 See Schofield, *Democracy and Utility*, 9.
213 *IPML* (*CW*), 12.
214 Ibid., 15.

to the sovereignty of pleasure and pain, and assumes this subjection as its 'foundation',[215] but the latter does not. The principle of sympathy and antipathy establishes as the standard the relevant persons' 'internal sentiments of approbation and disapprobation', and disclaims 'the necessity of looking out for any extrinsic ground',[216] or for 'something that points out some external consideration',[217] which for Bentham is 'the probable balance in the account of utility, whether of pleasure or of pain'.[218] These considerations are extrinsic and external, not because they are outside human experience, but because they do not exclusively belong to particular individuals' internal sentiments: they are shared or inter-subjective sentiments supported by evidence which particular individuals have no power to disbelieve. So the disputes between parties following the principle of sympathy and antipathy are 'childish altercation' and 'womanish scolding', whereas the principle of utility rests all disputes on the footing of 'matter of fact: that is, future fact – the probability of certain future contingencies', which help them to reach agreement, or at least to engage genuinely with 'the real grounds of dispute'.[219]

Second, whilst the interesting properties that natural arrangement looks for are interesting according to the principle of utility, they are not invented arbitrarily by human whim, like the fictions of natural lawyers. Natural lawyers may unconsciously rely on the human desire for pleasure and avoidance of pain in establishing their sets of rights, but when they do they are mistaking generic wants for existing means, hunger for bread, and reasons for rights for rights.[220] Instead, the interesting properties identified by natural arrangement are the experienced real properties of real materials. Bentham's principle of utility governs his natural arrangement by requiring the latter to point out – in copious, clear and simple language – the interesting properties of real legal materials, which exist as factual properties. Only in this way can natural arrangement serve the utilitarian project. So far as the relation between UEJ and morals is concerned, here might lie the important difference between Bentham and common law and natural lawyers.

215 Ibid., 11.
216 Ibid., 25.
217 Ibid.
218 'Rationale of Judicial Evidence', Bowring, vi. 209 (Bk. I, Ch. 1).
219 'Fragment', in *Comment/Fragment* (*CW*), 491.
220 Bentham, 'Nonsense upon Stilts', in *Rights, Representation, and Reform: Nonsense upon Stilts and Other Writings on the French Revolution*, eds. P. Schofield, C.P. Watkin, and C. Blamires (Oxford: Clarendon Press, 2002 (*CW*)), 317–401, at 330.

Postema correctly argues that Bentham's rejection of common law 'rest[s], at crucial points, on practical or normative considerations which can be traced to his fundamental Utilitarian political views'.[221] He is entirely right to say that Bentham's concern

> was not to develop a politically noncommittal and "purely sociological theory of law". . . . Bentham was concerned to construct the conceptual and technical machinery . . . needed for the construction of a complete body of law according to rational principles. . . . the formal theoretical work . . . is integral to that project.[222]

However, he goes too far when he says that utilitarian considerations determine Bentham's definition of 'a law'.[223] I do not mean that his claim is wrong, but the key is how to understand the import of the word 'determine'. Bentham's utilitarian considerations do not determine his definition of a law in the same way that for natural lawyers wants determine means, huger determines bread, and reasons determine rights. Unfortunately, Postema seems to suggest that this is what he means by the word 'determine'. According to Bentham's definition, a law is an authoritative general rule. Postema claims that this definition is based on Bentham's idea of a good constitutional structure.[224] He even contends that Bentham treats common law as a fiction or fabulous entity, and as non-law, 'only' because he thinks that common law is inefficient, open to great abuse, and obstructive to rational utilitarian reform, so that a legal system would be better off if it eliminated such law.[225] This interpretation in fact makes Bentham no different from the natural lawyers against whom he waged a life-long war, and cannot be reconciled with Bentham's constant emphasis on the status of even bad laws as law.

Postema's problem is that he does not pay due attention to the way in which natural arrangement serves the utilitarian project by means of abstracting and describing interesting truths. Utilitarian considerations do indeed determine Bentham's definition of 'a law', but the former determines the latter indirectly via natural arrangement. Bentham treats common law as a fiction, a fabulous entity, and non-law, not just because treating it this way is useful, but primarily because it is, according to Bentham's definition of a law, a fiction, a fabulous entity, and non-law, which

221 Postema, 'The Expositor, the Censor, and the Common Law', 647.

222 Ibid., 667.

223 Ibid., 666.

224 Ibid., 654.

225 See ibid., 659–61, 667–70.

is to say that it does not exist in the form of authoritative general rules. Once it does exist in this form, it ceases to be common law, and becomes judicial legislation: a bad form of law, but a form of law nonetheless.

As a general rule, natural arrangement promotes utility by abstracting and describing truths. However, being true and being useful, by definition, are still different. Even if truths were always potentially useful, telling truths might in some situations cause harm. Bentham's hope is that thanks to such contingent factors as the improvement of political discernment and the universal spread of learning, which have raised human beings to a relatively equal level with each other, the situation may approach his optimistic scenario:

> The indestructible prerogatives of mankind have no need to be supported upon the sandy foundation of a fiction. . . . But the season of *Fiction* is now over. . . . To attempt to introduce any *new* one, would be *now* a crime: for which reason there is much danger, without any use, in vaunting and propagating [fictions] . . . nor is any man now so far elevated above his fellows, as that he should be indulged in the dangerous licence of cheating them for their good.[226]

However, there are indeed some situations where dissimulation might be useful, and where declaring truths might be useless, impertinent or destructive. Bentham cares about truths only when they are interesting and thereby useful (although it is not always easy to tell the usefulness of a truth). For Bentham, being interesting does not only mean, as for some contemporary legal positivists,[227] being 'intellectually exciting' without any practical use. Truths are worth pursuing not for their own sake, but for the pay-off they can offer. What Bentham's natural arrangement seeks is useful or instructive truths. Nowadays, the situations where untruths are useful are very rare, but when faced with situations in which, after felicific

226 'Fragment', in *Comment/Fragment* (*CW*), 439–41.

227 Scott Shapiro, in an interview, says that 'Most legal philosophers (especially those of the positivistic persuasion) regard analytical jurisprudence as having little or no relevance for the practicing lawyer. This does not mean, of course, that they think it should not be pursued. Legal philosophers regard analytical jurisprudence as worth pursuing because it is intellectually exciting. It is good for its own sake.' Shapiro himself agrees with 'most legal philosophers', and he goes on to say 'I do not mean to suggest that the value of analytical jurisprudence is exhausted by its practical relevance. Nothing could be farther from the truth. I am a big fan of philosophy for philosophy's sake. Legal theory should be studied because it is interesting. It needs no other justification than that'. S. Shapiro, 'Planning Theory and the Nature of Law', *Legal Theory in China*, 1 (2011), 18. This electronic journal can be accessed at www.legal-theory.com.

calculation (which can be very difficult), lying would be useful, Bentham would not hesitate to lie. 'Remember, "no act can with propriety . . . be termed virtuous except in so far as in its tendency it is conducive to the sum of happiness". To rule out duplicity always and everywhere simply is to reject the calculation of the probable consequences of an action'.[228] As to Raz's and Gardner's 'necessary' claim, Bentham's rejoinder would be this: because of 'the inexorable nature of things', certainty, necessity, and impossibility are 'for ever out of our reach'.[229] They are only 'expressions of the degree of the persuasion', and the use of these words virtually involves 'the assumption of omniscience. – All things that are possible are within my knowledge'.[230] According to Bentham, all truths are inductive: they are provisional and fallible, asserting the best approximation at the current empirical and cognitive stage to 'things as they are'; they are always corrigible by further experience.

Part Three: Neutral Vocabulary versus Morally Neutral Vocabulary

Bentham's UEJ is not morally inert or indifferent, and thereby not morally neutral in that sense. It is guided by, and also serves, Bentham's utilitarian project indirectly, via natural arrangement which aims at abstracting and describing interesting properties of real legal material – useful truths – but also leaves room for useful lies. However, it does not necessarily follow from this that Hart is wrong when he interprets Bentham's UEJ as some kind of his MND, because the common understanding of 'morally neutral' seems at odds with Hart's real purport when he claims that his account is 'descriptive in that it is morally neutral'. Hart never thinks that his 'morally neutral' means 'purposeless' or 'useless'. He indicates that the 'purpose' of his own 'morally neutral' theory is 'to advance legal theory by providing an improved analysis of the distinctive structure of a municipal legal system and a better understanding of the resemblances and differences between law, coercion, and morality'.[231] He stresses that his choice of the positive conception of law is a lesson from the history of morals: this conception does not hide moral quandaries or 'cloak the true nature of the problems'; it warns us that the values we cherish

[228] Quinn, 'Bentham's Chicken of Utility or his Egg of Truth?'.
[229] 'Rationale of Judicial Evidence', Bowring, vii. 105 (Bk. V, Ch. 16).
[230] UC cii. 76 (*De l'ontologie*, 154; Bowring, viii. 211).
[231] Hart, *Concept of Law*, 17.

do not always 'fit into a single system', and some must be sacrificed or compromised to accommodate others; it is more sincere about moral dilemmas, and arms us with the 'simplest' and therefore 'most powerful' forms of moral criticism: a law may be law but too evil to be obeyed.[232]

In Hart's view, his theory is 'an important preliminary to any useful moral criticism of law'[233]; Bentham's 'protest', contained in his legal theory, 'against the confusion of what is and what ought to be, has a moral as well as an intellectual value.'[234] Hart emphatically stresses that his 'morally neutral' method is not the same thing as a 'morally neutral' method in the scientific or empirical sense, which he thinks useless for the understanding of law as a form of normative social structure,[235] and which he argues is not what Bentham means by science.[236] Quite the contrary, he seeks to give 'an explanatory and clarifying account of law' which focuses on law's rule-governed aspect.[237] When reviewing influential theses concerning the nature of law, Hart comments that they

> actually did in their time and place increase our understanding of it. . . . they are more like great exaggerations of some truths about law unduly neglected. . . . They throw a light which make us see much in law that lay hidden; but the light is so bright that it blinds us to the remainder and so leaves us still without a clear view of the whole.[238]

This remark applies to Hart's theory as well. Strictly speaking, 'a clear view of the whole' is unachievable, and also unnecessary. Like Bentham, Hart chooses what he wants to describe for his own purposes, and his choice cannot avoid being related to morality. This Hart concedes readily and frankly. He chooses to describe the normative aspect of law, which he supposes is important. For Hart, this normative aspect raises three major questions: 'How does law differ from and how is it related to orders backed by threats? How does legal obligation differ from, and how is it related to, moral obligation? What are rules, and to what extent is law an affair of rules?'[239] Hart invents conceptual tools to 'pick out [the] action-guiding

[232] See Hart, *Essays in Jurisprudence and Philosophy*, 72–8; and see also *Concept of Law*, Ch. 9.
[233] Hart, *Concept of Law*, 240.
[234] Hart, *Essays in Jurisprudence and Philosophy*, 78.
[235] See ibid., 13.
[236] See Hart, 'Bentham's Principle of Utility and Theory of Penal Law', lxxxiii.
[237] Hart, *Concept of Law*, 239.
[238] Ibid., 2.
[239] Ibid., 13.

and evaluation-guiding function' of social rules.[240] This means that Hart's description 'must itself be guided, in focusing on those features rather than others, by some criteria of importance'.[241] The analysis, therefore, 'will be guided by judgments, often controversial, of what is important and will therefore reflect such meta-theoretic values and not be neutral between all values'.[242] The chief meta-theoretic value is 'the explanatory power of what his analysis picked out'. The values lying behind 'judgments of what is important', which Hart does not make clear, surely cannot be purely meta-theoretic and epistemic. They are substantive practical values reflecting our moral and intellectual concerns.[243] However, Hart's purpose, choice, and description are very different from Bentham's. These differences arise from their different ontologies and philosophies of language. Hart accepts moral claims as essential, and moral beliefs and justificatory practices as important, although contingent, constituents of the existence of rules.[244] His legal theory, as an explanation of the internal conceptual framework of participants in legal order, has to make sense of moral factors or moral considerations involved in participants' legal practice. When describing the conversion of the regime of primary rules into a developed legal system, Hart says that, as a form of social control, the regime of primary rules which fared successfully in a small community 'must prove defective' in other conditions. It is defective in that, judged against its primary function of 'guiding the conduct of its subjects',[245] it is uncertain, static, and inefficient as 'a means of social control'[246] in a world other than that where it came into being. This analysis involves evaluation. In a word, Hart's 'morally neutral' cannot be equated with 'being morally inert, indifferent, or irrelevant' as commonly understood.

Compared with Bentham's crystal-clear declaration of the utility of his description, Hart's prevarication on the relationship between his theory and value indicates that he is hedging about his moral concerns or stance. Despite the fact that his own legal theory has moral concerns, treats, of moral factors and makes evaluations, and despite his awareness that

[240] Hart, 'Legal Theory and the Problem of Sense: Comment', in *Issues in Contemporary Legal Philosophy: The Influence of H.L.A. Hart*, ed. R. Gavison (Oxford: Clarendon Press, 1989), 35–42, at 38.

[241] Ibid., 39.

[242] Ibid.

[243] See G. Postema, 'Jurisprudence as Practical Philosophy', *Legal Theory*, 3 (1998), 329–57, at 334.

[244] See Hart, 'Legal Theory and the Problem of Sense: Comment', 39.

[245] Hart, *Concept of Law*, 249.

[246] Ibid. 40.

Bentham does not think his UEJ could be separated from his utilitarian social philosophy, Hart still insists repeatedly that his own theory is 'morally neutral description', and that Bentham was attempting something similar. If Hart is taken at his word, and is not simply contradicting himself, he must have meant something very different by 'morally neutral description'. In fact, Hart does offer an alternative way of understanding 'morally neutral description' which offers a resolution of the apparent contradiction. Occasionally, Hart regards 'morally neutral' as a requirement about 'vocabulary'. He even encourages this reading. As we have seen, one requirement of Bentham's natural language is that it should aspire to be as neutral as possible. Bentham emphasizes this as 'the only novelty' of his methodology of naming.[247] Hart picks out this idea as a 'very distinctive part of Bentham's general theory of law', and stresses that it is 'really part of something much wider' and manifests 'a very fundamental and original feature in Bentham's whole austere approach to the philosophy of law and politics'.[248] Understood in this sense, being 'morally neutral' is indeed one property of Bentham's UEJ.

However, this interpretation raises another more basic question: why does Bentham, who is very cautious about words and language, never use the phrase 'morally neutral'? A possible explanation is that, as has been argued, Bentham is fully aware that his UEJ is utilitarian. His requirement for a neutral vocabulary aims to ensure that the exposition is conducted with impartiality, and that the name expresses the idea in question only, and nothing more, and avoids bringing in any unwarranted prejudices, thereby avoiding any question-begging fallacy. Prejudiced emotions are emotions prompted by unevidenced assumptions. Such emotions, derived from such assumptions, are imposturous and question-begging. For Bentham, the effort to denominate without entailing unwarranted emotions, and to use neutral vocabulary is, strictly speaking, a requirement of his logic, which is always morality-(or value-)laden, and not morally neutral. Hart mistakes Bentham's neutral vocabulary for morally neutral description. One possible explanation might be linked with Hart's own meta-ethical theory. Although longing for some independent rational foundation for ethical thought, Hart is highly sceptical of objective moral standards or facts. He requires legal theory to 'avoid commitment to controversial philosophical theories of the general status of moral judgments', and to leave open the general question of whether they have

[247] *IPML* (*CW*), 102.
[248] Hart, *Essays on Bentham*, 27.

objective standing.[249] Hart seems to subscribe to some kind of non-cognitivism[250] concerning the nature of moral judgment. For him, moral judgment is a matter of attitude, feeling, and emotion, and so Bentham's naming without entailing unwarranted emotions is, understandably but mistakenly, equated by him with morally neutral description.

[249] Hart, *Concept of Law*, 253.

[250] See T. Campbell, 'The Point of Legal Positivism', *King's College Law Journal*, (9) 1998, 63–88, at 70–3.

8

Utility, Morality, and Reform

Bentham and Eighteenth-Century Continental Jurisprudence

EMMANUELLE DE CHAMPS[1]

The 1780s were a seminal decade in Bentham's legal and political thought. In 1780, he had the first copy of *An Introduction to the Principles of Morals and Legislation* printed for private circulation.[2] During the next couple of years, he drafted *Of the Limits of the Penal Branch of Jurisprudence.*[3] The originality of these works in English-language jurisprudence has been widely recognized, and their relation to contemporary British legal thought has been assessed.[4] But the context for debates on law reform in that decade was not a strictly British one. Indeed, one of the reasons why Bentham chose to have *IPML* privately printed in 1780 was that he was looking for a German translator. At that stage, he still thought of it as an introduction to a penal code.[5] But within three or four years he embarked on a broader plan, a *Projet d'un corps de loix complet* (*Project for a complete body of laws*), to be written in French. Although this work was finally abandoned and remained unpublished as such, it casts light on the philosopher's continental ambitions and on his solid knowledge of European legal matters. Indeed, as this chapter argues, many of his positions regarding legal and political reform can be better understood when placed

1 I thank Michael Quinn and Ann Thomson for their comments on this chapter.

2 See *An Introduction to the Principles of Morals and Legislation* (henceforth *IPML* (*CW*)), eds. J.H. Burns and H.L.A. Hart (London: Athlone, 1970 (*CW*)), 1.

3 J. Bentham, *Of the Limits of the Penal Branch of Jurisprudence* (henceforth *Limits* (*CW*)), ed. P. Schofield (Oxford: Clarendon Press, 2010 (*CW*)).

4 See G.J. Postema, *Bentham and the Common Law Tradition* (Oxford: Clarendon Press, 1986); D. Lieberman, *The Province of Legislation Determined: Legal Theory in Eighteenth-Century Britain* (Cambridge University Press, 1989); M. Lobban, *The Common Law and English Jurisprudence, 1760–1850* (Oxford: Clarendon Press, 1991).

5 See E. de Champs, 'An Introduction to Utilitarianism: Early French Translations of Bentham's Introduction to the Principles of Morals and Legislation', in *Cultural Transfers: France and Britain in the Long Eighteenth-century*, eds. A. Thomson, S. Burrows and S. Audidière (Oxford: Voltaire Foundation, 2011), 269–83.

against the backdrop of Continental debates in the late Enlightenment, in the years preceding the outbreak of the French Revolution.

Projet and Continental Legal Reform

Since the publication of Montesquieu's *The Spirit of the Laws* in 1748, calls for legal reform had been part and parcel of Enlightenment debates in Europe. Voltaire relentlessly attacked the barbarity of French criminal legislation, publicly defending the Protestant Calas and the Chevalier de La Barre in the 1760s. Together with D'Alembert, he also asked the abbé Morellet to translate a short treatise on *Crimes and Punishments* published by the Milanese Cesare Beccaria in 1764. *Des Délits et des Peines* was duly published in French in 1766, leading to passionate debates. The book went through seven editions within six months of its publication in French, and was soon translated into most European languages.[6] Bentham himself became aware of it during his years at Oxford, at the same time as Priestley's *Essay on the First Principles of Government.*[7] In many ways, Beccaria's book set the framework for all discussions of legal reform in the second half of the eighteenth century.

In an exchange of letters with Morellet, Cesare Beccaria stated his debt to the French *philosophes*, among whom he singled out Claude-Adrien Helvétius, author of *An Essay on the Mind* (*De l'esprit*). In that book, published to much scandal in Paris in 1758 among accusations of materialism, Helvétius sought to renew the science of man by resting it on strong psychological foundations.[8] Among his recommendations was that of applying the principle of utility to legal reform:

> [I]t is . . . on the uniformity of the legislator's views, and the dependence of these laws on each other, that their excellence consists. But in order to establish this dependence, it would be necessary to refer them all to one simple principle, such as that of the public utility; or to that of the greatest number of men, subject to the same form of government: a principle more extensive and more fruitful than imagination can conceive: a principle,

6 A.J. Draper, 'Cesare Beccaria's Influence on English Discussions of Punishment', *History of European Ideas*, 26 (2000), 177–99.

7 See the chronology established by R. Shackleton, 'The Greatest Happiness of the Greatest Number: The History of Bentham's Phrase', *Studies on Voltaire and the Eighteenth Century*, 90 (1972), 1461–82.

8 On Helvétius, see D. Smith, *Helvétius: A Study in Persecution* (Oxford: Clarendon Press, 1965); D. Wootton, 'Helvétius: From Radical Enlightenment to Revolution', *Political Theory*, 28 (2000), 307–36.

> that includes all the morality and all the legislations, of which many men discourse without understanding them, and of which the legislators themselves have yet but a very superficial idea, at least if we may judge from the unhappiness of almost all the nations on earth.[9]

In the posthumously published *Essay on Man* (*De l'homme*), Helvétius returned to the task awaiting legal reformers. On the one hand, their role was to establish 'laws proper to render men as happy as possible', while on the other, any violent upheaval of the existing social, political and legal order was bound to detract from the happiness of the greatest number. The legislator had to find 'the means by which a people may be made to pass insensibly from the state of misery they suffer, to the state of happiness they might enjoy'.[10] In *Of Crimes and Punishments*, Beccaria directly echoed Helvétius's words, and opened his essay on the dictum that the laws should 'conduce to the greatest happiness shared among the greatest number'.[11] He subsequently advocated a reform of criminal law along consequentialist and utilitarian lines:

> In order that punishment should not be an act of violence perpetrated by one or many upon a private citizen, it is essential that it should be public, speedy, necessary, and the minimum possible in the given circumstances, proportionate to the crime, and determined by the law.[12]

As is well known, Bentham closely followed on the path opened by Helvétius and Beccaria. In them he recognized the fathers of 'Censorial Jurisprudence' or 'the art of knowing what *ought* to be done in the way of internal Government'.[13] To them also can be traced the focus on criminal law evident in *IPML*. In 1778, he wrote to his friend John Forster:

> From [Helvétius] I got a standard to measure the relative importance of the several pursuits a man might be engaged in: and the result of it was that the way of all others in which a man might be of most service to his fellow creatures was by making improvement in the science which I had been engaged to study by profession.... That illustrious philosopher (whose principles however I am very far from adopting without distinction) at the

[9] C.-A. Helvétius, *De l'Esprit: Of Essays on the Mind, and Its Several Faculties* (London, 1759), 88.

[10] C.-A. Helvétius, *A Treatise on Man, His Intellectual Faculties and His Education*, 2 vols. (London: B. Law and G. Robinson, 1777), ii. 270.

[11] C. Beccaria, *On Crimes and Punishments and Other Writings*, ed. R. Bellamy (Cambridge University Press, 1995), 7.

[12] Beccaria, *On Crimes*, 113.

[13] 'Preparatory Principles Inserenda', UC lxix. 195, quoted in D.G. Long, 'Censorial Jurisprudence and Political Radicalism: A Reconstruction of the Early Bentham', *The Bentham Newsletter*, 12 (1988), 4–23, at 17.

> same time that he suggested incentives, furnished me with instruments, for making the attempt. From him I learnt to look upon the tendency of any institution or pursuit to promote the happiness of society as the sole test and measure of its merit: and to (rest all my ideas of right and wrong upon the single basis of utility) regard the principle of utility as an oracle which if properly consulted would afford the only true solution that could be given to every question of right and wrong. Much about the same time M. Beccaria's book of crimes and punishments, and the Empress of Russia's instructions for a Code of Laws, gave me fresh incentives and afforded me further lights.[14]

This extract is often quoted to illustrate the extent of Bentham's debt to Helvétius and Beccaria, and therefore to establish an intellectual and political genealogy of utilitarianism.[15] Seldom noted, however, are the strategic uses of these references in Bentham's early writings. In *IPML*, Bentham only mentioned Helvétius or Beccaria in indirect and roundabout ways: Helvétius was listed alongside La Rochefoucauld and Mandeville, all 'ingenious moralists' who had been attacked on the mistaken grounds of 'the unsoundness of their opinions' and 'the corruption of their hearts'.[16] Only one of Beccaria's maxims regarding punishment was quoted, and Bentham pointed out that the Milanese had limited himself to criminal law, without looking at the other branches of the law.[17]

Only in private correspondence did Bentham self-consciously present his own work in continuity with theirs. To Forster, a chaplain based in Russia, he cautiously pointed out that he was 'far from adopting [all of Helvétius's principles] without distinction', most probably an allusion to the Frenchman's supposed materialism, and stressed, by contrast, the relevance of Beccaria's work to his own. For although Helvétius remained a controversial figure, by the late 1770s Beccaria's fame on the Continent – including Russia – was well established. Indeed, in presenting himself as the direct heir to the Milanese, Bentham strongly increased his odds of making a name for himself in the Republic of Letters. The success of the

[14] *The Correspondence of Jeremy Bentham, Vol. 2, 1777–1780*, ed. T.L.S. Sprigge (London: Athlone, 1968 (*CW*)), 99.

[15] For Bentham and Helvétius, see Long, 'Censorial Jurisprudence', 7–12; D. Smith, 'Helvétius and the Problems of Utilitarianism', *Utilitas*, 5 (1993), 275–89; F. Rosen, 'Helvétius, the Scottish Enlightenment, and Bentham's Idea of Utility', *Classical Utilitarianism from Hume to Mill* (London: Routledge, 2003), 82–96; E. Pacaud, 'Sur l'une des sources de l'utilitarisme benthamien: la théorie de l'utilité de Claude-Adrien Helvétius', in *Deux siècles d'utilitarisme*, ed. M. Bozzo-Rey and E. Dardenne (Presses Universitaires de Rennes, 2011), 41–52.

[16] *IPML* (*CW*), 102n.

[17] Ibid., 166n, 298n.

book had been so prompt that just a year after the publication of the French translation, Beccaria had been invited to Russia to supervise work on a new code of laws. Catherine II, the empress, had also published an *Instruction* to the committee in charge of drafting a new code of laws in which she directly borrowed a number of key principles from him as well as from Montesquieu's *Spirit of the Laws*. This is precisely the document Bentham quoted in his letter to Forster.[18] Even if Beccaria's suggestions were far from being unanimously adopted by European writers on jurisprudence (his stance in favour of the abolition of the death penalty, for instance, was rarely followed), he directly contributed to set the agenda for any further discussion of criminal reform. For instance, in 1777 the Oeconomical Society of Bern (Switzerland) offered a prize for the best essay on the following topic under the sponsorship of Voltaire himself:

> The composition of a complete and finished plan of legislation, relative to criminal cases, under these three articles or points of view: 1st. A consideration of the nature of crimes, and of the proportion to be observed in the punishment of them. 2ndly, The nature and strengths of proofs and presumptions. 3rdly, the manner of obtaining evidence by a criminal process, so that clemency and mildness in the mode of trial and punishment may not be incompatible with the speedy and exemplary chastisement of the guilty, &c.[19]

Bentham briefly considered submitting his 'Introduction to a penal code', before abandoning the idea. In the same period, he envisaged advertizing his work to the most renowned of enlightened sovereigns on the European continent in the hope of receiving an invitation similar to that of Beccaria in Russia. He therefore drafted letters to Frederic II of Prussia, Leopold II Grand Duke of Tuscany, the King of Sardinia, the Secretary of State to the Kingdom of Naples, Gustavus III of Sweden, and, of course, Catherine II of Russia. None of these letters were, alas, sent.

About that time, in November 1782, Bentham met the Frenchman Jacques-Pierre Brissot in London. Brissot had been engaged in the publication of an anthology of recent legal writing, the *Bibliothèque du Législateur*, the object of which was to make available in French an extensive selection

18 Catherine II, *Instruction de Sa Majesté Impériale Catherine II, pour la Commission chargée de dresser le Projet d'un nouveau Code de Lois* (Petersburg: Imprimerie de l'Académie des Sciences, 1769). Prompted by D'Alembert, Beccaria turned down the Empress's offer.

19 This English translation appeared in *The Monthly Review, or Literary Journal*, 58 (Jan–June 1778), 546.

of recent works published in Europe on the reform of legislation.[20] Bentham's friendship with Brissot, whom he saw regularly over the two years the Frenchman spent in exile in the British capital, contributed to broaden the focus of his plans for legal reform beyond Britain.[21] Following his brother's departure and settlement in Russia, Bentham turned his eyes more specifically to Eastern Europe.[22]

But Bentham was also desirous to distinguish himself clearly from Beccaria, writing to Voltaire that his own system was 'neither borrow'd, nor pilfer'd'.[23] Some time in 1783 he changed his plans and took to writing directly in French in the hope of having a more substantial proposal for legal reform printed for the use of Catherine II, who could not read English. '*Projet d'un corps de loix détaillé et complet, à l'usage d'un état quelconque*' was to occupy him for a period of nearly five years, including his stay in Russia. This idea directly derived from the opportunities opened up by Beccaria's reputation in Eastern Europe. The number of references to Continental and Roman law in the manuscript shows that Bentham was versed in contemporary legal writing well beyond English sources. It is by turning to this text that the specificity of his position among contemporary legal reformers can be made clear.

The *Pannomion* and the Codification Movement

On the Continent, the tradition of Roman law and the prestige of Justinian's *Institutes* had long served to promote the ideal of a written body of law. But throughout the eighteenth century, in most French provinces and in Europe, legal practice combined references to statute law and to customs. From the 1750s, a general trend in favour of codification developed, as ruling monarchs tended to find fault with a complex body of local customs and strove to unite large countries under one common

[20] J.P. Brissot de Warville, *Bibliothèque du Législateur, du Politique, du Jurisconsulte, ou Choix des meilleurs discours, dissertations, essais, fragmens, composés sur la législation criminelle par les plus célèbres écrivains, en françois, anglois, italien, allemand, espagnol, &c. pour parvenir à la réforme des loix pénales dans tous les pays: traduits & accompagnés de notes & d'observations historiques* 10 vols., (Berlin, 1782–5), i. p. xxxvi. Unless otherwise stated, all the quotes from this collection are to Brissot's own commentaries.

[21] J.H. Burns, 'Bentham, Brissot et la science du bonheur', in E. de Champs and J.-P. Cléro (eds), *Bentham et la France: Fortune et Infortunes de l'utilitarisme* (Oxford: Voltaire Foundation, 2009), 3–19.

[22] On this episode, see I.R. Christie, *The Benthams in Russia, 1780–1791* (Oxford: Berg, 1993).

[23] *The Correspondence of Jeremy Bentham, Vol. 1, 1752–1776*, ed. T.L.S. Sprigge (London: Athlone, 1968 (*CW*)), 367.

authority.[24] Codification was also debated by philosophers, for it summed up a number of questions pertaining to the balance of powers in the state, the role of judges, and the rights of citizens. In *Spirit of the Laws*, Montesquieu highlighted both the need for digesting local custom into a written body of laws and the dangers that could arise from a general scheme of codification. Although a chaos of obscure laws favoured the despotic power of kings and judges, simplicity could also be a trap: 'the despot knows nothing and can attend to nothing; he must approach everything in a general way; he governs with a rigid will that is the same in all circumstances; all is flattened beneath his feet.'[25]

In the next decades, Voltaire chose to highlight the protection against the monarch's arbitrary power afforded by codified laws, be they civil or criminal. Under the entry 'Laws', the *Philosophical Dictionary* ridiculed the variety of customs in 1760s France. He also explicitly called for the codification of civil and criminal law on the grounds that fixed and written rules afforded protection against a despotic monarch.[26] Beccaria also believed that limiting the adjudicating powers of the courts would best serve the interests of subjects, but he introduced a new argument: not only would it serve as a security protecting citizens, but it would also, more positively, provide a guide for action. A written code was 'useful [to the citizens], because it allow[ed] them to evaluate exactly the drawbacks of wrongdoing'.[27] In Voltaire and Beccaria's books, judges held an ambiguous position, being too often the instruments of arbitrary rule. It is not surprising therefore that English common lawyers, proud of their judge-based tradition, should have seized on precisely this issue. Edward Wynne – a disciple of William Blackstone – defended the power of interpretation held by judges against Beccaria and Catherine II (who had taken up his proposals in her *Instruction*):

> The present Czarina has treated this in the same manner, Instruct. pour le code de la Russe [sic.], Art. 10, par. 142, and the Marquis de Beccaria, c. 4,

[24] See X. Rousseaux, 'Le droit pénal entre consolidation étatique et codification absolutiste au XVIIIe Siècle', in *Le pénal dans tous ses états. Justice, Etats et sociétés en Europe, XIIe-XXe siècles*, ed. X. Rousseaux and R. Lévy (Brussels: Publications des Facultés Universitaires Saint-Louis, 1997), 251–78.

[25] C.L. de Secondat Montesquieu, *The Spirit of the Laws*, eds. A.M. Cohler, B.C. Miller, and H.S. Stone (Cambridge University Press, 1989), 73 (Bk. VI, Ch. 1).

[26] See 'Lois' ('On Laws') in Voltaire, *Philosophical Dictionary*, ed. T. Besterman (Harmondsworth: Penguin Books, 1971), 281–8; and 'Republican Ideas. By a member of a public body', in Voltaire, *Political Writings*, ed. D. Williams (Cambridge University Press, 1994), 195–211, at 206.

[27] Beccaria, *On Crimes*, 16.

> p. 14, whom indeed the Empress evidently copies, because they both concur in the singular notion of taking from the Judge the power of interpreting Criminal Laws, notwithstanding his decision on those Laws implies it: for how can he draw that conclusion which is the result of the comparison of the Law with the Fact, if he does not know the precise meaning of the Law itself? How, in other words, can he conclude without premisses, for when the Law is in doubt, the major proposition of the Syllogism is evidently defective? If indeed the Prince is to explain Law by a new one in every instance, what kind of sense will such laws be?[28]

Beccaria also insisted on the fact that codification should not only be limited to setting down in print existing rules and customs, but rather entailed a substantial revision of the contents of legislation. Rousseau forcefully made a similar point. In *Considerations on the Government of Poland,* he called for 'three codes. One political, the other civil, the third criminal. All as clear, short and precise as possible'. He added: 'as regards Roman and customary law, all this, if it exists at all, has to be eliminated from the schools and the law courts. They should recognize no other authority than the Laws of the State'.[29]

Bentham's lifelong insistence on codification, from his early plans to digest the common law of England in the early 1770s to his attempts to reform property law in the last years of his life, is well known.[30] The early 1780s marked a turning point as he abandoned the idea that present laws could be simply digested into a written code and attempted to lay the foundations for a *Pannomion*, a complete code of new legislation based on utility. In *Limits* he had expressed his hopes that his writings would serve

> to frame for each nation a compleat code new in point of substance as well as form . . . with such alterations as shall be deemed requisite to adapt it to the particular manners, sentiments and exterior circumstances of each respective state.[31]

In *Projet*, he explained why contemporary attempts at codification had failed. The main target of his criticism was the Frederician code drafted

[28] E. Wynne, *Eunomus: Or, Dialogues Concerning the Law and Constitution of England. With An Essay on Dialogue*, 4 vols. (London, 1774), iv. 36–7.

[29] J.J. Rousseau, 'Considerations on the Government of Poland', in *The Social Contract, and Other Later Political Writings*, ed. V. Gourevitch (Cambridge University Press, 1997), 177–260, at 220.

[30] See Lobban, *Common Law*, 116–54; D. Lieberman, 'Bentham on Codification', in *Jeremy Bentham: Selected Writings*, ed. S.G. Engelmann (New Haven and London: Yale University Press, 2011), 460–77.

[31] *Limits* (*CW*), 232.

by Cocceji for Prussia in the 1750s. Although the title seemed to promise a *Corps de droit Frédéric*, or a *Code Frédéric*, Bentham argued that the code itself was elusive, being referred to in different places but never stated *in terminis*.[32] He also examined the Danish code of 1683, the Swedish code of 1734, the Sardinian code of 1770, and the Theresian code drafted for Austria, and concluded that all were little more than fragmentary digests of established customs.[33] Bentham was right: the first attempts at thoroughly reshaping civil and criminal law indeed took place in the late 1780s and 1790s, in a number of smaller states, precisely as he was writing *Projet*. A code was adopted in 1783 for Corsica, recently fallen under French rule. In Tuscany new penal laws came into force in 1786, soon known as the *Leopoldina* (after king Leopold II). One year later, Joseph II's Austria followed suit. The Austrian code was afterwards adapted to Lombardy, then under Austrian domination, where Beccaria was among the king's advisers. Meanwhile, Frederick II's second attempt at codification was taking shape. It bore fruit eight years after his death with the adoption of the *Allgemeines Landrecht für die Preussischen Staaten* in 1794.[34] Although new in point of form, all these new codes incorporated vast amounts of existing laws and customs.

Like Beccaria, and for similar utilitarian reasons, Bentham insisted that only a written code could provide a clear and precise guide for action. He was also wary of the adjudicating power of judges and strove to constrain it within precise bounds. He insisted on the protection afforded to the people by a good and clearly written system of legislation: 'the work I give the strong' (the drafters of codes) 'serves to ensure peace and rest to the weak'.[35] In *Limits* he had also presented the advantages of codification as a way of 'check[ing] the licence of interpretation' by judges: if his rules for the organization and wording of the code were followed, 'such a degree of comprehension and steadiness might one day perhaps be given to the views of the legislator as to render the allowance of liberal or discretionary interpretation on the part of the judge no longer necessary'.[36] In *Projet*, he developed this idea by proposing to insert alongside the laws proper a

[32] See UC xxxiii. 113. All quotes from Bentham's *Projet* are my translations from Bentham's French.

[33] See UC c. 65; UC xcviii. 189.

[34] For a thorough presentation of each of these codes, see Y. Cartuyvels, *D'où vient le code pénal? Une approche généalogique des premiers codes pénaux au XVIIIe siècle* (Presses de l'Université de Montréal, Presses de l'Université d'Ottawa, 1996).

[35] UC c. 68.

[36] *Limits* (*CW*), 227–8.

number of articles containing commentaries on the reasons for the laws: the legislator himself would therefore guide the judge's interpretations.[37] But nobody could apply a law, Bentham remarked, without interpreting it so some extent. Not excluding judicial interpretation altogether, he singled out 'corrective interpretation' as to be avoided at all costs: only the legislator could amend the text of the law.[38]

Bentham's interest in the wording of the law cannot be separated from his defiance of judicial interpretation. This explains why he chose to devote the first part of *Projet* to the 'form' of a complete code of laws, the second containing the 'matter' of civil, penal, and constitutional law. To Bentham, his work on the 'formal' aspect of legislation represented a major breakthrough: 'Montesquieu knew nothing about order. Beccaria, who has done so much regarding matter, said nothing of form.'[39] Indeed, Beccaria had done little more than insist in general terms on the 'clarity' of the laws. Likewise, Catherine II had devoted a section of her *Instruction* to the importance of an unambiguous wording of the laws, for which Brissot, for instance, commended her.[40] For Brissot and Bentham, questions of organization and expression were the areas in which the collaboration between jurists and philosophers was most crucial. Bentham devoted a large part of *Projet* to establishing precise rules for 'Composition' and 'Stile':

> The object of laws, as regards style, is that whenever they bear in one way or another on the citizen's conduct, this citizen should be able to conceive the will entertained by the legislator regarding [the action] in question.[41]

Bentham's utilitarian approach emphasized the intimate connection between the 'form' and the 'matter' of the law: the laws, no matter how good in substance, could neither be accurately known, understood, and

[37] UC xcviii. 208. The idea of giving a rationale for the laws was not new: Frederick II had published a *Dissertation sur les raisons d'établir ou d'abroger les loix* (Utrecht, 1770), in which he provided reasons supporting legal reform. However, Bentham was the first to propose that the rationale should be directly integrated within the code. This proposal was taken up in *Constitutional Code*, in which 'ratiocinative' articles stood alongside 'enactive' ones: see *Constitutional Code: Volume I*, eds. F. Rosen and J.H. Burns (Oxford: Clarendon Press, 1983 (*CW*)), passim.

[38] UC xcviii. 207–11.

[39] UC xxxiii. 92.

[40] 'The chapter on the style of laws is very philosophical. It is strange that among enlightened nations laws should still be drafted in a barbarous style and unintelligible words. The legislator resembles the sphinx, he seems to be proposing riddles to have the right to slaughter.' Brissot de Warville, *Bibliothèque du législateur*, iii. 175.

[41] UC c. 66.

memorized, nor interpreted, if the style in which they were expressed was faulty. In evaluating legal style, Bentham relegated 'strength', 'harmony' and 'nobility' to the second rank, and emphasized instead 'intelligibility', 'brevity', 'completeness', 'accuracy', 'precision' and homogeneity: the legislator had to be 'a consummate grammarian'. Bentham laid out a string of concrete rules: the code should be in the vernacular, it should exclude digressions or irrelevant matter, eradicate ambiguity, and be neither too specific nor too general.[42]

One of Bentham's most innovative proposals in *Projet* was to break down the complete code into 'general' and 'particular' codes. The 'general code' would contain the laws 'in which everyone has roughly an equal interest'. 'Particular codes', on the contrary, would assemble in single volumes all the laws relating to specific categories among the population, according to either their status (parent, tutor, child) or their profession, trade, or occupation ('tenant, shopkeeper, tobacco monger, citizen of one city or another').[43] The first advantage of this strategy, Bentham argued, was that it allowed the printing of short and handy volumes that could be carried and consulted on the spot whenever a doubt or a conflict arose. At any given point, anyone might find guidance about what should be done in the letter of the law. Bentham repeated the suggestion in the preface to *Constitutional Code*.[44]

Principles of Morals and Legislation

Personal codes could be carried in one's pocket, or, if they contained rules specific to a trade or a place, posted on the walls of shops, markets, or gardens. The universal code, however, would be taught in schools and read out in churches as a guide for moral conduct. Bentham explained further how morals and legislation coincided: 'Sacred books say, be just. A good Pandicaion shows in every way what it is to be just, in how many ways and in what ways one can fail to be.'[45]

Like Helvétius, Bentham held legislation to be a branch of morals, and sought to uncover the principles according to which each branch was organized. In so doing, he took up one of the most fruitful articulations in

42 See UC c. 66; UC xcviii. 180–95 and UC c. 63–78. These rules correspond to those set down in English in the 1810s: see 'Nomography; or the Art of Inditing Laws', Bowring iii. 231–83.

43 UC xcviii. 180.

44 *Constitutional Code: I* (*CW*), 5–6.

45 UC c. 38.

contemporary legal thinking. In the *Spirit of the Laws*, Montesquieu had devoted one chapter to examining '[h]ow laws can contribute to forming the mores, manners and character of a nation'.[46] In asking that question, Montesquieu immediately postulated that laws could and should be distinguished from mores (*mœurs*) and manners (*manières*). For legislators such a distinction was crucial: only by separating the contents of each sphere could they have a clear understanding of their field of action. He wrote: 'When a prince wants to make great changes in his nation, he must reform by laws what is established by laws and change by manners what is established by manners, and it is a very bad policy to change by laws what should be changed by manners.'[47] Montesquieu pointed out some limits to the power of the legislator.

Montesquieu's insistence that laws should be distinguished from morals was functional, for it served to delineate the obstacles that the legislator could encounter in the course of exercising his power, and provided him with a method in order to solve them: 'the means for preventing crimes are penalties, the means for changing manners are examples'.[48] It did not imply that the spheres of law and morals were entirely independent. In numerous passages, Montesquieu showed how good laws and good manners mutually reinforced each other in a way that varied according to the political constitution of a given state. In republics, manners prevailed upon laws, whereas despotic monarchs attempted to rule over the manners of the people by imposing autocratic laws. Montesquieu's preferred system, a limited monarchy, would avoid these pitfalls by wisely examining the cases in which reform would be better effected by enacting laws or by promoting good habits.[49]

During the 1780s, Bentham devoted a number of discussions to the central question of the respective boundaries of morals and legislation. As he had made clear in *A Fragment on Government*, the observance of laws depended on 'a habit of obedience' in the people, and habits were directly related to the *mores* of a nation.[50] The closing chapter added to *IPML* in 1789 summed up the conclusions of a decade of enquiry:

46 Montesquieu, *Spirit of the Laws*, 325 (Bk. XIX, Ch. 27).

47 Ibid., 315 (Bk. XIX, Ch. 14).

48 Ibid.

49 Ibid., 25–6 (Bk. III, Ch. 5).

50 Bentham, *A Fragment on Government; Being an Examination of What Is delivered, on the Subject of Government in General, in the Introduction to Sir William Blackstone's Commentaries* (London: T. Payne, 1776), published in the critical edition of Bentham's collected works in *A Comment on the Commentaries and a Fragment on Government*, eds. J.H. Burns and H.L.A. Hart (London:

> Private ethics has happiness for its end: and legislation can have no other. Private ethics concerns . . . the happiness and the actions of every member of any community that can be proposed; and legislation can concern no more. Thus far, then, private ethics and the art of legislation go hand in hand. . . . Where then lies the difference? In that the acts which they ought to be conversant about, though in a great measure, are not *perfectly and throughout* the same. . . . There is no case in which a private man ought not to direct his own conduct to the production of his own happiness, and of that of his fellow-creatures: but there are cases in which the legislator ought not . . . to attempt to direct the conduct of the several other members of the community.[51]

Utility served to 'draw the line' between the two fields, by excluding from the sphere of penal law conduct for which punishment was 'groundless', 'inefficacious', 'unprofitable' or 'needless'.[52] If utility was a discriminating principle, it also paradoxically served to unite the domains of morals and legislation, for Bentham explained in *Projet*:

> I had to find a principle, a strong and solid foundation on which the remainder of the fabric could rest. I embraced the principle of utility. This principle explained in the only intelligible manner led me of necessity to consider[?] pleasures and pains. Here are the foundations not only of legislation and government, but also of morals and of the most interesting part of metaphysics.[53]

In *Projet*, the role ascribed to the laws was not only to define the external boundaries of the field of morals but also to influence its contents. A legal code driven by utility would serve as an instrument for the reform of both manners and morals. The code itself, for Bentham, was an illustration of, as well as a plea for, the principle of utility: within the code, each provision would be justified by reference to this principle, especially in the commentaries published alongside the letter of the law. By explaining why murder should be punished, Bentham explained, the legislator not only stated the obvious, he also provided the intellectual tools that would allow the public to understand why cases such as suicide, duelling, and the infanticide of newborns by the parents were *not* to be punishable, and therefore should *not* be condemned on moral grounds. He continued:

Athlone, 1977 (*CW*)), 391–551 (henceforth 'Fragment', in *Comment/Fragment* (*CW*)), at 429–30n.

51 *IPML* (*CW*), 285.

52 Ibid., 286–93.

53 UC c. 80.

> If one must spell out the evil of stealing, it is not to convince men that stealing is a bad thing. It is to convince them of a variety of equally true statements regarding that topic, and that they have so far ignored: amongst other things, thefts that have been neglected or left entangled. It is also to rule others out, which have so far been singled out from the rest for specific punishment without any sufficient reason. Lastly, it is to bring together all its true and genuine modifications, to distinguish among them those that deserve to be so and to rule the spurious ones out.[54]

Inserting a rationale for each provision alongside the letter of the law served to promote a strictly utilitarian reasoning in the field of jurisprudence and of morals. On the contrary, for many of his contemporaries calls to utility and to natural law mutually reinforced one another. Bentham's exclusive appeal to utility set him apart. Beccaria, for instance, had indiscriminately used consequentialist arguments drawn from utility and natural-law principles founded on rights and humanity.[55] Bentham, however, hoped to exclude all appeals to jusnaturalist arguments. By defining offences according to utility, the utilitarian legislator forced his subjects to apply a different sort of moral reasoning: in so doing, Bentham hoped they could be convinced to 'break the sweet tyranny of instinct to substitute to it the often importunate yoke of reason'. In words that recall the language used in *IPML*, Bentham used the words 'instinct', 'prejudice', and 'caprice' interchangeably to reject appeals to nature or common sense.[56] It was by promoting the principle of utility to the exclusion of every other that Bentham hoped that 'a book of law' would provide 'without further work and besides the letter of the law, a guide for history and a handbook of philosophy and morals'.[57]

Stating the rationale for legislation within the code itself was a central tool in utilitarian pedagogy. Besides this moral function, it also had legal and political implications. As far as the distribution of legal power was concerned, it served further to limit the power of judges by guiding – and therefore constraining – the interpretation of laws.[58] In political terms, it allowed the contents of the code itself to be understood, and therefore appropriated both by the sovereign and by the people.[59]

54 UC c. 43.

55 See D. Ippolito 'La philosophie pénale des Lumières entre utilitarisme et rétributivisme', in *Lumières 20, Penser la peine à l'âge des Lumières*, eds. L. Delia and G. Radica (Presses Universitaire Bordeaux, 2012), 21–37.

56 UC c. 43.

57 UC c. 44; see also UC c. 38.

58 UC xcviii. 207, 208.

59 UC xxxiii. 93; UC clxx. 189.

Enlightened Sovereigns and Legal Change

In the decade immediately preceding the French Revolution, as arguments in favour of legal reform multiplied, the debate shifted to the means through which the proposed changes should be implemented. France, Prussia, and Russia remained absolute monarchies. Likewise, in smaller European states, reforms had been conducted by autocratic, if enlightened, monarchs. In that context, the dividing line amongst reformers did not consist in appealing to sovereigns as the main agents of change or refusing to do so, but rather in the details of the proposed reforms and in the steps envisaged as necessary to carry them into practice. A republican disciple of Rousseau, Brissot became more radical in the early 1780s as he was forced into exile because of his journalistic activities. But even in works published from London he continued to appeal to sovereigns and to praise their achievements. This implied a criticism of the French monarchy, which had proved itself unable to match the modernizing pace set by its enlightened neighbours. But the truly subversive features of his radicalism lay elsewhere, in the analysis of the legal system he proposed. In comparison, Bentham's political position can be examined anew. To assess Bentham's politics of reform, one must look first at the order in which he thought the branches of the laws should be reformed, and second at the role given to the people as agents of change.

In expressing his preference for the rule of law over that of virtue, Montesquieu had distanced himself from the republican model. In the second half of the eighteenth century however, the rising fortunes of republicanism had a direct impact on legal writing and more specifically on the debate on the respective boundaries of morals and legislation.[60] Rousseau, for instance, in reflecting on the government of Poland, argued that when subjects had become citizens, when their manners had been perfected by political responsibilities, fewer laws would be needed.

Rousseau and his republican followers thus reversed the order of priority set by Montesquieu: there could be no legal reform without a preliminary overhaul of corrupt political and civil institutions. As Brissot explained in 1780, crimes were especially numerous in France because of the depraved morals of corrupted rulers who perverted the political

[60] For the place of the vocabulary of 'manners' in the republican paradigm, see J.G.A. Pocock, 'Virtue, Rights and Manners. A Model for Historians of Political Thought', in *Virtue, Commerce and History, Essays on Political Thought and History, Chiefly in the Eighteenth Century* (Cambridge University Press, 1985), 37–50.

system, which, in turn, corrupted the manners of the people.[61] Likewise, in the essay he submitted to the Bern competition, Marat denounced a society in which the '[t]he unfair division of wealth would be odious enough, if almost everywhere governments themselves did not force their poorest subjects to commit crimes by depriving them of the means of subsistence'.[62] Brissot readily accepted these arguments, and they served as the basis for his reforming agenda: no overhaul of penal or criminal law could be attempted effectively before the foundations of civil and constitutional legislation had been thoroughly rebuilt according to moral principles. In *Moyens de prévenir les crimes en France*, he developed an argument he had already put forward in *Théorie des loix criminelles*:

> The more [civil law] tends to perfection, the less use there will be for criminal legislation. There will be almost none once civil law rests on its proper basis, which is fixed and immutable; once the monarch has been taught to respect the property and the liberty of subjects; once the unfortunate whom fate caused to be born without property, though with needs, can by his work correct the unfairness of his lot & level the unequal distribution of wealth.[63]

Once the civil arrangements had been overhauled, the reformation of morals would follow, the corruption of the wealthy would be exposed and the number of crimes would fall. Brissot's republican analysis clearly stressed the primacy of civil law reform over that of criminal law, and made it clear that political change was a necessary preliminary to both.

Such arguments were conspicuously absent from Bentham's early proposals. First, he followed Beccaria in reasserting the primacy of penal over civil law, working from the utilitarian premise that classification had to be organized with reference to pleasure and pain, and that there could be no law without a sanction. Defined as dealing primarily with the infliction of penalties as punishment for harm, penal law came first and provided the model according to which civil and constitutional laws were to be understood. In his words, penal matter was 'the most instructive, for it clearly brings to light the essence and the origin of the law, it expresses in the clearest way the authority from whence it issues'.[64] In so

[61] Brissot de Warville, *Bibliothèque du législateur*, vi. 15–16.

[62] J.-P. Marat, 'Plan de législation en matière criminelle', in Brissot, *Bibliothèque du Législateur*, v. 109–290, at 147. Marat's plan was republished separately in Paris in 1790.

[63] Brissot de Warville, *Bibliothèque du Législateur*, vi. 25.

[64] UC xxxiii. 117.

doing, he took up an argument Hobbes had, before him, directed against seventeenth-century republicans.

In the 'Matière' material, Bentham dealt with civil law at length. Although he advanced 'equality' as one of its 'subordinate goals', its utility was always to be balanced against the possible threat to 'security'.[65] Bentham did recognize that, other things being equal, a relative equality of property produced a greater mass of happiness than an unequal distribution. The means he proposed to reconcile these two diverging aims consisted in reforming the law so that in the absence of any direct heir (children, parents, or siblings), inheritances should return to the state. This avoided diminishing the legitimate expectations of property owners or of their close relatives while securing some revenue to the state, but this hardly provided the means of diminishing inequalities.[66] Bentham's reluctance to pursue redistributive policies was justified by the axiom according to which 'the evil of loss is greater than the profit of gain'.[67] Similar reasoning also applied to the enfranchisement of slaves. Opposing slavery on the utilitarian ground that the mass of unhappiness produced by it always outweighed any gains, Bentham nevertheless argued against immediate enfranchisement and proposed three measures: (1) that each slave should be entitled to purchase his freedom from the owner; (2) that slaves should be freed on the owner's death in the absence of direct heirs; and (3) that a tenth of all slaves should be freed on each succession, when there were direct heirs.[68] In their gradualism, these proposals were far removed from the immediate enfranchisement increasingly called for by Brissot and his friends in the same decade.

If Bentham disagreed with the most radical among his contemporaries, including Brissot, on the order of priorities for reform, he also differed on the role ascribed to the people themselves as agents of change. In the 1780s, echoing Montesquieu's arguments, most authors explained how to accommodate universal principles of reform to local circumstances, for instance by appointing local representatives, elected or not, who could have a voice in debating the laws and adapting them to national or local

[65] For a discussion of the four ends of civil law (subsistence, abundance, equality, and security) in *Projet*, see UC xxix. 11–13; UC xcix. 34–5; for the conflict between equality and security, UC xcix. 9–63.

[66] See UC xcix. 83–5.

[67] UC xcix. 53.

[68] UC xcix. 93–8. Bentham's hostility to slavery as an institution is discussed in F. Rosen, 'Jeremy Bentham on Slavery and the Slave Trade', in *Utilitarianism and Empire*, eds. B. Schultz and G. Varouxakis (Lanham MD: Lexington Books, 2005), 33–56.

manners. Catherine II suggested such a scheme in her *Instruction.* Bentham was fully aware of these arguments. In an essay entitled 'Place and Time', written slightly before *Projet,* he addressed precisely the issue of imposing a new (and supposedly good) code of law on a given country.[69] In the past, he argued, legislators did not pay much heed to local circumstances, but '[s]ince Montesquieu, the number of documents which a legislator would require is considerably enlarged'. Accepting Montesquieu's argument that manners were liable to vary almost infinitely on account of local factors, he proposed to list, for each country, the specific customs and habits of the people, so that a precise map of the 'circumstances influencing sensibilities' in each part of the country could be drafted.[70] Under 'circumstances', Bentham included not only 'purely physical causes' – that is, those derived from the climate or the nature of the soil – but also 'the circumstances of government, religion and manners', thereby presented as given, not as objects of change. The legislator should assess the mischief produced under the existing institutions and weigh it against the improvement expected from the introduction of the new system. Bentham then laid out the following rules to govern legal and moral reforms:

1. No law should be changed, no prevailing usage should be abolished, without special reason: without some specific assignable benefit [which] can be shewn as likely to be the result of such a change.
2. The changing of a custom repugnant to our own manners and sentiments, for no other reason than such repugnancy, is not to be reputed as a benefit.[71]

Where did that leave the possibility of change? In theory, Bentham's early political thought did not preclude it: in 'Fragment', he even provided a clear rule to identify the 'juncture for resistance' ('when the *probable mischiefs of resistance* (speaking with respect to the community in general) *appear less . . . than the probable mischiefs of submission*').[72] However, his opinion in the 1780s was that the dangers of civil war almost always outweighed the disutility of the existing institutions. This point was made clearly in the French manuscripts: popular revolutions led to civil wars, the greatest of all possible evils. The conclusion was unambiguous: 'No government can be so bad that a friend to mankind should be justified in

69 'Place and Time', in *Jeremy Bentham: Selected Writings*, ed. Engelmann, 152–219.
70 Ibid., 156n.
71 Ibid., 173–4.
72 'Fragment', in *Comment/Fragment* (*CW*), 484.

advising revolt in order to substitute to it any other form of government'.[73] This argument also applied retrospectively to the American Revolution. Bentham argued that, for each American, the cost of the revolt had been far higher than that of the taxes imposed under British rule.[74]

The subtitle to *Projet* was 'Offre faite par un Anglois aux Souverains de l'Europe'.[75] Bentham's praise of Catherine II and other enlightened rulers might have been tactical, but the rationale behind legal reform and the details of its application cut Bentham off from his republican contemporaries, as it had done previously during the controversy with Richard Price on the occasion of American Independence.

Rejecting republican arguments, Bentham however suggested an original path towards reform, one that pursued Helvétius's call for a gradual move towards the greatest happiness of the greatest number. In the offer to draft a code, Bentham conspicuously presented himself as 'an Englishman'. Indeed, as an English subject, he could claim to be familiar with a legal system that had banished torture, and with a constitution recognized throughout the eighteenth century as the freest in the world. Bentham was conscious of the advantages that could be derived from this position in debates over the best constitution. At the beginning of the 1770s, he had stressed what set Britain apart from the other countries, namely its respect for freedom of opinion:

> This age, say they, is the age of Philosophy. All the nations of Europe have produced men of genius in this walk. All seem to occupy themselves in our days in searching after moral truth. Be it so. But in what country can it with impunity be divulged? – There is but one: 'tis England . . .
>
> No, England any more than Portugal is not wanting in men who, as far as wishes can make them, are oppressors. But against the press what in London is their power? . . . Liberty is the Britons birthright – let them profit of that liberty to give light unto the world. Let him lift up his head: . . . to shed light among the nations.[76]

Bentham was, however, far from accepting the praise usually bestowed on the British constitution. In 'Fragment' he had ridiculed Blackstone's 'panegyric', which rested on the idea that the perfection of the British constitution derived from a harmonious synthesis of the three classical forms of government, or from the happy balance of the three main powers: the

[73] UC clxx. 199.
[74] UC clxx. 200.
[75] UC xcix. 156.
[76] UC xxvii. 4.

executive, the legislature, and the judiciary.[77] If 'Fragment' criticized Blackstone's method, it did not challenge the idea that the British constitution was far superior to all existing political arrangements. But its superiority, Bentham argued, resided in a set of factors that set it apart from 'despotic' governments: the distribution of power among the office-holders, the changes of position between rulers and ruled, the responsibility of office-holders, and the liberty of the press and public association.[78]

Though discussion of constitutional law in *Projet* was less developed than those of the civil and the penal branches, Bentham argued that it was indeed one of the three branches necessary in a complete code.[79] In the 'form' manuscripts, three chapters were devoted to 'elementary political powers', with a view to establishing a new nomenclature that would render the political institutions existing throughout the world comparable, whereas present titles failed to make political differences visible (the King of Poland's power, for instance, had little in common with the King of England's, despite their sharing the same title). This improved classification was Bentham's answer to the tripartite division of power that he had ridiculed Blackstone for adopting.

Moreover, *Projet* reasserted the idea, present in *Limits*, that there could be effective restraints on the power of the sovereign, even though the highest legislative authority could not be submitted to positive laws. 'Privileges' such as freedom of conscience, of worship, and of assembly could be granted to subjects or citizens or to provinces as a whole.[80] How could those privileges be enforced if the sovereign could not be held legally accountable? Bentham's answer was to invoke public opinion as the ultimate security against abuses on the part of the sovereign. The sanction of public opinion was the direct, the 'natural' consequence of the sovereign's misconduct:

> Natural punishments are far from being inefficacious: immediate punishments, dishonour on the part of the sovereign, discontent on the part of the subjects; subsidiary punishment, in last resort, revolt and lost sovereignty.[81]

[77] 'Fragment', in *Comment/Fragment* (*CW*), 461–74.

[78] Ibid., 485.

[79] UC xxxiii. 126.

[80] UC xxxiii. 79. On this point, see E. de Champs, 'Constitution and the Code: Jeremy Bentham on the Limits of the Constitutional Branch of Jurisprudence', *The Tocqueville Review/La Revue Tocqueville*, 32 (2011), 21–42.

[81] UC xxxiii. 79.

The important role given to public opinion was reasserted in the 'matter' manuscripts for *Projet*, in which Bentham presented the constitutional mechanisms required to make its exercise possible. These manuscript pages contain what could be the earliest reference from Bentham's pen to public opinion as a 'tribunal' – though not in French.[82] Under the heading 'Popular sanction tribunal', he referred to the check exercised by public opinion on the sovereign and on office-holders, and pointed to Jean-Louis De Lolme as the originator of this idea.[83] In his celebrated book, *The Constitution of England*, first published in French in 1771, the Genevan writer had identified the strength of the constitution in the provision it made for the non-legislative force of public opinion:

> As the evils that may be complained of in a State do not always arise merely from the defect of the laws, but also from the non-execution of them, and this non-execution of such a kind, that it is often impossible to subject it to any express punishment, or even to ascertain it by any previous definition, Men, in several States, have looked for an expedient that might supply the unavoidable deficiency in legislative provisions, and begin to operate, as it were, from the point at which the latter begins to fail: I mean here to speak of the Censorial power; a power which may produce excellent effects, but the exercise of which (contrary to that of the legislative power) must be left to the People themselves.[84]

Describing the English system in *Projet*, Bentham used the very same phrase to distinguish between the power deriving from the liberty of the press and the power of electing representatives, when he defined 'censorial power' as that of 'openly canvassing and arraigning the conduct of those who are invested with any branch of public authority', and remarked that this was one of the foundations on which English liberty was founded.[85]

Bentham went further than De L'Olme, and listed a number of 'expedients against bad governments', whose common purpose was to create the conditions for the exercise of public opinion in the state. These 'securities against misrule', as he later called them, were broadly similar to

[82] The shift from 'opinion' to 'public opinion' and then to 'the tribunal of public opinion' in French political discourse has been charted in K.M. Baker, *Inventing the French Revolution: Essays on French Political Culture in the Eighteenth Century* (Cambridge University Press, 1990), 167–99, and R. Chartier, *The Cultural Origins of the French Revolution* (Durham: Duke University Press, 1990), 20–37.

[83] UC xxxiii. 80.

[84] J.-L. De Lolme, *The Constitution of England; Or, an Account of the English Government*, ed. D. Lieberman (Indianapolis: Liberty Fund, 2007), 199.

[85] UC xxxiii. 80. This casts light on a passing mention of De Lolme in 'Fragment', in *Comment/Fragment* (*CW*), 473: '[Blackstone] has copied, Mr. De L'Olme has thought'.

those which had been stated in 'Fragment': laying out the reasons for the laws and all administrative measures, distributing power among several persons at each level of the chain of command, placing the powers of appointing and dismissing in distinct individuals, establishing short terms of office for official appointments, introducing strict rules of procedure to avoid the exercise of undue power, controlling the use of public money, and, lastly, 'all the rights left to the people in the view of giving public will the influence it should have: right to bear arms, right to assemble, right to confederate'. These included the liberty of the press, which had also been singled out by De Lolme as the main channel of 'censorial power'.[86] Bentham concluded that the difference between free and despotic governments was not so much due to the form of their institutions as to the degree of enlightenment of the people: 'Wherein does the difference between the state of things under the governments or states named monarchical and those named despotic lie, if not in the knowledge of the people?'[87] On this last point, Bentham concurred with his old friend Brissot, who had stated the idea of reform in an age of Enlightenment in similar terms. Republishing his 1781 essay *Le Sang innocent vengé* in *Bibliothèque du législateur* the following year, he introduced it with these words:

> Some people who believe that books are good for nothing have asked me whether our laws had not remained the same since this work was published. They do not want to see that the remedy to existing laws can only come from public opinion, and that the said public opinion can only be changed slowly. It is not from the present generation that one should expect a complete reform, unless it be directed by an active human genius, one combining power with love and knowledge of the good. Failing that, one must wait until the upcoming generation, enlightened by our books, has replaced the present one, rejected its prejudices and abolished its method.[88]

Bentham was a perceptive observer of the political situation on the European continent, as this chapter has shown. Not any more than Brissot, whose radicalism gradually developed throughout the 1780s, could he foresee that the old regime would be irreversibly brought down in France

[86] UC clxx. 202–5. These measures anticipate later provisions stated in *Securities against Misrule, and Other Constitutional Writings for Tripoli and Greece*, ed. P. Schofield (Oxford: Clarendon Press, 1990 (*CW*)), 80–6. See also F. Rosen, *Jeremy Bentham and Representative Democracy: A Study of the Constitutional Code* (Oxford University Press, 1983), 60–3.

[87] UC clxx. 197.

[88] Brissot de Warville, *Bibliothèque du législateur*, vi. 173–243, at 242n.

before the end of the decade. The summoning of the Estates-General in 1788, and the fall of the Bastille on 14 July 1789 markedly changed political expectations throughout Europe. Brissot, Bentham, and many others seized on the opportunities opened by the onset of the Revolution, even if their political trajectories remained distinct, and if their paths failed to meet again.[89]

As early as the winter of 1788–9, Bentham's Russian hopes receded into the background as he turned to France. His proposals to Revolutionary France did not break with his earlier position, as has sometimes been implied, but rather displayed continuity with *Projet*.[90] Despite the fact that he abandoned his calls for top-down reform engineered by an enlightened monarch, his proposals for a representative system rested on ideas that were already present in the earlier French work. They combined the people's direct political participation with a number of checks exercised by public opinion. Directions for extending the suffrage were thus combined with provisions for the publicity of debates, liberty of the press, and the revocability of representatives by petition.[91] His eventual estrangement from French revolutionary politics after the Terror was formulated in terms reminiscent of the high hopes he had placed on an enlightened public opinion taking part in politics: after the September Massacres in 1792, he regretted that 'as it is the bulk who govern, things will never go on well till even the bulk are well informed'.[92]

Well after the Revolution, the system worked out in *Projet d'un corps complet de loix* continued to provide inspiration. As has been pointed out, the philosopher drew on it extensively forty years later. In *Constitutional Code*, he put into practice the codification advice he had given in the French manuscripts as he embarked on the redaction of the first volume of a complete code, stating the reasons for each provision and

[89] See J.H. Burns, 'Bentham, Brissot and the Challenge of Revolution', *History of European Ideas*, 35 (2009), 217–39.

[90] The idea that Bentham 'converted' to democracy during the French revolution, initially put forward by Mary Mack, has been disproved. However, the continuity in his political views has been underestimated. See M. Mack, *Jeremy Bentham: An Odyssey of Ideas 1748–1792* (London: Columbia University Press, 1962), 412–17; Philip Schofield, *Utility and Democracy: The Political Thought of Jeremy Bentham* (Oxford University Press, 2006), 108. Schofield provides a useful summary of historiographical debates.

[91] The fullest presentation of Bentham's proposals over that period can be found in '*Projet* of a Constitutional Code for France', in Bentham, *Rights, Representation, and Reform: Nonsense Upon Stilts and Other Writings on the French Revolution*, eds. P. Schofield, C. Blamires, and C. Pease-Watkin (Oxford: Clarendon Press, 2002 (*CW*)), 227–61.

[92] Quoted in *Rights, Representation and Reform* (CW), 'Editorial Introduction', lviii.

weaving together imperative and explicative material.[93] One sign of his radicalization in the last decades of his life was that he by then believed that reformed constitutional and civil codes were necessary prerequisites for reform of the penal code, which reversed the order of priorities set out in the 1780s.

Rereading Bentham's early career as a dialogue with Continental and republican ideas, as has been suggested in this chapter, reveals that there could be no clear-cut opposition between laws and morals in Bentham's legal philosophy. Though this interpretation conflicts with positivist readings of classical utilitarianism, it is in line with recent studies.[94] Such a contextual approach also brings out the originality of Bentham's attitude towards legal, political, and social reform, the ambiguities of appealing to 'public opinion' as an agent of change, and the shifts in his views on democracy according to whether local and historical circumstances held – or did not hold – the promise of an enlightened public opinion.

[93] See Bentham's preface to *Constitutional Code: I* (*CW*), 3–9.

[94] See especially P. Schofield, 'Jeremy Bentham, Public Utility and Legal Positivism', *Current Legal Problems* 56 (2003), 1–39; Schofield, 'Jeremy Bentham and HLA Hart's "Utilitarian Tradition in Jurisprudence"', *Jurisprudence* 1 (2010), 147–67; and X. Zhai, 'Bentham's Natural Arrangement', Chapter 7 in this volume.

9

A Defence of Jeremy Bentham's Critique of Natural Rights

PHILIP SCHOFIELD

Introduction: Bentham's Three Types of Moral Theory

In 1795, Jeremy Bentham composed an essay with the title 'Nonsense upon Stilts'. It consisted of a clause-by-clause critique of the Declaration of the Rights of Man and the Citizen, which had been first issued by the French National Assembly in 1789. It contains what is arguably the most profound critique of the theory of natural rights ever written. By extension, its criticisms apply to modern theories of human rights.[1] From Bentham's point of view, any list of human rights was likely to be no more than a reflection of the personal or sectional interests of those promoting it, whereas the principle of utility represented a universal standard of right and wrong, and thereby provided the only basis for a meaningful exchange of views where there were competing moral claims.[2]

Bentham identified three broad types of moral theory: first, the principle of utility; second, its opposite, the principle of asceticism; and third, the principle of sympathy and antipathy. According to Bentham, the desire for pleasure and the aversion to pain were the sole motives to conduct. In other words, every action performed by a sentient creature was motivated by a desire either to experience some pleasure or to avoid some pain. In the field of human psychology, terms such as happiness and suffering

[1] See J. Griffin, *On Human Rights* (Oxford University Press, 2008), 1–2, 13, for a brief historical account of the transition that took place at the time of the American and French Revolutions from the language of natural rights to that of human rights. Griffin explains that the essential meaning of both a natural right and a human right – '*a right that we have simply in virtue of being human*' – remained unchanged, but links the change in language to the secularization of the concept.

[2] For the universalism of Bentham's utilitarianism in its historical context, see D. Armitage, 'Globalizing Jeremy Bentham', *History of Political Thought*, 32 (2011), 63–82; and for his extraordinary avoidance of bias in his assessment of foreign cultures (in this instance in relation to the transplantation of laws), see S.G. Engelmann and J. Pitts, 'Bentham's "Place and Time"', *The Tocqueville Review/La Revue Tocqueville*, 32 (2011), 43–66.

did not make sense unless they were explained in relation to sensations of pain and pleasure: an individual was happy when he or she was experiencing a balance of pleasure over pain, and in a state of misery or suffering when experiencing a balance of pain over pleasure. In the field of ethics or morality, terms such as good and evil did not make sense unless they were also explained in relation to pleasure and pain: hence, good consisted in pleasure and exemption from pain, and in nothing else, while evil consisted in pain and loss of pleasure, and in nothing else. An action was right and proper if it produced a balance on the side of pleasure or happiness, and wrong if it produced a balance on the side of pain or suffering. If an individual believed that he or she would gain pleasure from performing some action or seeing some state of affairs brought about, he or she was said to have an interest in performing that action or bringing about that state of affairs.

Each individual, then, was motivated to pursue his or her own happiness. Yet many actions affected not only the individual or individuals acting, but other individuals as well. When judging whether an action was right or wrong, one had to account for all the pleasures and pains produced by the action in question. This meant taking into account not merely the pleasures and pains of the actor or actors, but every single individual affected by the action. The right and proper course of action was that which promoted the most pleasure in the most people – in other words, 'the greatest happiness of the greatest number'. An action that produced such a state of affairs was said to be conducive to the general or universal interest. To accept this standard of right and wrong was to be an adherent of the principle of utility. In summary, an adherent of the principle of utility was someone who approved of those actions that increased pleasure and diminished pain.[3]

In contrast to an adherent of the principle of utility, an adherent of the principle of asceticism approved of those actions that increased pain and diminished pleasure. Bentham noted that if one-tenth of the inhabitants of the world pursued the principle of asceticism consistently, 'in a day's time they will have turned it into a hell'. It had nevertheless been pursued by two classes of people, neither of whom, however, were particularly concerned to impose it on the rest of society. The first were the Stoic philosophers, who had pursued the principle in the hope of furthering their reputation, which was in fact a source of pleasure. The

[3] See Bentham, *An Introduction to the Principles of Morals and Legislation* (henceforth *IPML* (*CW*)), eds. J.H. Burns and H.L.A. Hart (Oxford: Clarendon Press, 1970 (*CW*)), 11–16.

second were 'religionists', who had 'frequently gone so far as to make it a matter of merit and of duty to court pain', and who had been motivated by 'the fear of future punishment at the hands of a splenetic and revengeful Deity'. There was, therefore, a contradiction in the practice of those who adhered to the principle of asceticism: they took the view that by experiencing pain in the short term, they would either experience pleasure or avoid greater pain in the longer term or in the hereafter.[4]

There was a third principle – the principle of sympathy and antipathy. All other moral principles, whether called, for instance, natural law, right reason, common sense, or justice, were variants of this principle. The adherent of the principle of sympathy and antipathy raised his or her own likes and dislikes – his or her own desires and aversions – into a moral standard, in order to achieve his or her own ends, or the ends of the party or group to which he or she belonged, whatever the consequence for the greatest happiness of the greatest number. While an adherent of the principle of utility took into account the interests of all the persons affected by the action under consideration, an adherent of the principle of sympathy and antipathy took into account no more than his or her own interest, or at most the interests of some group or class smaller than that of the whole number of persons affected.[5] Typically, a privileged group would claim that it was morally right that its members should continue to enjoy their privileges.

Utility vs. Human Rights

The works of John Rawls, Bernard Williams, and Ronald Dworkin contain representative criticisms of classical utilitarianism from the perspective of modern rights-based legal and political philosophy. Rawls argues that utilitarianism does not take seriously the distinction between persons[6]; Williams argues that utilitarianism does not respect integrity[7]; and Dworkin argues that utilitarianism illegitimately counts 'external preferences' as part of its decision-making procedure. Dworkin famously

4 See ibid., 17–21.

5 See ibid., 21–31.

6 See J. Rawls, *A Theory of Justice* (Oxford University Press, 1972), 22–33.

7 See B. Williams, 'A Critique of Utilitarianism', in eds. J.J.C. Smart and B. Williams, *Utilitarianism For and Against* (Cambridge University Press, 1973), 75–150.

states that 'Individual rights are political trumps held by individuals'. In other words, an individual right takes precedence over any but the most urgent of policy considerations, that is measures designed to produce an increase in utility or welfare.[8] Bentham would argue that twentieth-century theories of human rights, like eighteenth-century theories of natural rights, are versions of the principle of sympathy and antipathy, because they take intuitions – internal feelings of right and wrong – as their starting point.[9] This is as much as to say that they take as their starting points our likes and dislikes, which may have their source in utility itself, but are just as likely to have their source in self-interest, prejudice, foolishness, or delusion. The principle of utility, in contrast, is founded on the universal nature of human beings – the fact that human beings, and indeed all sentient creatures, are motivated by a desire for pleasure and an aversion to pain. Instead of appealing to metaphysics as the basis for his system, or to a non-materialistic realm of moral norms, Bentham's theory is naturalistic.[10] If Bentham is correct, then the principle of utility provides a standard that every human being can understand, and a language in which every human being can talk sensibly to every other. We may disagree as to which course of action is best, or we may recognize conflicts of interest and, therefore, wish to pursue different courses of action, but at least our disagreements will be genuine, and we will be open to persuasion.[11] On the other hand, if we adhere to theories of human rights, one side will claim that a person has a particular right, and the other side will simply deny the claim; there is no common standard to which an appeal can be made to resolve the argument – or rather, the only appeal is to brute force.[12]

[8] See R. Dworkin, *Taking Rights Seriously* (London: Duckworth, 1977), 232–8.

[9] See ibid., 150–83, esp. 159, where Dworkin describes intuitions as 'beliefs about justice that we hold because they seem right, not because we have deduced or inferred them from other beliefs'. He goes on to say (ibid., 176–7, 182) that what he claims to be the foundational right to equality of concern and respect underpins both his own and Rawls's theories of justice, that this was 'a natural right of all men and women' that they possessed 'simply as human beings with the capacity to make plans and give justice', but that the term 'natural right' does not in this instance involve any 'metaphysically ambitious' assumptions.

[10] See P. Schofield, 'Jeremy Bentham, the Principle of Utility, and Legal Positivism', in *Current Legal Problems* 56 (2004), 1–39.

[11] See Bentham, 'A Fragment on Government', in *A Comment on the Commentaries and a Fragment on Government*, eds. J.H. Burns and H.L.A. Hart (London: Athlone, 1977 (*CW*)), 391–551 (henceforth 'Fragment', in *Comment/Fragment* (*CW*)), at 491.

[12] See Bentham, *Securities against Misrule and Other Constitutional Writings for Tripoli and Greece*, ed. P. Schofield (Oxford: Clarendon Press, 1990 (*CW*)), 23–4n.

'Nonsense upon Stilts'

Bentham's 'Nonsense upon Stilts' is a sustained criticism of natural rights theory. The main body of the essay consists of a series of remarks on the articles of the Declaration of the Rights of Man and the Citizen, attached to the French Constitution of 1791, in substance a reissue of the Declaration promulgated by the National Assembly in August 1789. Written in 1795, it was not published until 1816 when a French translation, prepared by Bentham's Genevan editor Étienne Dumont, appeared under the misleading title of 'Sophismes anarchiques'.[13] Dumont's French version was eventually followed by an English version, again with the misleading title of 'Anarchical Fallacies', for inclusion in the Bowring edition of Bentham's *Works* published in 1838–43.[14] An authoritative text, with Bentham's own title, was finally published in *The Collected Works of Jeremy Bentham* in 2002.[15] During Bentham's lifetime, the influence of 'Nonsense upon Stilts', like many of Bentham's political writings, was at least in his own country, negligible.[16] By 1795 when the essay was composed, the famous Burke-Paine controversy had petered out, with the conservative opponents of the rights of man and the associated doctrine of popular sovereignty winning their case both politically and intellectually.[17] Writers such as Edmund Burke, William Paley, William Cusac Smith, Edward Tatham,

13 See Bentham, *Tactique des assemblées législatives, suivie d'un traité des sophismes politiques*, ed. Ét. Dumont, 2 vols. (Geneva: J.J. Paschoud), ii. 269–392.

14 See 'Anarchical Fallacies', Bowring, ii. 489–534.

15 Bentham, 'Nonsense upon Stilts', in *Rights, Representation, and Reform: Nonsense upon Stilts and Other Writings on the French Revolution*, ed. P. Schofield, C. Pease-Watkin, and C. Blamires (Oxford: Clarendon Press, 2002 (*CW*)), 317–401. For full details of the history of the text, see the Editorial Introduction, ibid., xlv–liii.

16 Bentham had originally welcomed the French Revolution, seeing it as an opportunity to further his legislative schemes by putting himself forward as an unofficial adviser to the French political classes. From late 1792, however, in step with British opinion generally, he renounced the Revolution, and entered a phase of political conservatism. Following the effective rejection of the panopticon prison scheme by the government in 1803, he gradually came to recognize that the whole British establishment was infected by sinister interest, and in 1809 began to write in favour of radical parliamentary reform. By the time he began work on his constitutional code in 1822, he had become a republican. See J.H. Burns, 'Bentham and the French Revolution', *Transactions of the Royal Historical Society*, 16 (1966), 95–114; J.R. Dinwiddy, 'Bentham's Transition to Political Radicalism', *Journal of the History of Ideas*, 36 (1975), 683–700; P. Schofield, *Utility and Democracy: The Political Thought of Jeremy Bentham* (Oxford University Press, 2006), 78–170; and P. Schofield, 'Jeremy Bentham and the British Intellectual Response to the French Revolution', *Journal of Bentham Studies*, 13 (2011).

17 For a survey of the debate that raged in the wake of the French Revolution, see H.T. Dickinson, *Liberty and Property: Political Ideology in Eighteenth-Century Britain* (London: Methuen, 1977), 232–318.

Richard Hey, and Francis Plowden, had launched coherent attacks on rights-of-man doctrine from differing standpoints within the major traditions of eighteenth-century British political thought.[18] Had Bentham's essay been published in 1795, it would, perhaps, have constituted a major contribution to the conservative case – but while, as I have noted, Bentham's essay had no influence at the time it was written, it has had an enduring interest for moral, political, and legal philosophers.[19]

I outline Bentham's attack on the doctrine of natural rights as presented in 'Nonsense upon Stilts', then look at the way in which modern rights theorists, and in particular John Rawls, have responded to Bentham's critique of natural (and hence human) rights, and in turn offered their own critique of Bentham's utilitarianism. I will then suggest how Bentham might be defended against these criticisms. Of particular importance in this respect will be Bentham's account of the democratic process and his notion of security. But before turning to 'Nonsense upon Stilts' itself, I sketch briefly the theory of natural rights against which Bentham was directing his criticisms. In this respect, Thomas Paine's *Rights of Man* of 1791 offers an appropriate paradigm.[20]

Paine's *Rights of Man*

Paine began his account of natural rights by stipulating what he termed 'the unity of man' – the fact that man partook of a common nature.

[18] T.P. Schofield, 'Conservative Political Thought in Britain in response to the French Revolution', *Historical Journal*, 29 (1986), 601–22.

[19] See, for instance, W.L. Twining, 'The Contemporary Significance of Bentham's Anarchical Fallacies', *Archiv fur Rechts – und Sozial philosophie*, 61 (1975), 325–56; M.T. Delgano, 'The Contemporary Significance of Bentham's Anarchical Fallacies: A Reply to William Twining', *Archiv für Rechts – und Sozial philosophie*, 61 (1975), 357–66; R. Harrison, *Bentham* (London: Routledge and Kegan Paul), 1983, 77–105; H.L.A. Hart, 'Natural Rights: Bentham and John Stuart Mill', in Hart, *Essays on Bentham: Studies in Jurisprudence and Political Theory* (Oxford: Clarendon Press, 1983), 79–104; J. Waldron (ed.), *Nonsense upon Stilts: Bentham, Burke and Marx on the Rights of Man* (London: Methuen, 1987); G.J. Postema, 'In Defence of "French Nonsense": Fundamental Rights in Constitutional Jurisprudence', in *Enlightenment, Rights and Revolution: Essays in Legal and Social Philosophy*, eds. N. MacCormick and Z. Bankowsi (Aberdeen University Press, 1989), 107–33; P.J. Kelly, 'Constitutional Reform vs Political Revolution: Jeremy Bentham's Critique of Natural Rights', *Philosophische Schriften: Naturrecht und Politik*, 8 (1993), 49–67; N. Lacey, 'Bentham as Proto-Feminist? or An Ahistorical Fantasy on "Anarchical Fallacies"', *Current Legal Problems*, 51 (1998), 441–66; H.A. Bedau, '"Anarchical Fallacies": Bentham's Attack on Human Rights', *Human Rights Quarterly*, 22 (2000), 261–79; and P. Schofield, 'Jeremy Bentham's "Nonsense upon Stilts"', *Utilitas*, 15 (2003), 1–26.

[20] T. Paine, *Rights of Man: Being an Answer to Mr. Burke's Attack on the French Revolution* (London: J.S. Jordan, 1791).

When man was created by God, there were no artificial distinctions: 'Man was his high and only title, and a higher cannot be given him.' Each man was born equal and with equal natural rights. This principle remained true throughout all time, for human nature did not, and indeed could not, change. Natural rights were the origin of civil rights, and just as men remained equal in natural rights, so they ought to remain equal in civil rights. According to Paine, then, a man possessed natural rights just because he existed. What was the content of these natural rights? They consisted of intellectual rights and rights of acting in any way not injurious to the natural rights of others. Civil rights were those rights that a man possessed because he was a member of society – civil rights had their basis in natural rights pre-existing in the individual, but which the individual was incapable of securing through his own, unaided effort. Upon entering society, a man retained the natural rights that he was capable of exercising unassisted, and among these were all the intellectual rights. The natural rights not retained were those he could not exercise unassisted. For instance, a man had a natural right to judge in his own cause, and so far as the intellectual right was concerned, he never surrendered it. But the right of judgment was of no use without the power to redress. Man, therefore, relinquished the right of judgment to society, and looked to the power of society for redress. Society gave nothing to man which he did not already possess: each man was a 'proprietor' in the 'common stock of society', and he 'draws on the capital as a matter of right'. In short, man entered society to secure his natural rights, and its benefits belonged equally to each man.

According to Paine, a state of society meant a state where there was government. A state of nature, where there existed no government and each individual was sovereign, had to be given up, and the transition made into a state of society. This transition was achieved legitimately when there was a social contract, entered into by each individual acting in his own sovereign right. It was done illegitimately when achieved through superstition and conquest. A social contract was 'the only mode in which governments have a right to arise, and the only principle on which they have a right to exist'; such a government originated 'out' of the people, and not 'over' them, as did every other government that did not originate in this way. Under such a legitimate government, government was the product of a constitution, which was the product of the social contract: 'A constitution is a thing *antecedent* to a government, and a government is only the creature of a constitution. The constitution of a country is not the act of its government, but of the people constituting a government.'

The constitution laid down the way in which the government was organized, that is the principles on which it was to act and by which it was bound. The government was governed by the constitution. Governments, therefore, were either legitimate or illegitimate depending on their origin. Government was not the property of any one man or group of men, as the defenders of monarchy and aristocracy claimed, but of the whole community. The right of sovereignty belonged to the nation, which had at all times an inherent indefeasible right to abolish any form of government it found unsuitable, and establish one which accorded with its interest, disposition, and happiness.[21]

Article 2 of the French Declaration of Rights

Paine's doctrine was, in effect, an elaboration of the second article of the French Declaration of Rights: 'The final end of every political institution is the preservation of the natural and imprescriptible rights of man. These rights are those of liberty, property, security and resistance to oppression.' There were, according to Bentham, three important propositions implied by the first sentence – propositions that had been drawn out and elaborated, as we have seen, by Paine. (1) That natural rights existed prior to the establishment of government. A distinction was thereby drawn between natural rights and legal rights. Legal rights were acknowledged to be the product of government, and consequently came into existence only after the establishment of government. (2) That natural rights could not be abrogated by government – in other words, government acted wrongly insofar as it infringed any natural right. (3) That governments were founded upon an original contract, entered into by all the members of the community; a government with any other origin was illegitimate and it was, therefore, a duty to resist and attempt to overthrow it. Bentham's critique of natural rights can be seen in terms of a response to these three propositions.

(1) *That natural rights existed prior to government.* Bentham's response was that there were no such things as natural rights. He granted that it was possible to conceive of a state of nature where men lived without government, and, therefore, without laws – but in such a state there were no rights. In such a state, might was right – the stronger, more cunning, and more skilful would be able to get what they wanted at the expense of the weaker, less cunning, and less skilful. The Hobbesian view of the state

[21] See ibid., 43–54, 152–8.

of nature was brought forward time and again by opponents of natural-rights theory during the 1790s – the reality of the state of nature was not noble, but brutal. To believe otherwise was wishful thinking, as Bentham acidly remarked:

> In proportion to the want of happiness resulting from the want of rights, a reason exists for wishing that there were such things as rights. But reasons for wishing there were such things as rights, are not rights; – a reason for wishing that a certain right were established, is not that right – want is not supply – hunger is not bread.

Bentham was emphasizing the point that 'right is the child of law' – there was no right without a correspondent duty, and there could be no duty without a sanction, and no sanction without an authority to enforce it.

Bentham's view that natural rights simply did not exist, and that to talk about natural rights was to talk nonsense, was grounded on his ontology, which was characterized by his theory of real and fictitious entities. The name of a real entity represented an object existing in the physical world, and which was, therefore, capable of being perceived by the senses. The name of a fictitious entity did not represent an object to which it was intended to ascribe physical existence, but rather one which was spoken about as though it existed. An apple or a table, for instance, was a real entity, whereas a property of the apple or the table, such as sweetness, hardness, or colour, was a fictitious entity. It was possible, as it were, to strip away all the perceivable properties of a real entity, until all that was left was substance or matter. A fictitious entity did not have perceivable properties. Substantive nouns such as 'right', 'power', and 'obligation', represented fictitious entities – no one ever had or ever would perceive a 'right' or any property of a 'right'. A sentence containing a fictitious entity made sense if it could be translated into a sentence containing only real entities, in other words into a sentence containing, for instance, identifiable actors and the objects on which they acted. Bentham termed this technique of exposition 'paraphrasis'. It made sense to talk about legal rights, given that such rights existed in virtue of permissions or duties decreed and enforced by a legislator.[22] In the case of natural rights, there was no legislator, unless God was given that role. The problem in that case, according to Bentham, was that no human being could have

[22] For Bentham's exposition of the terms 'right' and 'duty', demonstrating his technique of paraphrasis, see 'Fragment', in *Comment/Fragment* (*CW*), 494–5n. For a brief account of Bentham's theory of real and fictitious entities, and its place in his ontology and epistemology, see P. Schofield, *Bentham: A Guide for the Perplexed* (London: Continuum, 2009), 50–3.

any knowledge whatever of the supernatural, and hence no knowledge of God and of his decrees. All knowledge was derived from sense perception, and the supernatural concerned those things that were supposed to exist outside or beyond sense perception. The supernatural, therefore, was a nonsensical basis for morals and legislation.[23]

(2) *That governments could not abrogate natural rights.* Bentham objected to the notion that governments could not abrogate natural rights on two grounds: first, such a view would encourage unjustifiable insurrection; and second, it violated the 'omnicompetence' of the legislature. First, Bentham noted that the object of a declaration of imprescriptible rights seemed to be to excite a spirit of resistance to all laws and against all governments. This was the creed of anarchy – seeing a law of which he did not approve, the anarchist denied its validity, and called on everyone else to resist it. This was in contrast to 'the rational censor' who, when faced with a law of which he disapproved, proposed its repeal to the legislator.[24] Bentham pointed to a difference between the logic of his own approach and that of the proponents of natural rights. The latter began with the general and proceeded to the particular, whereas Bentham began with the particular and proceeded to the general, in other words from an empirical investigation of what laws had been enacted to a statement of the general propositions, if any, that could be constructed from them. A general proposition was true because all the particular propositions under it were true; therefore, we should satisfy ourselves of the truth of the general by means of the particular. In contrast, the Declaration of Rights was a series of general propositions in the form of fundamental laws, from which its proponents attempted to draw the particular laws that they wanted to exist. The proponents of the rights of man, then, compared the particular laws enacted by a legislature with their own list of fundamental laws, and if the laws failed to accord with the list, they declared them not to be laws; 'the rational censor', on the other hand, constructed the fundamental laws as general propositions concerning the particular laws that he found had been enacted.

Second, Bentham argued that a legislature needed to have the power to respond to changing circumstances, for it could never be assumed that any particular law would always be in the universal interest. For a person

[23] See Waldron, *Nonsense upon Stilts*, 35–6; P. Schofield, *Jeremy Bentham: Prophet of Secularism* (London: South Place Ethical Society, 2012).

[24] This echoes what Bentham termed 'the motto of a good citizen', namely '*To obey punctually; to censure freely*': see 'Fragment', in *Comment/Fragment* (*CW*), 399.

to establish a set of imprescriptible laws at a particular juncture in history amounted to a claim that he was superior in wisdom to the whole of posterity, and betrayed a desire to rule unto eternity. Bentham argued that the legislature of any given time had to be able to provide for the needs of that time – legislation enacted by previous lawgivers was valid only because it was the will of the present legislature that it remained so – imprescriptible rights were a usurpation of that legislature's right to legislate.[25] Bentham brilliantly turned on its head Paine's argument against Burke that each generation must be free to act for itself – in other words, not be shackled forever to a government of monarch and aristocracy.[26] Paine's endorsement of natural rights simply contradicted this freedom. The proper question, according to Bentham, was not whether a law did or did not infringe a list of natural rights, but whether it promoted the general happiness.[27] Hence, to talk of 'natural rights' was 'simple nonsense', while to talk of 'natural and imprescriptible rights' – to say that something that did not exist could not be taken away – was nonsense added to nonsense: it was 'rhetorical nonsense, nonsense upon stilts'.[28]

(3) *That governments were founded on an original contract.* Bentham argued that the claim that governments originated in contract was a pure fiction – a falsehood. In fact, contracts, like rights, derived their binding force from governments, not governments from contracts. Governments had in general been gradually established by habit, after having been formed by force. What mattered was not how governments were formed, but only how far they were conducive to happiness.[29]

The second sentence of Article 2 of the French Declaration of Rights listed the 'natural and imprescriptible rights of man' as liberty, property, security, and resistance to oppression. According to Bentham, there could

[25] For a detailed discussion of this point, see M. Schwartzberg, 'Jeremy Bentham on Fallibility and Infallibility', *Journal of the History of Ideas*, 68 (2007), 563–85.

[26] See Schofield, *Utility and Democracy*, 103 and n.

[27] See 'Observations on the Draughts of Declarations-of-Rights presented to the Committee of the Constitution of the National Assembly of France', in Bentham, *Rights, Representation, and Reform* (*CW*), 177–92, at 184–9. This essay was written in the summer of 1789, but anticipates some of the arguments put forward in 'Nonsense upon Stilts'.

[28] *Rights, Representation, and Reform* (*CW*), 330.

[29] See ibid., 331–2. Following David Hume, Bentham had attacked the fiction of the original contract in his first major published work, the anonymous *A Fragment on Government: Being an Examination of What Is delivered, on the Subject of Government in General, in the Introduction to Sir William Blackstone's Commentaries* (London: T. Payne, 1776). His point was that a contract of government, like a promise, should only be kept if it was conducive to utility to do so: see Bentham, 'Fragment', in *Comment/Fragment* (*CW*), 439–48.

be no right to liberty because rights were created at the expense of liberty. Liberty could result from the establishment of rights, but that was because the restrictions imposed on all, through the threat and eventual application of coercion, preventing each one from interfering with everyone else in relation to the performance or non-performance of certain actions, created in each a greater liberty than the liberty they lost from the imposition of the restrictions: an individual gained more liberty from a right to walk down the street without fear of interference than he or she lost from being prohibited from interfering with others performing the same activity. The same was true of property – property was created by laws which took away the liberty of everyone else to use the article in question except the party to whom the law had given the title. The Declaration's right to security, Bentham surmised, referred to the security of the person – but by such a right the whole penal law, which appointed punishment, for instance, or laws which conscripted men for military service, would be rendered null and void. The addition to the list of a right of resistance to oppression was gratuitous. Oppression was the misapplication of power to the prejudice of an individual, but the three preceding rights to liberty, property, and security made provision against all possible sorts of oppression – there was no form of oppression that was not an infringement of the right to liberty, property, or security. Though the right of resistance amounted in substance to nothing more than the other three, Bentham suggested that its purpose was different:

> To prevent the mischief in question, the endeavour of the three former clauses is to tie the hand of the legislator and his subordinates by the fear of nullity, and the remote apprehension of general resistance and insurrection: the aim of this fourth clause is to raise the hand of the individual concerned to prevent the apprehended infraction of his rights at the moment when he looks upon it as about to take place.

In other words, when it suited a man's caprice to resist the government, it told him that he was entitled to act accordingly.[30] The rights to which the members of the community were entitled were those that were conducive to the general interest:

> the exercise of the rights allowed to and conferred upon each individual ought to have no other bounds set to it by the law than those which are necessary to enable it to maintain every other individual in the possession

30 See *Rights, Representation, and Reform* (*CW*), 332–7; and compare the discussion of the principle of sympathy and antipathy in *IPML* (*CW*), 21–33.

> and exercise of such rights as the regard due to the interests or greatest possible happiness of the whole community taken together admitt of his being allowed.[31]

Contemporary Anti-Utilitarianism

Bentham has, in turn, come in for criticism from modern rights theorists, who have argued that human rights should take precedence over the good of the community as a whole – in Dworkin's words, that rights should be 'trumps'. This is, in effect, a return to Paine's view that government exists to protect natural rights, though the basis of this approach tends now to be some form of intuitionism rather than natural law. The great advantage of recognizing and respecting human rights, it is claimed, is that, within certain essential areas of life, the individual is guaranteed freedom from interference, and may lay claim to certain positive services, from other individuals, groups of individuals, and, most importantly perhaps, the state. On this view, Bentham's utilitarian doctrine pays insufficient regard to the individual. In the calculus of utility, the individual is not important for his or her own sake, but only as a repository of pains and pleasures. When the utility (the balance of pleasure over pain) of any action which affects the community is being worked out, the significant factor is the sum total of pains and pleasures, and not the pains and pleasures of any particular individual. This may bring about a state of affairs in which each individual in a majority receives a very small increase in pleasure, but at the cost of each individual in a minority suffering some great pain – for instance, an innocent individual might be tortured and executed if the blood lust of a group of people out for revenge was thereby satisfied. Rights theorists might concede that a utilitarian system could be constructed in such a way that such a consequence could be averted, but they would still argue that even to make a calculation of this sort is morally reprehensible. Generally speaking, rights theorists give an absolute – or, if not an absolute, a special – priority to human rights which they see as protecting the integrity or dignity of the individual in areas vital to his or her well-being. They will accept the value of utility calculations in certain areas of social life, for instance in the determination of economic policy, once a framework of human rights has been established, but a utility calculation is not used to determine what those rights should be.

[31] *Rights, Representation, and Reform* (*CW*), 340.

In a political context, the issue between utilitarians and rights theorists is joined on the question of the power afforded to a legislature in a democratic state. Rights theorists argue that human rights should operate as constraints upon the actions of a democratically elected legislature – for instance, any legislation which violates human rights, at least those regarded as foundational, should be held to be void by a judicatory appointed for the purpose of deciding such cases. Rights theorists accept that on most issues (in Dworkin's terminology, those concerned with 'policy' as opposed to those concerned with 'principle') democratic procedure offers an appropriate method for resolving conflicts, but there are certain areas of social life which should be placed outside the scope of majoritarian decision making. In contrast, the Benthamite utilitarian who accepts democratic procedure (modern utilitarianism is usually associated with democratic political theory, though the connection is not a necessary one),[32] will argue that rights are valid only insofar as they contribute to happiness, and whether they do so or not is a decision to be left to the legislature (the distinction between 'policy' and 'principle' disappears). In other words, no right is free from the possibility of interference or abrogation from the legislature provided that such an action, according to the best estimate that can be made, will increase utility.[33]

These criticisms of utilitarianism are particularly associated with John Rawls's *A Theory of Justice*. Rawls does not confine his attack to utilitarianism, nor does he conflate all strands in utilitarian thought, but is careful to distinguish between the 'classical utilitarianism' (sometimes termed 'aggregate utilitarianism') that he correctly attributes to Bentham, and more particularly to Henry Sidgwick,[34] and the 'principle of average utility'. The distinction is broadly between a principle that calls for the maximization of the total amount of pleasure in the community, and one that calls for the maximization of the number of individuals in the community who enjoy a given amount of pleasure, that given level itself to be maximized. My concern here is with Rawls's comments on classical utilitarianism. As a teleological doctrine, says Rawls, utilitarianism defines the right in terms of the good: in other words, it stipulates the good (the satisfaction of rational desire), and then proposes that the right consists in maximizing whatever has been stipulated to be good: 'The appropriate terms of social cooperation are settled by whatever in the circumstances

32 See R. Harrison, *Democracy* (London: Routledge, 1993), 89–112.

33 See Waldron, *Nonsense upon Stilts*, 202–3.

34 Rawls, *Theory of Justice*, 32.

will achieve the greatest sum of satisfaction of the rational desires of individuals.' The way in which the sum of satisfaction is distributed amongst individuals does not matter – only that the distribution in question yields the maximum fulfilment.

> Thus there is no reason in principle why the greater gains of some should not compensate for the lesser losses of others; or more importantly, why the violation of the liberty of a few might not be made right by the greater good shared by many.

According to Rawls, an important feature of the utilitarian approach is that, in working out the balance of satisfactions, a moral idea with its basis in the desires of the individual is extended to the whole of society – all persons are conflated into one, the community personified. Just as an individual has a motive to act when he or she calculates that the action in question will produce a preponderance of pleasure over pain for himself or herself, so the community will act when it calculates that the action in question will produce a similar preponderance. This gives rise to the notion of the 'impartial sympathetic spectator' – a being who is said to sympathize with all the individuals in the community in calculating the likely effect on them in the aggregate of any particular action – in effect an all-knowing legislator. The problem is that certain individuals may suffer enormously, providing that some vastly greater number make what might be an almost intangible (though it does need to be tangible) gain. Paradoxically, in what appears to be an individualist creed, the individual is lost sight of at the critical moment – the utilitarian, therefore, refuses to take seriously any distinction between persons.[35]

In developing his conception of 'justice as fairness', Rawls aims to distinguish between the claims of liberty and right on the one hand, and the desirability of increasing aggregate social welfare on the other, and then to assign priority to the former. Each member of the community should possess an inviolability founded on justice, which cannot be overridden by considerations of the welfare of any one – or even everyone – else. The precepts of justice are, therefore, accorded priority. The conceptual device from which the rights of the individual emerge is a version of the social contract which, instead of being in the traditional sense an agreement to enter a particular society or set up a particular form of government,

35 See ibid., 25–7. In passing, it is unclear how far Rawls himself can be said to take seriously the distinction between persons in his original position – individual personality is stripped away and only a sort of human essence remains.

sets down the substantive principles of justice that will order the basic structure of society. Rawls thereupon constructs the device of the 'original position', in which the basic principles of justice are agreed, 'once and for all', by representative, abstracted individuals. The outcome of this process is 'justice as fairness' – the assignment of certain inviolable rights and duties – and the justice of any existing political system may be determined by comparing it with the result expected from the hypothetical original position. If the members of a society accept that the institutions of their existing society meet this criterion, they can be said to have voluntarily entered into a social contract.[36]

In order finally to dismiss utilitarianism, Rawls argues that persons in the original position would not choose a utilitarian conception of justice as their starting point. A rational man – that is one who desires to protect his own interests – who has been placed behind 'the veil of ignorance', where he is unaware of the state of the actual society to which he belongs and of his personal circumstances within it, would not agree to live in a society structured in such a way that it merely maximized the sum of satisfactions without guaranteeing him certain basic rights and protecting certain basic interests. The losers would not agree to cooperate in such a society.[37] Rawls notes that in contrast to utilitarianism, justice as fairness is deontological in the sense that it does not interpret the right as that which maximizes the good; the persons in the original position, Rawls claims, would choose a principle of equal liberty and restrict social and economic equalities to those in everyone's interests, and there is no reason to think that in such a society the good would be maximized. There is a further important contrast. To Bentham, all pleasure is good, but justice as fairness regards certain pleasures as wrong: limits are placed on which satisfactions have value: 'in justice as fairness the concept of right is prior to that of good' – thus any desire that requires the violation of justice has no value.[38]

Bentham's three major criticisms of natural rights may then be answered in the following way. (1) *Natural rights do not exist prior to government.* Rights do in a sense exist prior to government – they are founded on a conception of justice, and, therefore, have a moral validity even if they do not have a legal existence. (2) *To speak of natural rights that cannot be abrogated is to speak nonsense.* Acceptance of the claim that

[36] See ibid., 11–13.
[37] See ibid., 118–50.
[38] See ibid., 27–33.

certain rights are imprescriptible, and, therefore, beyond the scope of government interference, far from being a danger to civil society, is necessary to obviate a much greater danger – the oppression of the individual by the state, or the oppression of a minority by a majority. (3) *Government is not founded on an original contract.* The historical truth of the social contract is irrelevant; its importance is as a conceptual device that helps determine which conception of justice and what sorts of rights should be established.

A Defence of Bentham's Critique of Natural Rights

Can Bentham be defended from the charge that his theory offers insufficient protection to the individual against oppression on the part of the state, or to a minority against oppression on the part of a majority? Does Bentham have a response to Rawls? In Rawls's *Theory of Justice*, the starting point for his criticism of classical utilitarianism is the role of the 'impartial sympathetic spectator' in working out the felicific calculus, with the result that the distinction between persons is lost. On a cursory view, Bentham's legislator, deciding on policy by aggregating pains and pleasures, appears to fit the model of the impartial spectator. However, Bentham's theory of representative democracy shows that such a characterization is inaccurate. Axiomatic to Bentham's political thought was the view that human beings were motivated predominantly by self-interest, which, when opposed to the interest of the community as a whole, became a sinister interest. The point of political arrangements was to ensure that the gratification of the particular and sinister part of the interest of each individual was frustrated, but that that part of his or her interest that accorded with the general or universal interest was promoted. Government was to be structured in such a way that the universal interest was promoted, and not any person's particular and sinister interest. The administrative machinery of government was to be made subordinate to – that is subject to the will of – the legislature, and the legislature subordinate to the people in the character of electors. The legislature was to be elected by universal suffrage, which secured the promotion of the universal interest in the following way. The state would be organized into single-member constituencies, and elections would be held annually. Each constituent would vote for the candidate who promised to sacrifice the interests of all other persons to his; each candidate, rather than not be elected, would promise to perform this 'sinister sacrifice'. This was the case with every constituent in each electoral district. With the exception, however, of certain common points, the interest of each of these constituents was in a state of opposition to that of every other. The strategy adopted by the candidate, in order to obtain the votes of all, was to promote the interests of each on those points where it was unopposed by any other interest. The candidate most successful in this operation would be elected.

Meanwhile, the interest of the inhabitants of a certain district might vary on a certain matter with the interest of those of all the other districts, and the deputy of that district would bring forward a measure promoting that interest in the representative assembly. No harm would result because the deputies from all the other districts would vote against the measure, and the endeavour to promote the particular interest would fail. Arrangements favourable to the inhabitants of all districts, or at least to a majority of them, would be adopted. In this way, that part of the happiness of each individual which did not conflict with the happiness of any other would be secured to him.[39]

Legislation, then, was not the product of some all-knowing, all-seeing, and all-feeling mind, but a compromise to which each individual in the community would have a right to contribute. Indeed, one of the points made by Bentham was that the interests of the members of the community were best known by the members themselves, and not by some impartial spectator: 'The will of the people is determined by the interest of the people; so far as that interest is understood by them. Its not being understood is not to be presumed: for if not by them, by who else is it understood?'[40] Bentham did not lose sight of the individual at the critical moment, if by that is meant the moment when political decisions are taken. Rather, he recognized that each individual had his or her own distinctive interest – his or her own distinctive pains and pleasures – which were likely to be in conflict, and that some decision procedure that gave appropriate weight to those interests needed to be devised.

It may, nevertheless, be argued that the distinction between individuals does not ultimately matter in Bentham's thought, because each individual is viewed only as a receptacle of pains and pleasures, and it is the aggregate sum of pains and pleasures, and nothing else, that is morally valuable.[41] There is no doubt that Bentham would, and indeed did, advocate policies

[39] Bentham, *First Principles Preparatory to Constitutional Code*, ed. P. Schofield (Oxford: Clarendon Press, 1989 (*CW*)), 135–6.

[40] UC xliv. 17.

[41] Bentham did in fact refer to individuals as 'receptacles' for pleasures and pains: see Philip Schofield, 'Jeremy Bentham on Taste, Sex, and Religion', Chapter 5 in this volume, 102.

that would have been detrimental to certain minorities in society, such as monarchs, aristocrats, 'fee-fed' lawyers, and rich clergymen. But what could Bentham's utilitarianism offer to the unprivileged or underprivileged individual or minority who were subject to, or were threatened with, oppression in its various guises?[42] In the first place, consider one of Bentham's 'axioms of . . . *mental pathology*': 'The suffering, of a person hurt in gratification of enmity, is greater than the gratification produced by the same cause.'[43] Bentham's axiom weighted the scale against the imposition of suffering on some in order to benefit others. In the next place, Bentham identified four subordinate ends of the principle of utility: subsistence, abundance, security, and equality. It was in the promotion of the subordinate ends that the legislator created legal rights for the protection of certain vital interests of the individual.[44] Each individual had a basic right to subsistence, while abundance – the creation of wealth – was valuable both for its own sake and as a security for subsistence. Material possessions were instruments of felicity – means of pleasure – and so they were to be increased to the greatest extent possible. Insofar as an inequality of wealth guaranteed subsistence to all, such an inequality would be justifiable. But were such an inequality not necessary to subsistence – and leaving out of the account security for existing expectations – then equality became a significant, and perhaps predominant, factor in promoting utility. The rationale here was Bentham's notion of diminishing marginal utility:

> To him who has lived all his life upon £100 a year and no more, £150 a year is opulence: reduction to £50 a year is ruin. To him who has £10,000 a year it requires £5,000 a year to produce a sensation equal in intensity to that produced in the case of him who has but £100 a year by an accession of £50 a year.[45]

Though a proportionate increase in income might produce a proportionate increase in pleasure, it cost the community much more to increase

42 For Bentham's attitude towards sexual non-conformists, Jews, colonial peoples, slaves, and women, see L.C. Boralevi, *Bentham and the Oppressed* (Berlin: Walter de Guyter, 1984). On slavery more particularly, see F. Rosen, 'Jeremy Bentham on Slavery and the Slave Trade', in *Utilitarianism and Empire*, eds. B. Schultz and G. Varouxakis (Lanham, MD: Lexington Books, 2005), 33–56.

43 *IPML* (*CW*), 3n.

44 For detailed accounts of Bentham's notion of security, see G.J. Postema, *Bentham and the Common Law Tradition* (Oxford: Clarendon Press, 1986), 147–90, and P.J. Kelly, *Utilitarianism and Distributive Justice: Jeremy Bentham and the Civil Law* (Oxford: Clarendon Press, 1990).

45 UC clx. 31.

the pleasure of the rich man than it did that of the poor man: for the £5,000 needed to increase the pleasure of the rich man with an income of £10,000, one hundred men with an income of £100 might receive a proportionate increase. Since every man was to count for one, and no one for more than one,[46] the general utility would be increased by a factor of a hundred times in the latter case compared to the former. Here, indeed, the interests of a minority would be sacrificed to those of a majority, but it would be a more affluent and advantaged group who would suffer some sacrifice (or rather fail to make some gain) for the sake of a poorer and disadvantaged group.

The fourth subordinate end was security which, noted Bentham, concerned evil, 'and can no otherwise be understood than by reference to it: security is security against Evil'.[47] Evil might arise from the operations of nature, from the operations of 'internal adversaries' (criminals and other malefactors), or from the operations of 'external adversaries' (foreign enemies). Misdeeds could be committed by government officials or by private persons. Now, 'It is the interest of every member of the community to possess in the compleatest degree security against evil from all these several sources: against misdeeds by individuals at large and against misdeeds of functionaries'.[48] The security of some was not to be bartered away for the security of others – it was the interest of each member of the community to possess security, and by means of the democratic structure of society, security would be guaranteed to all. This, according to Bentham's analysis, would work as follows. The individual understood that the satisfaction of a certain desire of his own would be detrimental to the happiness of all other individuals, and, therefore, its satisfaction would be opposed by them – the individual did not, therefore, have the power to achieve the satisfaction of this purely selfish desire. He or she also understood that the satisfaction of the same desire in another would be harmful to himself or herself, so along with everyone else he or she opposed that person in his or her attempt to satisfy the desire. In this way, with each member of the democratic state checking and being checked by the others, certain securities were established and maintained. The

[46] See *Rationale of Judicial Evidence, Specially Applied to English Practice*, ed. J.S. Mill, 5 vols. (London: Hunt and Clarke, 1827), iv. 475 (Bk. VIII, Ch. 29) (Bowring, vi. 189–585, and vii. 1–644, at vii. 334): 'every individual in the country tells for one; no individual for more than one'.

[47] *First Principles Preparatory* (*CW*), 153.

[48] Ibid.

securities usually listed by Bentham consisted in legal protections for person, property, reputation, and condition in life.

There is, in fact, little substantive difference between the rights and duties that Rawls derives from the first of his two principles of justice and those Bentham derives from the greatest happiness principle. Rawls lists the 'basic liberties' as political liberty, liberty of conscience and freedom of thought, freedom of the person along with the right to hold personal property, and freedom from arbitrary arrest and seizure as defined by the concept of the rule of law.[49] In *Securities Against Misrule*, while calling for a system of representative democracy – equivalent to Rawls's notion of political liberty – Bentham listed, amongst others, the following securities: security against religious persecution; security against secret confinement, banishment, and homicide; security against official oppression; and security against obstruction of intellectual communication. Bentham's democratic state would provide further protection for the individual by its encouragement of an extra-legal security in order to secure the legal ones – the operation of public opinion.[50]

According to Bentham, the greatest infringement of security was likely to occur where there existed in the state an individual who was not subject to the will of all the others – a person such as a monarch. A monarch had the desire, like every other member of the community, to further his or her own interest to the detriment of the universal interest. The difference in the situation of the monarch was that, added to the desire, he had the power to satisfy his or her wants. Bentham explained in detail how 'the external instruments of felicity' – money, power, and prestige – were used by the monarch to corrupt other members of the state in order to gratify his or her desires. The desires of the monarch could not be checked, and security was lost.[51] One answer which Bentham could make to the perceived dangers of majoritarian democracy would be to say that the dangers of minority rule were much greater: the interest of the few was

49 See Rawls, *Theory of Justice*, 61.

50 See *Securities Against Misrule* (*CW*), 79–102. For the importance of publicity, and public opinion, in Bentham's thought, see F. Rosen, *Jeremy Bentham and Representative Democracy: A Study of the Constitutional Code* (Oxford: Clarendon Press, 1983), 19–40, 111–29; O. Ben-Dor, *Constitutional Limits and the Public Sphere: A Critical Study of Bentham's Constitutionalism* (Oxford: Hart, 2000), 191–233; D. Lieberman, 'Economy and Polity in Bentham's Science of Legislation', in *Economy, Polity, and Society: British Intellectual History 1750–1950*, eds. S. Collini, R. Whatmore, and B. Young (Cambridge University Press, 2000), 107–34; and Schofield, *Utility and Democracy*, 250–7.

51 See, for instance, *First Principles Preparatory* (*CW*), 152, 160–5, 183–9.

much more opposed to that of the many than the interest of the many to that of the few.[52]

Conclusion

The theory of 'justice as fairness' put forward by John Rawls, with its notions of the social contract, the priority of rights, and infallibility (the principles of justice being decided 'once and for all' in the original position), is, in its essentials, a return to Thomas Paine's theory of the rights of man, which in turn is an extended commentary on the second article of the French Declaration of Rights of 1789. Bentham's criticisms of that second article have as much purchase against Rawls's theory of human rights as they did against Paine's theory of natural rights. Bentham's utilitarianism has been criticized because it does not provide absolute or near-absolute guarantees for the individual, or for a minority of individuals, against oppression, particularly when inflicted by the state. For Bentham, there were no absolute guarantees, that is true. Bentham's utilitarianism, however, has the advantage of avoiding the claim to infallibility that is implicit in declarations of human rights. Having said that, in practice, the content of human rights, in both their theoretical and legal aspects, is far from settled. On the one hand, Bentham might argue that, if human rights are regarded as definitively established in a declaration of rights, they represent a claim to infallibility. On the other hand, if they are changed over time in response to new circumstances or fashions in legal and political theory, they do not provide a settled basis on which to build expectations. In this latter case, moreover, the supposedly imprescriptible rights are seen to be anything but imprescriptible.

It should be remembered that liberal individualism was, from a historical point of view, as much the product of classical utilitarianism as any other political and moral theory – a reference to John Stuart Mill's *On Liberty* should be enough to remind us of that.[53] Bentham's utilitarianism, like theories of human rights, is a form of individualism. It recognizes that actual individuals benefit enormously from living in social groups, where they have interests that in some respects overlap, but in others conflict,

52 For a more extensive discussion see F. Rosen, 'Majorities and Minorities: A Classical Utilitarian View', in *Majorities and Minorities: Nomos 32*, eds. J.W. Chapman and A. Wertheimer (New York University Press, 1990), 24–43.

53 J.S. Mill, 'On Liberty', in *Essays on Politics and Society*, ed. J.M. Robson (Toronto and London: University of Toronto Press/Routledge & Kegan Paul, 1977) (*The Collected Works of John Stuart Mill*, vol. xviii), 213–310.

and that there needs to be some rational method of settling the disputes that arise in consequence. Bentham had an enormously strong, perhaps an overriding, commitment to freedom (which meant not being subject to restraint or constraint), because freedom constituted a vital element of the individual's happiness: when people were free, they were more likely to be happy. In Bentham's view, the most important contribution to the creation of such freedom was the establishment of the rule of law, and with it the introduction of legal rights providing security for each individual's basic needs. Bentham regarded the rule of law, and through it security, as the basis for a civilized and hence a happy life – and the desirability of a happy life was something on which, so Bentham believed, we would all agree. Bentham's commitment to the rule of law is a theme explored elsewhere in the present volume.[54]

[54] See Gerald Postema, 'The Soul of Justice: Bentham on Publicity, Law, and the Rule of Law', Chapter 3 in this volume.

BIBLIOGRAPHY

I. Manuscript Collections

Grote Papers, British Library Additional Manuscripts 29,806–9.

University College London collection of Bentham manuscripts (UC), boxes i–clxxvi.

II. Works by Jeremy Bentham

1776 *A Fragment on Government; Being an Examination of What Is delivered, on the Subject of Government in General, in the Introduction to Sir William Blackstone's Commentaries* (London: T. Payne).

[1790] 'Draught of a New Plan for the organisation of the Judicial Establishment in France: proposed as a Succedaneum to the Draught presented, for the same purpose, by the Committee of Constitution, to the National Assembly, December 21st, 1789'.

1811 *Théorie des peines et des récompenses*, 2 vols. ed. É. Dumont (London: Vogel and Schulze).

1816 *Tactique des assemblées législatives, suivie d'un traité des sophismes politiques*, ed. É. Dumont, 2 vols. (Geneva: J.J. Paschoud).

1823 'Leading Principles of a Constitutional Code, for any state', *The Pamphleteer* 22 (44), [476]–86.

1823 *Not Paul, but Jesus* (London: John Hunt).

1825 *The Rationale of Reward*, ed. R. Smith (London: John and H.L. Hunt).

1827 *Rationale of Judicial Evidence, Specially Applied to English Practice*, ed. J.S. Mill, 5 vols. (London: Hunt and Clarke).

1843 *The Works of Jeremy Bentham*, published under the Superintendence of his Executor, John Bowring, 11 vols. (Edinburgh: William Tait).

1968 *The Correspondence of Jeremy Bentham, Vol. 1, 1752–1776*, ed. T.L.S. Sprigge (London: Athlone (*CW*)).

1968 *The Correspondence of Jeremy Bentham, Vol. 2, 1777–1780*, ed. T.L.S. Sprigge (London: Athlone (*CW*)).

1970/1996 *An Introduction to the Principles of Morals and Legislation*, ed. J.H. Burns and H.L.A. Hart (London: Athlone (*CW*))/republished with a new introduction by F. Rosen (Oxford: Clarendon Press (*CW*)).

1970 *Of Laws in General*, ed. H.L.A. Hart (London: Athlone (*CW*)).

1977 *A Comment on the Commentaries and a Fragment on Government*, ed. J.H. Burns and H.L.A. Hart (London: Athlone (*CW*)).

1983 Chrestomathia, ed. M.J. Smith and W.H. Burston (Oxford: Clarendon Press (*CW*)).

1983 *Constitutional Code, Volume* I, ed. F. Rosen and J.H. Burns (Oxford: Clarendon Press (*CW*)).

1983 Deontology, *A Table of the Springs of Action, and Article on Utilitarianism*, ed. A. Goldworth (Oxford: Clarendon Press (*CW*)).

1989 *First Principles Preparatory to Constitutional Code*, ed. Philip Schofield (Oxford: Clarendon Press (*CW*)).

1990 *Securities Against Misrule, and Other Constitutional Writings for Tripoli and Greece*, ed. P. Schofield (Oxford: Clarendon Press (*CW*)).

1993 *Official Aptitude Maximized, Expense Minimized*, ed. P. Schofield (Oxford: Clarendon Press (*CW*)).

1997 *De l'ontologie, et autres textes sur les fictions*, ed. P. Schofield, trans. J.-P. Cléro and C. Laval (Paris, Seuil).

1998 *Legislator of the World: Writings on Codification, Law, and Education*, ed. P. Schofield and J. Harris (Oxford: Clarendon Press (*CW*)).

1999 *Political Tactics*, ed. M. James, C. Blamires and C. Pease-Watkin (Oxford: Clarendon Press (*CW*)).

2002 *Rights, Representation, and Reform: Nonsense upon Stilts and Other Writings on the French Revolution*, ed. P. Schofield, C. Pease-Watkin and C. Blamires (Oxford: Clarendon Press (*CW*)).

2010 *Of the Limits of the Penal Branch of Jurisprudence*, ed. P. Schofield (Oxford: Clarendon Press (*CW*)).

2012 *Of the Liberty of the Press, and Public Discussion, and Other Legal and Political Writings for Spain and Portugal*, ed. C. Pease-Watkin and P. Schofield (Oxford: Clarendon Press (*CW*)).

[2013] 'Not Paul, But Jesus Vol. III', ed. P. Schofield, M. Quinn and C. Pease-Watkin, www.ucl.ac.uk/Bentham-Project/publications/npbj/npbj.html (Bentham Project).

2014 *Of Sexual Irregularities, and Other Writings on Sexual Morality*, ed. P. Schofield, C. Pease-Watkin and M. Quinn (Oxford: Clarendon Press (*CW*)).

III. Works by Other Authors

Agrast, M., Botero, J., Ponce, A. and Pratt, C. 2013 *World Justice Project Rule of Law Index 2012–2013* (Washington, DC: World Justice Project).

Androff, Jr., D.K. 2012 'Can Civil Society Reclaim Truth? Results from a Community-Based Truth and Reconciliation Commission', *International Journal of Transitional Justice*, 6, 296–317.

Annan, K. 2004 *The Rule of Law and Transitional Justice in Conflict and Post-Conflict Societies – Report of the Secretary-General* (United Nations Security Council, 23 August 2004, S/2004/616).

Aquinas, T. 1966 *Summa Theologiæ: Volume 28 Law and Political Theory*, ed. T. Gilby (Cambridge: Blackfriars).

Aristotle 1946 *The Politics of Aristotle*, trans. and ed. E. Barker (Oxford: Clarendon Press).

Armitage, D. 2011 'Globalizing Jeremy Bentham', *History of Political Thought* 32, 63–82.

Austin, J. 1885 *Lectures on Jurisprudence*, 5th edn., ed. Robert Campbell, 2 vols. (London: John Murray).

Bain, A. 1882 *James Mill: A Biography* (London: Longmans, Green & Co.).

Baker, K.M. 1990 *Inventing the French Revolution: Essays on French Political Culture in the Eighteenth Century* (Cambridge University Press).

Barry, B. 2001 *Culture and Equality: An Egalitarian Critique of Multiculturalism* (Cambridge: Polity).

Beccaria, C. 1995 *On Crimes and Punishments and Other Writings*, ed. R. Bellamy (Cambridge University Press).

Bedau, H.A. 2000 '"Anarchical Fallacies": Bentham's Attack on Human Rights', *Human Rights Quarterly* 22, 261–79.

Ben-Dor, O. 2000 *Constitutional Limits and the Public Sphere: A Critical Study of Bentham's Constitutionalism* (Oxford: Hart).

Bingham, T. 2010 *The Rule of Law* (London: Penguin).

Birks, P. and McLeod, G. (trans.) 1987 *Justinian's Institutes* (London: Duckworth).

Blackstone, W. 1765–9 *Commentaries on the Laws of England*, 4 vols. (Oxford: Clarendon Press).

Boralevi, L.C. 1984 *Bentham and the Oppressed* (Berlin: Walter de Guyter).

Bracton, H. de 1968–77 *Bracton on the Laws and Customs of England*, ed. and trans. S.E. Thorne, 4 vols. (Cambridge, MA: Belnap Press).

Brissot de Warville, J.P. (ed.) 1782–5 *Bibliothèque philosophique du Législateur, du Politique, du Jurisconsulte, ou Choix des meilleurs discours, dissertations, essais, fragmens, composés sur la législation criminelle par les plus célèbres écrivains, en françois, anglois, italien, allemand, espagnol, &c. pour parvenir à la réforme des loix pénales dans tous les pays: traduits & accompagnés de notes & d'observations historiques*, 10 vols. (Berlin).

Burke, E. 1997 'A Philosophical Enquiry into the Origin of our Ideas of the Sublime and Beautiful', in *The Writings and Speeches of Edmund Burke. Volume I: The Early Writings*, ed. T.O. McLoughlin, J.T. Boulton and W.B. Todd (Oxford: Clarendon Press), 185–320.

Burns, J.H. 1966 'Bentham and the French Revolution', *Transactions of the Royal Historical Society* 16, 95–114.

——— 1973 'Bentham on Sovereignty: An Exploration', *Northern Ireland Legal Quarterly* 24, 399–416.

——— 2005 'Happiness and Utility: Jeremy Bentham's Equation', *Utilitas* 17, 46–61.

——— 2009 'Bentham, Brissot et la science du bonheur', in *Bentham et la France. Fortune et Infortunes de l'utilitarisme*, ed. E. de Champs and J.-P. Cléro (Oxford: Voltaire Foundation), 3–19.

——— 2009 'Bentham, Brissot and the Challenge of Revolution', *History of European Ideas* 35, 217–39.

Campbell, T. 1998 'The Point of Legal Positivism', *King's College Law Journal* 9, 63–88.

Cartuyvels, Y. 1996 *D'où vient le code pénal? Une approche généalogique des premiers codes pénaux au XVIIIe siècle* (Presses de l'Université de Montréal, Presses de l'Université d'Ottawa).

Catherine II, Empress of Russia 1769 *Instruction de Sa Majesté Impériale Catherine II, pour la Commission chargée de dresser le Projet d'un nouveau Code de Lois* (Petersburg: Imprimerie de l'Académie des Sciences).

Chartier, R. 1990 *The Cultural Origins of the French Revolution* (Durham: Duke University Press).

Christie, I.R. 1993 *The Benthams in Russia, 1780–1791* (Oxford: Berg).

Crompton, L. 1978 'Jeremy Bentham's Essay on Paederasty' in *Journal of Homosexuality* 3, 383–405, and 4, 91–107.

Dabhoiwala, F. 2010 'Lust and Liberty', *Past and Present* 207, 89–179.

de Champs, E. 2011 'Constitution and the Code: Jeremy Bentham on the Limits of the Constitutional Branch of Jurisprudence', *The Tocqueville Review/La Revue Tocqueville* 32, 21–42.

——— 2011 'An Introduction to Utilitarianism: Early French Translations of Bentham's Introduction to the Principles of Morals and Legislation', in *Cultural Transfers: France and Britain in the Long Eighteenth-Century*, ed. A. Thomson, S. Burrows and S. Audidière (Oxford: Voltaire Foundation), 269–83.

Delgano, M.T. 1975 'The Contemporary Significance of Bentham's Anarchical Fallacies: A Reply to William Twining', *Archiv für Rechts – und Sozial philosophie* 61, 357–66.

Dickinson, H.T. 1977 *Liberty and Property: Political Ideology in Eighteenth-Century Britain* (London: Methuen).

Dinwiddy, J.R. 1975 'Bentham's Transition to Political Radicalism', *Journal of the History of Ideas* 36, 683–700.

Draper, A.J. 2000 'Cesare Beccaria's Influence on English Discussions of Punishment', *History of European Ideas* 26, 177–99.

Dworkin, R. 1977 *Taking Rights Seriously* (London: Duckworth).

Dyzenhaus, D. 1998 *Judging the Judges, Judging Ourselves* (Oxford: Hart).

Ecenbarger, W. 2012 *Kids for Cash* (New York: The New Press).

Engelmann, S.G. (ed.) 2011 *Jeremy Bentham: Selected Writings* (New Haven & London: Yale University Press).

Engelmann, S.G. and Pitts, J. 2011 'Bentham's "Place and Time"', *The Tocqueville Review/La Revue Tocqueville* 32, 43–66.

Ferguson, A. 1995 *An Essay on the History of Civil Society*, ed. F. Oz-Salzberger (Cambridge University Press)

Finnis, J. 1980 *Natural Law and Natural Rights* (Oxford: Clarendon Press).

Frederick II, King of Prussia 1770 *Dissertation sur les raisons d'établir ou d'abroger les loix* (Utrecht).

Fuller, L. 1969 *The Morality of Law*, revised edn. (New Haven: Yale University Press).

Gagarin, M. and Woodruff, P (eds.) 1995 *Early Greek Political Thought from Homer to the Sophists* (Cambridge University Press).

Gardner, J. 2012 *Law as a Leap of Faith: Essays on Law in General* (Oxford University Press).

Goldsmith, N.M. 1998 *The Worst of Crimes: Homosexuality and the Law in Eighteenth-Century London* (Aldershot: Ashgate).

Griffin, J. 2008 *On Human Rights* (Oxford University Press).

Hamilton, A., Madison, J. and Jay, J. 2008 *The Federalist Papers* (Oxford University Press).

Hampton, J. 1994 'Democracy and the Rule of Law', in I. Shapiro (ed.) *Nomos 36: The Rule of Law* (New York University Press), 13–45.

Harris, J. 1765 *Three Treatises: The First Concerning Art: the Second Concerning Music, Painting and Poetry: the Third Concerning Happiness*, 2nd edn. (London: J. Nourse and P. Vaillant).

Harrison, R. 1983 *Bentham* (London: Routledge and Kegan Paul).

Hart, H.L.A. 1954 'Introduction', in Austin, *The Province of Jurisprudence Determined* (London: Weidenfield and Nicholson), ed. H.L.A. Hart, vii–xviii.

______ 1961/1994 *The Concept of Law* (Oxford: Clarendon Press). (2nd edn., 1994).

______ 1982 *Essays on Bentham: Studies in Jurisprudence and Political Theory* (Oxford: Clarendon Press).

______ 1983 *Essays in Jurisprudence and Philosophy* (Oxford: Clarendon Press).

______ 1985 '*Bentham.* by Ross Harrison', *Mind* 94, 153–8.

______ 1989 'Legal Theory and the Problem of Sense: Comment', in *Issues in Contemporary Legal Philosophy: The Influence of H.L.A. Hart*, ed. R. Gavison (Oxford: Clarendon Press), 35–42.

Helvétius, C.-A. 1759 *De l'Esprit: Of Essays on the Mind, and Its Several Faculties* (London).

______ 1777 *A Treatise on Man, His Intellectual Faculties and His Education*, 2 vols. (London: B. Law and G. Robinson).

Hobbes, T. 1998 *On the Citizen*, ed. R. Tuck and M. Silverthorne (Cambridge University Press).

______ 2012 *Leviathan*, 3 vols., ed. N. Malcolm (*The Clarendon Edition of the Works of Thomas Hobbes: Vols. III–V*) (Oxford: Clarendon Press).

Hooker, R. 1989 *Of the Laws of Ecclesiastical Polity*, ed. A. S. McGrade (Cambridge University Press).

Hume, D. 1983 *The History of England, from the Invasion of Julius Caesar to the Revolution in 1688*, 6 vols. (Indianapolis: Liberty Classics).

Hunton, P. 1643 *A Treatise of Monarchy* (London).

Ippolito, D 2012 'La philosophie pénale des Lumières entre utilitarisme et rétributivisme', in *Lumières 20, Penser la peine à l'âge des Lumières*, ed. L. Delia and G. Radica (Presse Universitaire Bordeaux), 21–37.

Jennings, I. 1959 *The Law and the Constitution*, 5th edn. (University of London Press).

Juvenal (Decimus Iunius Iuvenalis) 2004 *Satires, in Juvenal and Persius*, ed. and trans. S.M. Braund (Cambridge, MA: Harvard University Press), 127–511.

Kaino, M. 2008 'Bentham's Concept of Security in a Global Context: The Pannomion and the Public Opinion Tribunal as a Universal Plan', *Journal of Bentham Studies* 10.

Kant, I. 1996 *Practical Philosophy*, trans. and ed. M.J. Gregor (Cambridge University Press).

Kelly, P.J. 1990 *Utilitarianism and Distributive Justice: Jeremy Bentham and the Civil Law* (Oxford: Clarendon Press).

______ 1993 'Constitutional Reform vs Political Revolution: Jeremy Bentham's Critique of Natural Rights', *Philosophische Schriften: Naturrecht und Politik* 8, 49–67.

Kenney, C.D. 2003 'Horizontal Accountability: Concepts and Conflicts', in *Democratic Accountability in Latin America*, ed. S. Mainwaring and C. Welna (Oxford University Press), 55–76.

Kleinfeld, R. 2012 *Advancing the Rule of Law Abroad: Next Generation Reform* (Washington, DC: Carnegie Endowment for Peace).

Kotterman-van de Vosse, I. 1994 'Hayek on the Rule of Law', in *Hayek, Co-ordination and Evolution*, ed. J. Birner and R. van Zijp (New York: Routledge), 255–72.

Krüger, P (ed.) 1877/1998 *Codex Iustinianus* (Berlin: Weidmann/Goldbach: Keip).

Krygier, M. 2000 'The Rule of Law: Legality, Teleology, and Sociology', in *Re-locating the Rule of Law*, ed. G. Palombella and N. Walker (Oxford: Hart), 45–70.

______ 2011 'Four Puzzles About the Rule of Law: Why, What, Where? And Who Cares?', in *Nomos 50: Getting to the Rule of Law*, ed. J.E. Fleming (New York University Press), 64–104.

Lacey, N. 1998 'Bentham as Proto-Feminist? or An Ahistorical Fantasy on "Anarchical Fallacies"', *Current Legal Problems* 51, 441–66.

Lieberman, D. 1989 *The Province of Legislation Determined: Legal Theory in Eighteenth-century Britain* (Cambridge University Press).

______ 2000 'Economy and Polity in Bentham's Science of Legislation', in *Economy, Polity, and Society: British Intellectual History 1750–1950*, ed. S. Collini, R. Whatmore and B. Young (Cambridge University Press), 107–34.

______ 2008 'Bentham's Democracy', *Oxford Journal of Legal Studies* 28, 605–26.

______ 2011 'Bentham on Codification', in *Jeremy Bentham: Selected Writings*, ed. S. G. Engelmann, 460–77.

Lobban, M. 1991 *The Common Law and English Jurisprudence, 1760–1850* (Oxford: Clarendon Press).

Locke, J. 1988 *Two Treatises of Government*, ed. P. Laslett (Cambridge University Press).

Lolme, J.-L. De 2007 *The Constitution of England; Or, an Account of the English Government*, ed. D. Lieberman (Indianapolis: Liberty Fund).

Long, D.G. 1988 'Censorial Jurisprudence and Political Radicalism: A Reconstruction of the Early Bentham', *The Bentham Newsletter* 12, 4–23.

Luban, D. 1989 'Difference Made Legal: The Court and Dr. King', *Michigan Law Review* 87, 2152–2224.

Mack, M. 1962 *Jeremy Bentham: An Odyssey of Ideas 1748–1792* (London: Heinemann).

Maine, H.S. 1905 *Lectures on the Early History of Institutions*, 7th edn. (London: John Murray).

Malthus, T.R. 1798 *An Essay on the Principle of Population, as It Affects the Future Improvement of Society. With Remarks on the Speculations of Mr. Godwin, M. Condorcet, and Other Writers* (London: J. Johnson).

Marat, J.-P. 1782 *Plan de législation en matière criminelle*, in *Bibliothèque du Législateur*, ed. Brissot, v. 109–290.

Mill, J.S. 1969 *Essays on Ethics, Religion and Society*, ed. J.M. Robson (Toronto and London: University of Toronto Press/Routledge & Kegan Paul) (*The Collected Works of John Stuart Mill*, general editor J.M. Robson, 33 vols. (Toronto and London: University of Toronto Press/Routledge & Kegan Paul, 1963–91, vol. x)).

______ 1972 *The Later Letters of John Stuart Mill, 1849–73*, ed. F.E. Mineka and D.N. Lindley (Toronto and London: University of Toronto Press/Routledge & Kegan Paul) (*Collected Works of John Stuart Mill*, vol. xv).

______ 1974 *A System of Logic Ratiocinative and Inductive: Being a Connected View of the Principles of Evidence and the Methods of Scientific Investigation – Books IV–VI*, ed. J.M. Robson (Toronto and London: University of Toronto Press/Routledge & Kegan Paul) (*Collected Works of John Stuart Mill*, vol. viii).

______ 1977 *Essays on Politics and Society*, ed. J.M. Robson (Toronto and London: University of Toronto Press/Routledge & Kegan Paul) (*The Collected Works of John Stuart Mill*, vol. xviii).

Miller, Jr., F.D. 2010 'The Rule of Law in Ancient Greek Thought', in *The Rule of Law in Comparative Perspective*, ed. M. Sellers and T. Tomaszewski (Dordrecht: Springer), 11–18.

Montesquieu (Secondat, C.L. de) 1989 *The Spirit of Laws*, trans. and ed. A.M. Cohler, B.C. Miller, and H.S. Stone (Cambridge University Press).

Orsi, F. 2012 'Sidgwick and the Morality of Purity', *Revue d'études benthamiennes* 10.

Pacaud, E. 2011 'Sur l'une des sources de l'utilitarisme benthamien: la théorie de l'utilité de Claude-Adrien Helvétius', in *Deux siècles d'utilitarisme*, ed. M. Bozzo-Rey and E. Dardenne (Presses Universitaires de Rennes), 41–52.

Paine, T 1791 *Rights of Man: Being an Answer to Mr. Burke's Attack on the French Revolution* (London: J.S. Jordan).

Peerenboom, R. 2002 *China's Long March toward Rule of Law* (New York: Cambridge University Press).

Perry, S.R. 2001 'Hart's Methodological Positivism', in *Hart's Postscript: Essays on the Postscript to The Concept of Law*, ed. J. Coleman (Oxford University Press), 311–54.

Pettit, P. 1997 *Republicanism: A Theory of Freedom and Government* (Oxford University Press).

——— 2009 'Republican Legal Theory', in *Legal Republicanism*, ed. S. Besson and J.L. Martí (Oxford University Press), 39–59.

——— 2013 *On the People's Terms* (Cambridge University Press).

Pitts, J. 2010 '"Great and Distant Crimes": Empire in Bentham's Thought', in *Jeremy Bentham: Selected Writings*, ed. Engelmann, 478–99.

Plato 1926 *Laws*, trans R.G. Bury, 2 vols. (London: Heinemann).

Pocock, J.G.A. 1985 'Virtue, Rights and Manners. A Model for Historians of Political Thought', in Pocock, *Virtue, Commerce and History, Essays on Political Thought and History, Chiefly in the Eighteenth Century* (Cambridge University Press), 37–50.

Postema, G.J. 1979 'The Expositor, the Censor, and the Common Law', *Canadian Journal of Philosophy* 9, 643–70.

——— 1986 *Bentham and the Common Law Tradition* (Oxford: Clarendon Press).

——— 1989 'Bentham on the Public Character of Law', *Utilitas* 1, 41–61.

——— 1989 'In Defence of "French Nonsense": Fundamental Rights in Constitutional Jurisprudence', in *Enlightenment, Rights and Revolution: Essays in Legal and Social Philosophy*, ed. N. MacCormick and Z. Bankowsi (Aberdeen University Press), 107–33.

——— 1998 'Jurisprudence as Practical Philosophy', *Legal Theory* 4, 329–57.

——— 2006 'Interests, Universal and Particular: Bentham's Utilitarian Theory of Value', *Utilitas* 18, 1–25.

——— 2008 'Conformity, Custom, and Congruence: Rethinking the Efficacy of Law', in *The Legacy of H.L.A. Hart: Legal, Political, and Moral Philosophy*, ed. M. Kramer, C. Grant, B. Colburn and A. Hatzistavrou (Oxford University Press), 45–65.

——— 2010 'Law's Ethos: Reflections on the Public Practice of Illegality', *Boston University Law Review* 90, 101–22.

——— 2011 *Legal Philosophy in the Twentieth Century: The Common Law World* (Dordecht: Springer).

——— [In press] 'Fidelity in Law's Commonwealth', in *Private Law and the Rule of Law*, ed. D. Klimchuck (Oxford University Press).

Quinn, Malcolm 2012 *Utilitarianism and the Art School in Nineteenth-Century Britain* (London: Pickering and Chatto).

Quinn, Michael 2012 'L'archetypation et la recherche d'images significantes: significant et signifié dans la logique de Bentham', *Essaim* 28, 171–81.

——— 2012 'Which Comes First, Bentham's Chicken of Utility or His Egg of Truth?' *Journal of Bentham Studies* 14.

——— 2013 'Fuller on Legal Fictions: A Benthamic Perspective', *International Journal of Law in Context* 9, 466–84.

Rawls, J. 1972 *A Theory of Justice* (Oxford University Press).

Raz, J. 1979 *The Authority of Law* (Oxford: Clarendon Press).

——— 2005 'Can There Be a Theory of Law?', in *Blackwell Guide to the Philosophy of Law and Legal Theory*, ed. M.P. Golding and W.A. Edmundson (Oxford: Wiley-Blackwell), 324–42.

Rees, J. 1985 *John Stuart Mill's* On Liberty, ed. G.L. Williams (Oxford: Clarendon Press).

Reid, J.P. 2004 *Rule of Law: The Jurisprudence of Liberty in the Seventeenth and Eighteenth Centuries* (DeKalb: Northern Illinois University Press).

Riley, J. 1991 'One Very Simple Principle', *Utilitas* 3, 1–35.

Rosen, F. 1983 *Jeremy Bentham and Representative Democracy: A Study of the Constitutional Code* (Oxford: Clarendon Press).

——— 1990 'Majorities and Minorities: A Classical Utilitarian View', in *Nomos 32: Majorities and Minorities*, ed. J.W. Chapman and A. Wertheimer (New York University Press), 24–43.

——— 2003 *Classical Utilitarianism from Hume to Mill* (London: Routledge).

——— 2005 'Jeremy Bentham on Slavery and the Slave Trade', in *Utilitarianism and Empire*, ed. B. Schultz and G. Varouxakis (Lanham MD: Lexington Books), 33–56.

——— 2013 *Mill* (Oxford University Press).

Rousseau, J.J. 1997 'Considerations on the Government of Poland', in *The Social Contract, and Other Later Political Writings*, ed. V. Gourevitch (Cambridge University Press).

Rousseaux, X. 1997 'Le droit pénal entre consolidation étatique et codification absolutiste au XVIIIe Siècle', in *Le pénal dans tous ses états. Justice, Etats et sociétés en Europe, XIIe-XXe siècles*, ed. X. Rousseaux and R. Lévy (Brussels: Publications des Facultés Universitaires Saint-Louis), 251–78.

Schofield, P. 1986 'Conservative Political Thought in Britain in Response to the French Revolution', *Historical Journal* 29, 601–22.

______ 2003 'Jeremy Bentham's "Nonsense upon Stilts"', *Utilitas* 15, 1–26.

______ 2003 'Jeremy Bentham, the Principle of Utility, and Legal Positivism', *Current Legal Problems* 56, 1–39.

______ 2006 *Utility and Democracy: The Political Thought of Jeremy Bentham* (Oxford University Press).

______ 2009 *Bentham: A Guide for the Perplexed* (London: Continuum).

______ 2010 'Jeremy Bentham and HLA Hart's "Utilitarian Tradition in Jurisprudence"', *Jurisprudence* 1, 147–67.

______ 2011 'Jeremy Bentham and the British Intellectual Response to the French Revolution', *Journal of Bentham Studies* 13.

______ 2012 *Jeremy Bentham: Prophet of Secularism* (London: South Place Ethical Society).

Schwartzberg, M. 2007 'Jeremy Bentham on Fallibility and Infallibility', *Journal of the History of Ideas* 68, 563–85.

Selznick, P. 1999 'Legal Cultures and the Rule of Law', in *The Rule of Law after Communism*, ed. M. Krygier and A. Czarnota (Aldershot: Ashgate), 21–38.

Shackleton, R. 1972 'The Greatest Happiness of the Greatest Number: The History of Bentham's Phrase', *Studies on Voltaire and the Eighteenth Century* 90, 1461–82.

Shapiro, S. 2011 'Planning Theory and the Nature of Law', *Legal Theory in China*, 1, www.legal-theory.com.

Sidgwick, H. 1884 *The Methods of Ethics*, 3rd edn. (London: Macmillan).

Simmonds, N. 2007 *Law as a Moral Idea* (Oxford University Press).

Smith, D. 1965 *Helvétius: A Study in Persecution* (Oxford: Clarendon Press).

______ 1983 'Helvétius and the Problems of Utilitarianism', *Utilitas* 5, 275–89.

Smulovitz, C. and Peruzzotti, E. 2003 'Societal and Hortizontal Controls: Two Cases of a Fruitful Relationship', in *Democratic Accountability in Latin America*, ed. Mainwaring and Welna (Oxford University Press), 309–31.

Sokol, M. 2011 *Bentham, Law and Marriage: A Utilitarian Code of Law in Historical Context* (London: Bloomsbury).

Stromseth, J., Wippman, D. and Brooks, R. 2006 *Can Might Make Rights? Building the Rule of Law after Military Interventions* (New York: Cambridge University Press).

Tamanaha, B. 2002 'The Rule of Law For Everyone', *Current Legal Problems* 55, 97–122.

______ 2012 'The History and Elements of the Rule of Law', *Singapore Journal of Legal Studies* 2012, 232–47.

Ten, C.L. 1980 *Mill on Liberty* (Oxford: Clarendon Press).

______ 1991 'Mill's Defence of Liberty', in *J.S. Mill* On Liberty *in Focus*, ed. J. Gray and G.W. Smith (London: Routledge), 212–38.

Thompson, E.P. 1977 *Whigs and Hunters* (Harmondsworth: Penguin).

Tierney, B. 1963 '"The Prince Is Not Bound": Accursius and the Origins of the Modern State', *Comparative Studies in Society and History* 5, 378–400.

——— 1982 *Religion and the Growth of Constitutional Thought 1150–1650* (Cambridge University Press).

Twining, W.L. 1975 'The Contemporary Significance of Bentham's Anarchical Fallacies', *Archiv fur Rechts – und Sozial philosophie* 61, 325–56.

Urbina, I. 2009 'Despite Red Flags About Judges, a Kickback Scheme Flourished', *New York Times*, 27 March.

Voltaire (Arouet, J.-M.) 1971 *Philosophical Dictionary*, ed. T. Besterman (Harmondsworth: Penguin Books).

——— 1994 'Republican Ideas. By a member of a public body', in *Political Writings*, ed. D. Williams (Cambridge University Press), 195–211.

Waldron, J. (ed.) 1987 *Nonsense upon Stilts: Bentham, Burke and Marx on the Rights of Man* (London: Methuen).

——— 2002 'Is the Rule of Law an Essentially Contested Concept (in Florida)?', *Law and Philosophy* 21, 137–64.

——— 2008 'The Concept and the Rule of Law', *Georgia Law Review* 43, 1–61.

——— 2011 'The Rule of Law and the Importance of Procedure', in *Nomos 50: Getting to the Rule of Law*, ed. J.E. Fleming (New York University Press, 2011), 3–31.

Williams, B. 1973 'A Critique of Utilitarianism', in *Utilitarianism For and Against*, ed. J.J.C. Smart and B. Williams (Cambridge University Press), 75–150.

Winston, K. 2005 'The Internal Morality of Chinese Legalism', *Singapore Journal of Legal Studies* 2005, 313–47.

Wolff, J. 1998 'Mill, Indecency and the Liberty Principle', *Utilitas* 10, 1–16.

Wollheim, R. 1973 'John Stuart Mill and the Limits of State Action', *Social Research* 40, 1–30.

Wootton, D. 2000 'Helvétius: From Radical Enlightenment to Revolution', *Political Theory* 28, 307–36.

Wynne, E. 1774 *Eunomus: Or, Dialogues Concerning the Law and Constitution of England. With An Essay on Dialogue*, 4 vols. (London: B. White).

IV. Cases

Marbury v. *Madison*, 5 U.S. (1 Cranch) 137 (1803)

United States v. *United Mineworkers*, 330 U.S. 258, 67 S. Ct. 677 (1947)

Walker v. *Birmingham*, 388 U.S. 307, 87 S. Ct. 1824 (1967)

Whitney v. *California*, 274 U.S. 357, 47 S. Ct. 641 (1927)

INDEX